OECD Territorial Reviews

D1298386

Siena, Italy

OECD

ORGANISATION FOR ECONOMIC CO-OPERATION AND DEVELOPMENT

ORGANISATION FOR ECONOMIC CO-OPERATION AND DEVELOPMENT

Pursuant to Article 1 of the Convention signed in Paris on 14th December 1960, and which came into force on 30th September 1961, the Organisation for Economic Co-operation and Development (OECD) shall promote policies designed:

- to achieve the highest sustainable economic growth and employment and a rising standard of living in Member countries, while maintaining financial stability, and thus to contribute to the development of the world economy;
- to contribute to sound economic expansion in Member as well as non-member countries in the process of economic development; and
- to contribute to the expansion of world trade on a multilateral, non-discriminatory basis in accordance with international obligations.

The original Member countries of the OECD are Austria, Belgium, Canada, Denmark, France, Germany, Greece, Iceland, Ireland, Italy, Luxembourg, the Netherlands, Norway, Portugal, Spain, Sweden, Switzerland, Turkey, the United Kingdom and the United States. The following countries became Members subsequently through accession at the dates indicated hereafter: Japan (28th April 1964), Finland (28th January 1969), Australia (7th June 1971), New Zealand (29th May 1973), Mexico (18th May 1994), the Czech Republic (21st December 1995), Hungary (7th May 1996), Poland (22nd November 1996), Korea (12th December 1996) and the Slovak Republic (14th December 2000). The Commission of the European Communities takes part in the work of the OECD (Article 13 of the OECD Convention).

Publié en français sous le titre :
EXAMENS TERRITORIAUX DE L'OCDE
Sienne, Italie

Foreword

The globalisation of trade and economic activity is increasingly testing the ability of regional economies to adapt and exploit or maintain their competitive edge. There is a tendency for performance gaps to widen between regions, and the cost of maintaining cohesion is increasing. On the other hand rapid technological change, extended markets and greater use of knowledge are offering new opportunities for local and regional development but demand further investment from enterprises, reorganisation of labour and production, skills upgrading and improvements in the local environment.

Amid this change and turbulence, regions continue to follow very different paths. Some regions are doing well in the current phase of the growth cycle and are driving growth. Others are less successful at capturing trade and additional economic activities. Many territories with poor links to the sources of prosperity, afflicted by migration, notably of young people, and lagging behind with respect to infrastructure and private investment are finding it difficult to keep up with the general trend. At the same time central governments are no longer the sole provider of territorial policy. The vertical distribution of power between the different tiers of government needs to be reassessed as well as the decentralisation of fiscal resources in order to better respond to the expectations of the public and improve policy efficiency. All these trends are leading public authorities to rethink their policies and strategies

The Territorial Development Policy Committee (TDPC) was created at the beginning of 1999 to assist governments with a forum for discussing the above issues. Within this framework, the TDPC has adopted a programme of work that puts its main focus on reviewing Member countries' territorial policies and on evaluating their impact at regional level. The objectives of Territorial reviews are: *a*) identify the nature and scale of territorial challenges using a common analytical framework; *b*) assist governments in the assessment and improvement of their territorial policy, using comparative policy analysis; *c*) assess the distribution of competencies and resources among the different levels of governments; and *d*) identify and disseminate information on best practices regarding territorial policy.

The Committee produces two types of reviews:

Territorial reviews at the national level. Requested by national authorities, they analyse trends in regional performances and institutional settings, focus on policies to reduce territorial disparities and to assist regions in developing competitive advantages. They also concentrate on the governance framework, on the impact of national non-territorial policies on subnational entities and on specific aspects of fiscal federalism. The final report proposes territorial policy recommendations.

Territorial Reviews at the regional level. Requested by subnational authorities (local or regional) with the agreement of national ones, they concentrate on strategies for development of the respective entity. They in particular identify the role of key demographic, socio-economic, environmental, technological and institutional factors in explaining the performance of regions. Comparative analysis with regions of the same type is undertaken using the typology elaborated by the Secretariat. The final report proposes development policy recommendations.

Bernard Hugonnier,
Director,
Territorial Development Service

Acknowledgements

The project was co-sponsored and co-financed by the Province of Siena and by the OECD.

Socio-economic background information was collected and provided by the SMP consulting firm. Additional information was provided by Professor Guido Pellegrini and Professor Luigi Burroni.

The team of international experts who contributed their reports to the preparation of this review was comprised of Mr. Nicola Crosta, OECD Secretariat, Mrs. Sabrina Lucatelli, OECD Secretariat, Ms. Elke Loeffler, Bristol Business School, Specialist in Public Administration, and Mr. Edward Inskeep, International Consultant, Specialist in Tourism.

Invaluable assistance was provided by Mr. Albino Caporale, of the Provincial Administration of Siena.

This review was produced and co-ordinated by Mr. Timothy Wojan and Ms. Arantzazu Aramburu, Administrators, and it was directed by Mr. Mario Pezzini, Head of the Territorial Reviews and Governance Division of the OECD Territorial Development Service.

4

Table of Contents

List of Tables

List of Figures

Assessment and Recommendations

Siena's experience
contrasts general
trends of
predominantly
rural areas...

Siena, a predominantly rural province in central Italy, has enjoyed robust performance in the principal indicators of income and employment growth and in-migration. Even against the backdrop of impressive national gains in the post-war period, Siena has been able to improve its position relative to other Italian provinces in terms of per capita income. During this same period, predominantly rural Italian provinces as a whole fell in rank. Employment creation has also been impressive with the province demonstrating high rates of labour force participation for men and women. Labour shortages have emerged recently, replacing the more typical rural problem of persistent unemployment. A strong indicator of the opportunities available in a territory is the rate of in-migration, and here too Siena has bucked rural trends, registering positive net migration since the 1970s. Most importantly, the composition of gross migration flows has stemmed the "brain drain" evidenced by a higher share of college graduates than the national or regional Tuscany average. Empirically, Siena is representative of the upper-tail for most of the principal indicators of performance in predominantly rural areas. The conceptual task is to determine whether this experience points to emergent possibilities of rural areas or is merely an outlier reliant on irreproducible factors.

... providing insight
into the advantages
of specific rural
characteristics...

The commonality Siena shares with many other rural areas is its limited engagement with industrialisation. Between 1953 and 1971, the population fell by more than 7% following the crisis in sharecropping that afflicted the province. The migration story is typical of many predominantly rural areas in OECD Member countries that had also failed to generate sufficient employment in industry to compensate for the labour shedding in agriculture. What differentiates the experience in Siena is the relatively early shared realisation that this limited engagement would add value to a substantial endowment of amenities – a range of natural, man-made and cultural features recognised as having specific societal or economic value. This realisation resulted from a combination of civic obligation, the number and quality of these amenities and early success in the symbolic attachment of the territory to goods sold in the market. Siena is thus illustrative of a largely unappreciated potential in many rural areas and the social and collective orientation required for tapping it.

... and the necessity for co-ordination and a long-term vision.

However, the success that Siena has enjoyed has sensitised its residents to the need of sustaining these advantages into the future. Indeed, a part of this initial success was dependent on the significant endowment in place rather than their purposive co-ordination and valorisation. It is this current stage in Siena's development that is most informative for rural development policy more generally. Instead of relying on the attractive pull of a small number of renowned sites, the province must further its efforts to make the totality of cultural, natural and built amenities visible and accessible. The dual challenge is to control congestion in the most popular sites and direct more visitors to under-utilised areas in the province. Sustainable development will thus require greater co-ordination both within and between interdependent activities in sectors such as tourism, agriculture and public services with the integration of economic, social and environmental goals. In turn, this raises new needs of governance and long-term strategic planning. These sectoral challenges and policy alternatives are outlined before turning to an assessment of governance instruments required for addressing them.

The tourism strategy should appeal to more sustainable visitor profiles,...

A significant share of the more than five million visitors annually matches a mass tourism profile where the tourist views a limited number of sites included on the must-see list. This contributes to the territorial concentration of flows in a few areas of the province: three UNESCO World Heritage sites in the province – the city centres of Siena and Pienza and of San Gimignano – risk erosion due to over congestion, exceeding their maximum carrying capacity during peak periods. This in turn generates resentment among the local population, and ends up transforming the identity of historical centres, which gradually lose their traditional functions and inhabitants. Additionally, visitor congestion usually affects the quality of the tourism offer and creates high infrastructure and management costs, which exceed the financial resources of municipalities. At the same time, Siena possesses an exceptional wealth of less renowned attractions that are currently under-utilised – heritage, landscape, farm tourism, gastronomy, spas – and that are found throughout the province. Beautiful landscapes already attract numerous foreign tourists to stay in renovated farm houses that at one time sheltered the large contingent of labour required of modest holdings. The experience of rural tourism is aided by high quality wine and olive oil along with many typical products, all contributing to a rich culinary tradition. This element should allow the province to build a strategy harnessing its multiple tourism resources. The opportunity for tourists to create their own customised itineraries combining countryside, cultural visits, gastronomy and other interests would enhance the tourism experience, leading to longer stays. Appealing to this tourism profile would generate more sustainable tourism.

... which will require addressing weaknesses in quality and regulatory compliance of farm tourism...

The weaknesses in farm tourism should be addressed to ensure referral and return business and that incentives accrue only to accommodations that provide a substantive connection to farming. Standards of quality in accommodation and catering are highly variable; that, unsurprisingly, reflects the lack of professional hospitality experience of most Sienese farmers. A general plan for establishing and implementing a more consistent level of quality within these constraints should be developed. The degree of compliance with the current regulatory framework of farm accommodation is a growing concern, with some *agriturismo* failing to satisfy the legal requirements of commercial accommodation, and an increasing number of unauthorised farms operating as accommodation units. This situation demands stricter enforcement by public authorities. In terms of promoting the sector, co-ordination of integrated regional promotion networks with enhanced Internet

11

information and online reservation capability would substantially augment competitiveness.

... and the spa sector...

The spa sector, once an extremely prosperous one, is today adapting unevenly to changing conditions. Public subsidies to thermal therapies were reduced in the national health plan that halved occupancy rates in many of the spas. Concurrent to this crisis a new opportunity appeared in the increased interest of consumers in health and well being, manifest in the health tourist willing to finance his or her own treatments. This type of visitor demands curative or preventive therapies along with relaxation, fitness and beauty treatments, accompanied by quality accommodation. Notwithstanding some smaller spas, the spa sector should re-orient its product to meet new demands for therapies, fitness and well being as well as complementary tourism activities. The bigger spas of Chianciano could exploit their higher reception capacity in order to develop a complementary offer of conference and seminar tourism, and develop new types of attractions. Smaller spas could envisage a strategy of combining their own offers of high quality services with the other tourism resources of the province.

... and improving synergies with other sectors.

A tourism strategy should envisage more integrated efforts aiming to increase linkages between tourism and the craft and traditional food sectors. There is in Siena a wealth of "minor", high quality agro-food products, which can both find additional markets through tourism and also be used in the promotion of the province, as these products are strongly linked to the history and traditions of Siena. There are opportunities to improve and expand local production of craft items for sale to tourists, and reinforce its links with tourism, increasing thus the local benefits of tourism.

Siena agriculture presents a mix of market-driven and subsidised activity...

Despite the considerable economic success of many agricultural producers in the province, the majority of cultivated land area is dependent on Common Agricultural Policy (CAP) subsidies to remain economically viable. The combination of market-driven and subsidised agriculture highlights the policy dilemma regarding the relative value of commodity and non-commodity outputs of the sector. The integral rural landscape that is a considerable asset to the province would be different in the absence of agricultural subsidies. But, the logic of mono-cropping supported by the CAP has no claims to authenticity. This fact challenges the value of preserving the current cropping patterns over all others if landscape amenities are deemed an important non-commodity output of agriculture. More contentious are the environmental services in the form of reduced erosion risk that allegedly provide another valuable non-commodity output supported by the subsidy scheme. This argument does not consider agriculture's negative contribution in the form of increased nutrient or pesticide leaching or lower-cost land use alternatives that would provide the same protection against erosion. What is clear is that the link between the level of agricultural production and the various positive non-commodity outputs associated with this production is quite weak. Maintaining production subsidies at their current level to ensure adequate non-commodity provision fails to envision the entrepreneurial capacity of farmers or the possibility of better-targeted policy instruments.

... with the majority of cultivated land area dependent on CAP support.

Consortia, farmer associations and co-operatives can support an entrepreneurially dynamic sector.

The various associative institutions for farmers and agricultural producers in the province have demonstrated their value and will become increasingly important in a shift to market-oriented agriculture. Through the co-ordination of marketing and distribution activities, supporting research that would be beyond the means of individual producers, providing a menu of real services, and increasing the buying and selling power of collections of co-ordinated smallholders, the various organisations increase the viability of farming at a human scale. The possible diversification of individual holdings will make greater demands on the organisations' ability to co-ordinate, market and provide real services to an increasingly heterogeneous membership. One likely impact of CAP reform will be to extend the qualification of typical products such as wine and olive oil to qualify cereals and animal husbandry based on a quality or organic certification. However, the organisations also have a potentially important role to play in fostering the entrepreneurial activities of farmers. Increasingly, it will be the ability to follow emerging market trends that will allow farmers to realise viable opportunities.

13

Non-commodity outputs of agriculture are best assured by increased market viability.

The experience with farm tourism has demonstrated a successful means of diversifying farm income that also allows for the internalisation of some of the returns from the positive externalities of agricultural production. Indeed, farm tourism is the clearest way that consumers can express their demand for amenity attributes of farming through direct purchase of farm accommodations. The current incentive of taxing farm tourism as an agricultural activity should be maintained if the current legal requirement that not more than half of farm revenue comes from tourism is effectively enforced. Geographic indications of origin have been another strategy for internalising returns by connecting the product to the territory. Popular images of Tuscany and the large number of visitors each year to the region suggest that a winning strategy is one that links agricultural goods to the territory. The market success of Controlled Designation of Origin (DOC and DOCG) wines from the province is the clearest indication of this. However, various constraints suggest that any enlargement of the current DOC areas would proceed quite slowly, if at all, and certainly much too slowly to compensate for area that may be brought out of production in response to eventual CAP reform. In light of these constraints, efforts to diversify the range of typical products should be actively promoted. Although the range of labelled products currently extends to olive oil, and includes some meats and cheeses, there are currently a number of other traditional products that could also benefit from the legal protection and consumer information embodied in a label. Any such initiative would be facilitated by better co-ordination in the sale of authentic Sienese products so that the added value consumers derive from a product attached to the territory is represented in price premiums.

Internalising the returns from the positive externalities of agriculture has a long history in the province that should be encouraged further.

The European model of agriculture requires better consumer information and the reintegration of farming into the vitality of rural communities.

The province's intention to build support for the creation of an International Centre on Labelling of Typical Products should be encouraged. The mission of enhancing consumer information regarding typical products and developing strategies for maximising the contribution of typical products to rural development objectives would be a pure public good that has lacked substantial provision at the national or subnational level given an understandable preoccupation with "promotion". Especially in light of the concerns regarding a high-quality food supply, information on the justifiable claims of typical products would provide a valuable service to European consumers, as well as insight into how agricultural production can be reintegrated into the cultural, natural and economic systems of rural communities.

Specifying a transition period for reform of agricultural policies would mobilise the greatest range of creative resources.

In the pursuit of market-driven agriculture, the parallel costs of traditional agricultural policies are both the resulting misallocation of resources along with the strong disincentives it creates for agricultural venturing. The objectives and solutions for an economically competitive agriculture sector are inherently complex in stark contrast to the much simpler problem of increasing agricultural yields to ensure food security. Finding policy solutions in a complex environment must recognise the importance of enabling experimentation at the local level to mobilise the rich information sources and creativity of a diverse set of actors. Unfortunately, "wait-and-see" is the rational economic response in the current environment that squanders immense human resources, many of which are well disposed to "explore-and-endeavour". The implicit penalty on innovative behaviour should be removed by defining a transition period that would allow farmers to revert back to pre-transition activities if they find these to be more remunerative after reform.

Experience with public-private consultation suggests an ideal test case for experimenting with new instruments to support provision of non-commodity outputs.

More amenable to direct local policy action is the potential for local instruments to underwrite the provision of non-commodity outputs currently provided by agricultural production. Substantial transfers have dulled the true interdependence of other sectors with agriculture. This interdependence needs to be explicitly examined. The fact that many of the beneficiaries of the non-commodity outputs of agriculture are physically present and experience these outputs directly suggests that the *beneficiary pays principle* may be an appropriate and highly efficient way of ensuring a desirable level of provision. A tourism tax or means for soliciting voluntary contributions should be investigated. However, as the relationship between the level of non-commodity outputs and agricultural produc-

15

tion is weak these discussions should also investigate those non-commodity outputs that are valued and how they can be produced at lowest cost. In this respect, provincial experience with consultation and negotiation across public and private sectors would be a valuable resource in the constitution and specification of service contracts for the provision of non-commodity outputs.

Mutual interdependence of the farm and non-farm economy recommends territorial over sectoral approaches.

Sienese farmers maintain a keen – but by no means unique – interest in proactively responding to the internal and external forces that are driving the need for reform. The need to reduce distortions from subsidies to meet trade liberalisation obligations as well as reductions required by Eastern enlargement to meet EU budgetary targets are generally understood. As the resources for sectoral support become more constrained, the policy synergies in an integrated approach to rural and agricultural development become more persuasive. This suggests that farmers may be an allied interest in pursuing a territorial approach to "a living countryside" rather than a blocking coalition bent on maintaining sectoral subsidies. Given that alignment of these interests will become increasingly difficult at larger territorial scales, Siena may provide a unique opportunity for a pragmatic test of the advisability of redirecting a larger share of agricultural funds to non-farm activities. Such a test recognises the importance of pluriactivity to farm household income, thereby enhancing the quality of the rural milieu and ensuring adequate service provision in sparsely populated areas.

Administrative decentralisation should have a positive effect on service provision, although Siena faces a challenging situation.

For what concerns both tourism and agriculture, efficient service delivery at the local level is crucial. The far-reaching process of administrative decentralisation in Italy changed the institutional framework for service delivery. It also produced a number of managerial reforms for local authorities. Taken together these changes should make local service provision more efficient and citizen-oriented. Mayors are now directly accountable to citizens for a wide range of public services provided at municipal level. This accountability is re-enforced by a new regime of local taxation that has given municipalities the right to collect local taxes and user fees. Reforms have also increased municipal oversight, prompting a more efficient use of human resources in the civil service, and renewing attention to the implementation of management control at the local level. The main challenge for service provision lies in Siena's settlement pattern of small, scattered municipalities. Moreover, institutionalised forms of co-operation between the municipalities have been hindered by the pride attached to locally maintaining a wide range of public services. Nonetheless, this costly municipal autarky will no longer be possible in the future. Due to demographic changes, costs of public services will increase as demand for some withers and demand for others increases. At the same time, local authorities will find it still harder to compete with private companies in a tight labour market.

Options to increase the efficiency of service delivery include joint provision with other municipalities...

In order to increase the efficiency of service delivery, the province should consider the different approaches followed in OECD Member countries, where several possibilities seem particularly appropriate. Small size combined with considerable variation in demand suggests many municipalities in Siena could benefit from joining up service production in local consortia. Municipal partnerships are formal agreements in which at least two local authorities pool resources to deliver services. Flexibility is required of participants, as well as the ability to relinquish their former level of control over operations. Small municipalities in rural areas seem especially suitable for this intergovernmental arrangement, which is designed to enable joint service delivery and to maximise benefits in terms of potential cost savings and a wider range of high quality services than would be available to each local authority, acting alone. An appropriate "corporate governance" of municipal partnerships is essential in order to ensure transparency and accountability and thus guarantee an efficient service delivery. For instance, service partnerships with municipalities lacking major tourist attractions may help to deal with shortage of staff in the congested municipalities at peak times. Medical or policing staff from surrounding municipalities could be seconded to the tourist locations for a fixed period of time. But central government policies need to provide financial incentives for joint service delivery between small-sized local authorities to outweigh their reluctance to co-operate.

... one-stop shops and multifunctional service shops.

The strong municipal culture is also an obstacle for the realisation of one-stop shops (front offices for all the services of one public agency with different geographically dispersed departments, or for several public agencies). Given the small size of municipalities throughout the province, the best option would be to share one-stop shops between municipalities. Nonetheless, parochialism does not encourage local authorities to share their data. This resistance to co-operate could be overcome by bringing in external actors. This makes the relatively new approach of *Multifunctional service shops* an interesting alternative for the province; it goes one step further than one-stop shops, integrating public and private services delivered at the "front" office (service shop), which should be co-ordinated with service providers from the "back" office. Integrating private actors has the advantage of not only diluting rivalry between municipalities but also bringing in know-how and specific skills which are often lacking in small communities.

Siena should speed up managerial reforms and induce a cultural change within the administration

The above mentioned policy tools can have a strong impact on the province if applied in a co-ordinated manner. Still, they require at the same time that a crucial effort be made in the province: Siena needs to reinforce managerial reforms that were started only in 1999. In particular, the implementation of the Strategic Development Plan discussed below will require operational information and management control systems, which at present are at an embryonic stage. More worrying is the limited capacity of small municipalities to respond to the management reforms brought about by the Bassanini reforms in a positive way. However, the most urgent need across all levels of government in the province is for cultural change "to train" public managers and elected officials to talk to their citizens. Public authorities should set the example for increased customer satisfaction by ascertaining the needs, preferences and perceptions of citizens through surveys and other forms of market research.

The poor infrastructure endowment of the province today results from deliberate choice. ICTs may offer opportunities to enhance competitiveness and combat social exclusion...

Compared to other Italian provinces, Siena has rather poor infrastructure. This is particularly true with respect to airports and the railway network. The province also has large deficits regarding electric plants and services for enterprises. This situation has not emerged due to the lack of capital but rather the conscious choice of the provincial administration to prioritise the protection of landscape over new infrastructure projects. The picture is different regarding telecommunications infrastructure with the Province of Siena doing almost as well as the Region of Tuscany as a whole. And the province shows the will to put a stronger emphasis on ICT infrastructure; an ambitious project was recently initiated with the declared aim of bringing broadband infrastructure to all areas of the province. This project would add to the existing best practices in e-government (the *Siena Card*) and in the promotion of local products on the Net.

... but investments require a more comprehensive strategy.

However, optimising the social returns of investments in broadband, along with other interesting initiatives in Siena, requires a clear and widely shared strategy for the development of the Information Society integrated with the global strategic plan for the province . This should cover objectives of both competitiveness and social cohesion. ICTs offer new delivery channels for public services of particular interest in isolated rural areas. In addition to e-government initiatives, tele-medicine and tele-education should be developed in order to fight social exclusion. More generally, the development of such a strategy should include conducting a territorial analysis in order to identify precisely the areas that are likely to make better use of technologies, as well as providing appropriate training to increase computer literacy and language skills.

Participatory planning instruments support Siena's drive towards sustainable development,...

Governance reforms appear to be conducive to meeting the needs of sustainable development as administrative decentralisation in Italy has mixed the cards anew. In particular, local authorities gained new administrative functions and new political accountability. Through this process the province obtained an unprecedented planning authority, demonstrated by recent initiatives in participatory planning. At the same time, a new dimension of co-ordination

19

between different levels of government is required by this decentralisation or "administrative federalism". The dual learning process requires the central government level "to let loose" while local levels integrate municipal and provincial actions vertically. In other words, the hard test of local autonomy is integrated action. As a result, Siena provides a fertile ground for examining participatory planning along the lines of strategic management practices in the public sector elsewhere in OECD Member countries. In particular, Siena is predisposed to apply the new legislation in participatory planning given its high level of social capital. This helps a proactive provincial administration to mobilise private and social actors within short periods of time and to agree on large-scale projects. Many relevant stakeholders in the province are taking an active interest in different sustainable initiatives.

... addressing land use...

The process used in developing the Provincial Territorial Co-ordination Plan or PTCP is indicative of the comprehensiveness and inclusiveness required of sustainable development. Drafting of the document eschewed the traditional reliance on a single source of technical expertise in favour of the input and expertise from a wide range of actors and stakeholders in a consultation process that spanned three years. Developing a sense of ownership was critically important for a planning tool that makes the permanence and reproducibility of territorial capital – that may be exploited or enhanced but never dissipated for personal gain – the overarching principle. Going beyond the various formal and informal initiatives for valorisation of amenities to a systematic discipline of programming and policy will be necessary to ensure the sustainable utilisation of these territorial assets.

... and strategic planning.

While the PTCP co-ordinates programming and policy with respect to *land use*, it does not directly address the co-ordination of economic activities and social objectives with respect to the territory that are often critical means for achieving development objectives. The provisional Strategic Plan being developed at the time of writing should address this deficiency, providing a long-term strategic vision to guide initiatives and defining performance targets for the concrete monitoring of progress. If the process for developing the Strategic Plan is successful it will secure the commitment of an inclusive collection of stakeholders and frame efforts for the productive reorganisation and redesign required for better programme and organisational performance. As a "work in progress" there is a significant opportunity for comment on and appraisal of the process.

All planning processes reveal weaknesses with respect to transparency and public consultation.

The "Siena success story" shows that a high stock of social capital supports "good government". But the reverse is also true: "good governance" increases social capital. The fact that the Province of Siena has the historical advantage of a high-level of social capital makes Siena a unique case. Nevertheless, sustainable development will only be a realistic goal if real efforts are made to ensure that individuals and organisations co-operate in an effective, associative way. Accountability and increased public participation are key elements of any sustainable development policy framework. Nonetheless, the design processes of the PTC and the Strategic Plan show deficiencies in the consultation processes; in the PTC the consultation was not yet a genuine dialogue between all stakeholders, and the consultation in the Strategic Plan largely ignores the importance of engaging civil society. Moreover, the Monte dei Paschi Bank, one of the five largest Italian banks, headquartered in Siena, has created an autonomous foundation with a directive to fund projects solely within the territory of the province, constituting a unique development tool. In order to commit all the stakeholders in the Province of Siena to the strategic plan, the decision-making process concerning the grants of the foundation should be related, through an inclusive consultation, to the objectives of the Strategic Plan.

Public actors should improve their strategic capacities.

Nonetheless, the definition of the Strategic Plan should not end with its drafting, nor should the involvement of local actors end after initial consultation. Strategic management should be seen as a continually evolving process of mutual learning, where public and private stakeholders are committed to advancing the development of the community. Reporting systems and related sanction/premium mecha-

21

nisms are a way of both engaging stakeholders and ensuring better performance. Finally, such planning requires a substantive cultural change, as the different stakeholders need to act *strategically*. This requires individual and organisational learning and monitoring.

Chapter 1

Siena as Representative Rural Region or Archetype?

Introduction

The Province of Siena provides an exemplary case for examining the changing role of predominantly rural regions in this age of unparalleled affluence, interconnectivity and globalisation. The most evident support for this statement comes from prolonged and robust performance in employment creation and income growth. At a time when many other rural areas are suffering from economic stagnation and concomitant outmigration, Siena is illustrative of local rural features that have been able to spur new growth. By examining the structures and behaviours that have contributed to this success, the analysis endeavours to provide productive insight into how this experience might be reproduced in other places. The advantage of examining real world examples is the insight it provides regarding those rural challenges that are particularly intractable. Siena still struggles with many of the traditional rural challenges along with newly emerging ones that are also examined in turn. The wider implication of this is that the binding constraints of rural areas are brought into sharper focus. This perspective is particularly valuable for understanding the limits of current rural policy and options for its improvement.

It is now widely acknowledged that the province's limited engagement with industrialisation has become a considerable asset in the valorisation of its rich endowment of both cultural and natural amenities. Siena shares this characteristic of limited engagement with many other rural areas. What differentiates the experience in Siena is the shared realisation that these amenities are valuable. This realisation has resulted from a combination of civic obligation, the number and quality of these amenities and early success in the symbolic attachment of the territory to goods sold in the market. Siena is thus illustrative of a largely unappreciated potential in many rural areas and the social and collective orientation required for tapping it. But importantly, local actors believe that there is still substantial potential for adding value to products and services by linking these to the territory, providing provocative examples of unexploited opportunities.

Sustainable tourism development also presents unexploited opportunities that have strong parallels with rural tourism more generally. However, whereas the main interest in promoting rural tourism is usually the creation of income and employment opportunities, the critical objective of a rural tourism strategy in Siena is to alleviate congestion in its most renowned sightseeing spots. Substantial increases in mass international tourism and inclusion of Siena's most celebrated attractions on tour operators' "Tuscany must-see list" threatens the physical and social carrying capacity of these destinations. The ramparts of the hill towns that provided security against marauding foreign armies may eventually be undone by seemingly genial tourist coaches. The strategy being followed for solving this problem attempts to redirect these tourist flows to less congested areas by appealing to experiential agendas of a substantive connection to a destination's people, culture and environment. Farm tourism, which has already demonstrated considerable success in the province, is one component of this strategy along with strategies to facilitate access to the totality of the province's rich cultural heritage.

Against this backdrop of vibrant economic activities, the Province of Siena also presents several serious challenges owing to sparse population density in much of the province – exacerbated by a negative natural balance – and the continued reliance on agricultural subsidies affecting the majority of cultivated land area. Deficiencies in scale and scope economies will require administrative, technological or entrepreneurial innovations in service delivery. The province is following an ambitious program in pursuit of various technological innovations available in the Information Society, informing the efficacy of finding solutions to challenges of rural service delivery. More mundane solutions in the form of horizontal partnerships, privatisation and third sector initiatives also hold promise. With regard to agriculture, more than 70% of the utilised agricultural area produces cereals, oilseed, fodder and protein crops that generate roughly an equal split between market and subsidy revenue for many of its farmers. By comparison, vineyards that produce renowned wines from denominations such as Montalcino, Montelpuciano and Chianti account for only 9% of the cultivated land area. The integral rural landscape that is a considerable asset to the province would be dramatically different in the absence of agricultural subsidies. Local actors recognise the necessity of increasing the competitiveness of producers dependent on subsidies and fostering entrepreneurial efforts to uncover new sources of value. Siena thus provides an instructive test case for assessing the replacement of subsidies to declining sectors with an approach based on strategic investments to develop new activities.

The topics discussed above are instructive for finding solutions to rural problems in many areas. From a historical perspective, it is only relatively recently that a prolonged period of net outmigration was reversed. While it would be easy to dismiss the relevance of the Siena experience as being dependent on irreproducible factors, the danger of such reduction is to overlook the preponderance of rural resources capable of driving future growth. Uniqueness and differentiation that contribute to a heightened quality-of-life are becoming the main sources of rural comparative advantage in industrialised countries. The critical factors in Siena directing these new sources of growth have not been the abundance of amenities but rather the development of consultation and associative relations among local actors that have allowed for their sustainable valorisation. This experience is thus directly relevant to many rural areas. Viewing development as a continual process, it is only natural that past success has also opened up a new set of territorial challenges. The creation of new instruments of governance to address the challenges of sustainable development along with the rich history of associative relations provides an ideal laboratory for envisioning the future possibilities of a significant number of rural areas. These future possibilities are likely to be reliant on those rural features that make a unique contribution to the capabilities of people, who live, work or visit there.

Evolution of the territory

The historical origins of the Sienese provide numerous examples of increased human capability that has been reliant on novel combinations of local resources. The most lasting marks of the early Etruscan civilisation originated in the vast works of drainage of the land and distribution of water. In addition to the construction of navigable canals, outlets and a network of funnels to systematically drain extended areas, the Etruscans also constructed the first roads built on a wholly artificial foundation. Wealth accumulated from skilful cultivation of the land and craftsmanship that lead inevitably to trade. The so-called "orientalising age" (7th century BC) witnessed investment by the urban aristocracy in the production of olive oil and, above all, wine, whose surplus was eventually exported to meet the great demand of western barbarian peoples. Bronze-ware, toreutics and ceramics eventually became important exports leading to a specialisation in skills and the consequent birth of full-time artisans. The international dimension was thus well established in ancient times with Greek artisans responsible for much technology transfer, and many innovations in primary activities – such as the rotation of crops, new viticultural methods – having Greek or Oriental origin.

The Roman "globalisation" was particularly disastrous for Etruria, which then went through a period of economic decline, the reconversion of production and the social disintegration of the urban and rural organisation, from which it was to recover only during the Middle Ages. Of course, many of the indelible marks on the Province of Siena that are now highly prized come from this period, most evidently the man-made objects, such as urban structures, architectural monuments and art, but also rich cultural traditions, such as the renowned festival of Il *Palio*. In addition, three institutions fundamental to contemporary Siena economy and

25 |

society emerged in these times: the university, the bank and the hospital. The Santa Maria della Scala Hospital was founded before the year 1000, constituting one of the first examples in Europe. The institution grew rapidly thanks to legacies, donations and alms, above all on the part of the important families in Siena. The second institution of international importance was the university, founded shortly after the universities in Bologna and Paris. A decree emanating from the Siena Podestà in 1240 testifies to the existence of a study centre in Siena that applied a tax on students' lodgings to be transferred to the salaries of the Masters of the Siena Studium. Law, grammar and medicine were the main subjects taught. The emergence of Monte dei Paschi Bank completed the triad. A period of serious economic difficulty in Siena prompted the council magistrates to establish a *monte di pieta* in 1472 in line with clerical groups in Tuscany that were establishing funds for the needy. The bank soon extended its services beyond providing under-collateralised loans to the poor. Guarantees to the bank's depositors would eventually be provided by setting aside the income from the pastures (*paschi*) south-west of the city, cementing the strong links to Siena and providing an evocative name for a financial institution that would gain international importance. Throughout central and northern Italy, bankers provided both the economic impetuses along with civic leadership that were important to the flourishing of the Renaissance. At this time, Monte dei Paschi established its enduring role as patron of the arts, with its philanthropy extending to scientific research, health, education and welfare. These obligations were defined by statute that to this day governs the distribution of a share of profits.

The other important historical legacy comes from the system of sharecropping that originated as early as the 9th century in signed contracts by the Abbotts of Mount Amiata. *Mezzadria*, a system that split all yields evenly between the peasants tilling the soil and their mainly urban-based landlords, became dominant throughout central Italy in the 13th and 14th centuries. As late as 1947 nearly two-thirds of farmland in four Tuscany provinces was operated as *mezzadria* (Pratt, 1994). The most enduring impact on the present landscape is the collection of large farmhouses found throughout the countryside that often accommodated large extended families that would be necessary to work the modest-sized farms. The size of these old farmhouses contributes to an agrarian landscape that maintains a human scale even if most of the farm labour has since been shed. Multi-cropping was necessitated by the reliance on draught power for ploughing, to meet the subsistence needs of the farm families and to provide diversification for the benefit of both landlord and tiller. The commercialisation of the sector that began in the late 19th century saw the emergence of the *fattoria* – the manager of the collection of farms in an estate that specified cultivation of the individual farms, who operated the capital equipment of the estate including mills and presses and eventually tractors and threshers. However, the economic rationalisation of farming activities by *fattoria* diffused gradually with the main impact being that the landlord housed and controlled the production factors that were becoming more important to the modernisation of agriculture.

The weak response to the crisis in sharecropping after 1953, combined with the peripheral status in the Tuscan economy – both in terms of limited infrastructure links and a symbolic distance from the neighbouring regional capital in Florence – all contributed to Siena's limited encounter with industrialisation. Siena and Florence, as the locations of the main wine producing estates in Tuscany, were excluded from the redistributive land reform that affected the rest of the region. Although there were government programs in place to help tenants finance the purchase of the farms they tilled, this was often not an economically viable option given substantial deferred investment and the lack of important means of production that resulted from the *fattoria* system. In addition, the lack of an active land reform agency meant that many of the collective inputs required for the transformation from estate agriculture to family farm agriculture were not provided. Not surprisingly, the rural exodus from the province was immense with Montalcino and its surrounding areas losing half its population in the 1950s and early 1960s. In contrast to other predominantly rural areas where the transformation of agriculture released labour – often with good mechanical skills – to the local light manufacturing industry, this dynamic in Siena was for the most part absent. The exception to this was the northern part of the province (Poggibonsi-Colle area) where traditional activities, such as furniture, upholstery and glassmaking, along with carpentry and small mechanics aimed at meeting local markets were absorbed into the industrial system of small and medium concerns coming from the Florence-Pistoia area. In stark contrast to the rest of the province, the Poggibonsi-Colle area saw its population increase from 14 000 to 32 000 between 1951 and 1971.

Transportation infrastructure is also indicated as a critical factor in the province's limited encounter with industrialisation. However, as an enabling rather than propulsive factor of economic growth, its role as a determining factor must be assessed with caution. Certainly, the timing of various investments does not support the hypothesis that a relative deficiency in infrastructure caused the partial and weak response to industrialisation. Until the beginning of the 1960s, the Province of Siena was crossed by the main road connection between Florence and Rome (the Via Cassia, SS 2, which followed the route of the Mediaeval Via Francigena) and was skirted by the main railway line (then one of the few electrified, twin-track lines) which ran along the Val di Chiana with a minor line (single track, diesel traction) which connected many of the municipalities in the province. It was not until the construction of the A1 motorway in the 1960s (the "Sunshine Highway") and a few years later the Rome-Florence high-speed railway line, that the relative accessibility of the province was more seriously constrained. The frail response to industri-

27

alisation in the two decades following the war when relative accessibility was good would appear as confirmation of the weak industrial aspirations of the province. The eventual routing of the Sunshine Highway and high speed rail line – rather than being a cause of Siena's limited engagement with industrialisation – might be regarded as reinforcement of an alternative path to which it was predisposed.

In fact, the most compelling argument for a determinative role of infrastructure is the extent to which this marginalisation of accessibility locked in an alternative that was more dependent on enhanced quality-of-life rather than augmenting productive capacity. The reconfirmation of its peripheral position, the partial and weak industrial answer, the necessity to conform to EC agricultural directives that required leaving more "marginal lands" out of the production circuit, focused attention on quality agriculture that began to emerge in the 1970s. These developments would soon be followed by the first experiments of agri-tourism activities. The former crises in estate agriculture facilitated the infusion of non-local capital into the wine industry that could merge the local conditions to produce world class wines with an evocative image of the Tuscan countryside. In the town of Siena, the importance of the three venerable institutions discussed above increased in step with the growing importance of service industries. The Monte dei Paschi, which had emerged from the 1929 crisis in a position of strengthened national importance, maintained headquarters operations of an increasingly international operation in town. Demand for college education increased dramatically at this time in Italy, to the benefit of the university. Several important pharmaceutical industries have long-established operations in Siena that have benefited from the research capabilities of the university.

The culmination of these distant and more recent epochs has resulted in a Sienese model of development that draws on a diverse set of economic systems that have co-evolved with the natural and cultural systems of the province. It is the diversification into a number of often interdependent activities rather than the exploitation of single resources that provides the main source of resilience that has become increasingly evident since the 1970s and creates the main challenges for sustainable development. This is probably most evident in agriculture where the very survival of the vocation of farming is dependent on the ability to "close the loop" of the modern agri-alimentary system that currently provides an insufficient market income to primary producers, subsidised by the State. Closing the loop is dependent on local processing, marketing and distribution that is able to connect final products to a quality orientation made most evident to potential consumers by the integrity of the Siena countryside, which itself is most dependent on the production decisions of farmers. But clearly, the success of such a strategy is also dependent on the viability of tourism, service provision and the complex interaction of activities that intervene on the countryside. Similar interdependencies are evident within and between the manufacturing sector, services-producing sectors, hospitality industry and the cultural patrimony of the province. The risk is that critical systems that are not directly valued in the market will not be maintained at a level necessary for fully exploiting their contribution for adapting to change. One expression of this sentiment emerged in the meetings with local actors:

"A strong linkage of the various stages of production provides the unique opportunity to explore interaction of culture, ideas and skills. From ancient times the people were capable of finding solutions to problems that are dependent on local resources. There has always been this ability to analyse and adjust to economic trends. This is part of the cultural reality. This is extremely important as it allows us to understand how we can create microeconomies that are capable of adjusting to change." (OECD mission to Siena, April 2001)

The requisite task in meeting this challenge is to identify and make visible the whole complex of resources and the activities underpinning the territorial economies of the province. Sustainable development of the province can then emerge from public consultation and design of rules that ensure the permanence and reproducibility of the identified factors. We thus arrive at the current stage in the province, which is taking stock of its recent past success and trying to construct a governance framework that will allow the durable contribution of these territorial assets to development into perpetuity. Both the Provincial Territorial Co-ordination Plan (PTCP) and Strategic Plan are directed to the objective of sustainable development. Documenting provincial experience at this point thus provides insight into other areas implementing or planning similar initiatives, the opportunity for outside experts to critically assess and comment on the substance of these instruments and the processes used in developing them, and allows us to draw upon the experience in other regions that may be particularly instructive as regards the improvement of these instruments.

Taken together, the challenges and opportunities currently facing Siena delineate an archetype of sustainable development for territories defined by low population density, a diverse set of economic activities and a substantial endowment of natural and cultural amenities. It is in this regard that the "exceptional" characteristics of Siena may be most productive in suggesting productive reform to rural policy. Rural policies cannot be homogenous. In the past, public policies have tended to focus on rural areas as a block – assuming a uniform set of problems and opportunities defined principally by supposed contrasts with urban areas. Such an approach no longer reflects the present development opportunities for rural areas, if it ever did. Rather, different types of rural areas will present different problems to be addressed by public policies and different possibilities for development. A comparison exercise presented later in the Review, matching Siena to other structurally similar rural provinces in Europe, demonstrates the considerable policy leverage of a more targeted approach. The surprising result of this exercise demonstrates that half of the comparison provinces exceeded the employment creation performance of their respective countries while the other

29 |

half lagged behind. Policies designed to improve the opportunities for sustainable development of the laggard provinces are likely to be more efficacious if they are instructed by the experience of structurally similar areas that can reasonably share similar objectives. In this respect, the experience of Siena will be most useful for those rural areas that recognise an affinity for amenities-based rural development strategies. Before elaborating on the possibilities for sustainable development in rural areas with a rich endowment of amenities, it is instructive to examine the problems of reproduction that are arguably more common across the diversity of rural areas.

Problems of reproduction

As the lattice critical to both cultural and economic systems in the province, ensuring environmental integrity is essential to the reproduction of the Sienese model. There are currently two principal threats to meeting this objective. The first is that created by the large tourist flows that stream into the province, most evident at the renowned attractions but extending to traffic congestion during peak summer months in the countryside. However, as a repository of a considerable amount of Western cultural heritage, exclusion is not seen as a constructive option for addressing this problem. As the location of three UNESCO World Heritage sites, actors in the province perceive an obligation of ensuring access to all of its cultural treasures. Viable means of tackling the problem include initiatives for the better management of tourist itineraries, making the logistics for meeting these itineraries more sustainable, and by promoting the supply of services that appeal to quality cultural tourism as opposed to mass tourism perceived as more harmful to preservation efforts. Attempts to alter demand patterns are also being pursued; this has been reliant on the co-operation of tour operators and the educational efforts of UNESCO and the World Tourism Organisation. The second threat comes from economic pressures on the agriculture sector that may promote unsustainable farming practices, a widespread concern across rural areas. It is generally agreed that the subsidy scheme under the Common Agricultural Policy has not promoted sustainable farming practice, with mono-cropping in cereals, oilseeds, and protein crops advantaged by a high degree of mechanisation, relatively low labour input and reliance on industrial inputs for controlling pests and weeds and to bolster degraded soil fertility. Incentives for whole farm conversions to organic agriculture have helped to reduce the most harmful environmental practices but take-up has been modest. In the market-oriented wine sector, there have also been efforts to reduce variable input costs through increased mechanisation that often degrade the landscape and create erosion problems. Linking products sold on the market to the authentic integrity of the territory is clearly one way to provide incentives for more desirable farm practices, but this will also require collective agreement as to the responsibilities of the agriculture sector.

Current demographic trends that foreshadow long-term implications for the reproduction of the Sienese model must be assessed with respect to potential points of policy leverage. Indeed, a critical resource for ensuring preservation of the landscape or restoration of architectural and artistic treasures is the availability of skilled human capital. To date, the majority of this has been supplied indigenously, with its future supply threatened by a negative natural balance. While there is evidence that more of these functions are being filled by non-natives – especially the restoration efforts that have taken on international importance – there is considerable uncertainty regarding the long-term impacts on these traditional vocations. While aspirations of the school-age generation cannot be definitively known or regulated, there is some evidence that a Siena birthright is an important factor in economic activities that help to preserve traditional practice. For example, multi-cropping by wine-growers in Montalcino is practised almost exclusively on locally owned vineyards. More generally, in-depth knowledge of the local cultural patrimony is a salient characteristic of the Sienese. While the demographic factors impacting the rate of natural balance are no doubt complex, finding ways to reconcile the demands of work and family life may alter the reproductive choices of couples. This is the most direct way to correct age imbalances that are becoming more pronounced in the province, and which also pose threats to the sustainability of the Siena model.

Immigration may provide another means of moderating the effects of an ageing population, dependent on the composition of migrants. However, even migrants of child-bearing age, which consistently demonstrate a tendency toward greater fertility than their native peers, will only have a modest effect on the age balance. This is because the migration process adds persons to the middle of the age distribution who inevitably age, eventually joining the ranks of the elderly. The current composition of in-migrants to Siena is dominated by non-EU nationals of child-bearing age who should make just such a modest contribution to the age balance. They are currently filling labour shortages in routine services, manufacturing and farm wage-labour. Unfortunately, the investments required to actively assimilate them into the life of the province are currently lacking, especially with respect to housing and language training. As this component of the labour market is critically important to a large number of economic activities, inattention to the problems of easing their transition may impose significant economic costs on the province.

These demographic trends will also have implications for service provision throughout the province, with the more intractable phenomena requiring technological or organisational innovations. The tendency towards a fall in the birth-rate nearly everywhere weakens the prospects of any great demand in the future for all the lower grade schools. In the case of the offer of the service of schools, it is therefore clear that it is very difficult to compensate for the lack of an urban effect on the territory. Unfortunately, schools are more widespread in those areas where alternative solutions would be more logical: in the belt surrounding Siena, that is to say where the urban effect is sufficient and residence in the outskirts is often the result of individual "choice", there are a large number of municipal junior high schools, which, at least partly, could be replaced by the easy access to the administrative centre, which is also where the commuters work and shop. In any case, outside the larger urban centres access to the service becomes increasingly more expensive, given the unquestionable hypothesis that the school system as currently configured would become even more sparse throughout the territory in the future.

Despite this gloomy forecast, ways must be found to ensure provision of traditional educational services that will become even more essential to meeting human resource needs of the province. The relatively new requirements of the provision of opportunities for lifelong learning may provide needed room for manoeuvre. The empirical evidence suggesting a strong educational ethic in the province should also facilitate finding a solution. Strong foundations in literacy and numeracy will become increasingly important with the advent of the knowledge society requiring citizens and workers to comprehend and adapt quickly to new developments. Coupled with pervasive diffusion of ICT, globalisation and increased cross-border movement of people and ideas, education policy will, however, be required to move beyond developing competence in the basic skills. Lifelong learning strategies can serve as a key instrument for nurturing the knowledge society. They take account of learning over the whole course of a person's life, whether it takes place in formal or informal settings, and recognise the multiplicity of objectives for which it is undertaken – personal, social and economic. Increased capabilities for distance learning come naturally to mind in the more sparsely populated areas that characterise much of the province. As delivery nodes for diversified and specialised educational services, the minimum efficient scale of the traditional school may decline as it comes to serve a broader segment of the community. Especially in light of the ambitious plans for high-speed electronic connections throughout the province, Siena could provide considerable opportunity for demonstrating an augmented role for traditional educational institutions.

The necessity for bolstering the capabilities of economic actors is embodied in the single overarching strategy for maintaining competitiveness identified across economic sectors; namely, an emphasis on quality and continuous improvement as the indigenous sources of comparative advantage that should facilitate the required insertion into global economic networks. The acknowledgement that customer satisfaction comprises the only durable criteria for evaluating rival alternatives defines two spheres of ignorance: an understanding of what customers desire and an understanding of the processes in the production and distribution of an enterprise's goods and services that affect the ability to meet these desires. This in turn defines a set of required competencies including the ability for substantive communication with customers, systematic thinking of production and distribution forming the basis of incremental innovation and the ability to learn about possible advantages of alternative systems. These generic requirements extend from agriculture, to industry, to tourism and services, including public administration. Of course, the necessity of this ambition may be questioned, given the large and growing number of captive customers who come as tourists to the province. This raises three important points regarding reproduction of the Siena model: 1) Siena is not synonymous with tourism; 2) tourism premised on opportunism is not sustainable; and 3) excessive economic dependence on tourism would undermine the local identity and sociability that has been essential to current economic success. In short, insertion into global economic networks will be required to avoid degeneration into a souvenir economy.

The challenge of development

Solving the problems of reproduction assures the continuation of current activities, but it is the challenge of development – expanding the opportunity set and the human capability required to fill these new spaces – that animates local actors. These challenges are most easily summarised as those related to spatial disparities, those related to new opportunities in both emerging and venerable economic sectors, and those related to the social and political life of the province. As the central concern of territorial development, it is important to note that spatial disparities persist in the province and provide the most obvious opportunities for development. Finding means for the diffusion of greater economic opportunity throughout the province will have the dual benefits of increased equity and hopefully relieving pressures on the most popular tourism sites. There is also the expectation that the diverse set of economic activities currently located in the province will expand into emerging opportunities in biotechnology and information technology. An incubator has been established to promote the commercialisation of biotechnology while several firms are pursuing innovation in electronic security. In addition, the province is at the forefront in Italy in investigating the broader possibilities of the Information Society. Innovation also characterises the traditional activities in the province. Technologies to improve the interpretative content of museums and other exhibits are being actively developed while the status of wines from the area continues to improve in world markets as a result of innovation that better exploits the potential inherent in the climate, soil and vines. Finally, the province continues to improve democratic processes for defining social purpose along with the capabilities of governance for fulfilling these objectives.

33

This promising horizon is a stark contrast to the possibilities commonly envisioned for predominantly rural areas. Rural development in the industrialised world has been plagued by the successive lowering of expectations, most recently by conjectures on the implications of globalisation. However, the origins of the thesis of declining rural advantage are premised on the relationship between primary production and consumption. If comparative advantage of rural areas is limited to primary production of food and fibre then rising levels of affluence will result in an inexorable decline in the relative share of consumer expenditures as demand for these products grows much slower than income. Productivity increases have bolstered the income level of farmers but decimated the number of workers employed in the sector. Although employment losses in agriculture have been taken up to some extent by employment in manufacturing and services industries, it is widely believed to be limited to those activities requiring the significant cost advantages offered by rural areas. Like primary production, these industries will also face declining relative demand. Worse still, with increasing globalisation such industries will have greater incentive to find lower cost production sites in less developed countries. Lacking the agglomeration economies of urban areas, it is believed that rural areas will be unable to compete on economic grounds, necessitating subsidies to rural industry or permanent regional transfers if the settlements are to be maintained. Growing demand among urban residents to experience quaint, bucolic and charming rural areas, reminiscent of simpler times, flowing at a slower pace, provides a brighter forecast. In this scenario, some rural areas will be maintained by increasing demand for the unique attributes available there. Rural areas are reconceived primarily as locations for nostalgic experience, landscapers come to fill the role of farmers and the village square becomes the marketplace for traditional crafts, foodstuffs and *bric-à-brac* produced in the surrounding countryside. The values that can be appropriated from rural areas thus come to be defined wholly from the "consumption" of rural attributes. To be sure, most rural areas do not possess the wealth of amenities, easily accessible to urban populations that could support a significant share of the current population. Those rural areas proximate to cities are increasingly likely to be absorbed into those conurbations.

The consumption basis of the scenarios presented above mirrors the ambiguous objectives of modern conceptions of development concerned in some way with satisfying wants, that are being resolved in the new approaches to territorial development. The Italian District model offers a rejoinder to this earlier confusion by making heightened capabilities an end in themselves, independent of any enhanced ability to satisfy wants. This is not immediately apparent from the international attention that has focussed mainly on their ability to generate employment, promote innovation and provide above average incomes. However, more comprehensive ethnographic studies, both by Italian and international research-

34

ers, confirm the central role that demonstrable competence plays in aligning the seemingly contradictory objectives of co-operation and competition. Inside an industrial district it is not enough to simply "build a better mousetrap" and collect any deserved acclaim in the market. Instead, collective tests of capability through sub-contractor or co-production relations both solidify inter-firm co-operation and prod a controlled competition – within as well as between firms. Market tests will ultimately determine the monetary value of this capability serving as a complement to the collective test. The important point is that there is a social valuation of capability independent of its economic valuation:

> "The common solution [for the reconciliation of competition and co-operation and regeneration of resources required by the collectivity] is the fusion of productive activity, in the narrow sense, with the larger life of the community. The same experiences that teach people who they are teach them skills to acquire; how to collaborate; and what they may not do in their competition for honour in the community." (Piore and Sabel, 1984, p. 275)

As a province that already enjoys low unemployment and high income, the challenges in Siena are ill-defined with respect to the traditional preoccupations of rural development. A focus on augmenting the capabilities of citizens as both an end and means of development – in many ways parallel to augmenting the capabilities of workers in an industrial district – provides a clearer vision than incremental additions to the conventional indicators of income or job creation. Reinforcing this ambition are the ongoing discussions regarding the sustainable use of territorial capital linked to strategic planning, suggesting an ideal laboratory for elaborating this emerging vision of development. Indeed, this view of development that is more inclusive than a concern solely with economic outcomes is implicit in the debates regarding the impacts of infrastructure investment on the territory or, for that matter, the platitudes of sustainable development. Envisioning the public concern regarding development as an increased *"ability to lead the lives they have reason to value"* (Sen, 1999) would provide debatable criteria for assessing the efficacy of proposed programming and policy. Unfortunately, the confirming market test that is provided in the industrial district model is not readily available. In this respect, the rural dimensions of the province in combination with a "Tuscan way of thinking" that gives public consultation a privileged role are critical to the pragmatic application of these criteria. Development objectives directed to enlarging human capability would give clearer definition to the value of, say, expanding the feasible reproductive choices of families, or of being a farmer, or of preserving cultural heritage.

New requirements of governance

The preceding discussion makes explicit the tacit motivation that has helped direct the new tools for planning and development: planning and development

35

should contribute to citizens' ability to lead the types of lives they have reason to value. More generally, the current preoccupation with sustainable development of interdependent environmental, social and economic systems embodies this same inclusiveness. The confirmation that "sustainable policies" cannot be evaluated solely with respect to quantitative indicators – whether simple or composite – dismisses the usefulness of purely bureaucratic or technocratic solutions. Rather, new instruments of governance and planning must explicitly recognise the need to jointly assess the value of various ends and the efficacy of various means. For example, the debate over agricultural reform illuminates the interdependence of ends and means with the interests of various actors in the community. Is the end that is most valued the preservation of current cropping patterns sustained to now by Common Agricultural Policy subsidies? Is it generally believed that this policy has resulted in the development of human capabilities that are critical to sustaining the Sienese model? If so, are there viable means for achieving this end in the likely event that the level of supranational support will be reduced? If not, what should be the ends of policy directed to agriculture at the local level? Is the central interest augmenting the entrepreneurial capacity of farmers, or preserving an authentic Tuscan landscape or contributing to the gastronomic traditions of the territory or a combination of these and other ends? It is only when the ends of policy are discussed and agreed upon that the effectiveness of measures to achieve them can be debated, implemented and assessed.

The co-determination of ends and means presumes that territorial development can only proceed through shared guidance by relevant stakeholders. This is because each of the partners brings to the discussion different understandings of opportunities available, different risk assessments, different creative abilities for problem solving, and different types of resources that can be directed to realise agreed upon objectives. In addition, stakeholders who do not actively participate in the choice of strategy are unlikely to participate wholeheartedly in its implementation. Indeed, they may be hostile and even obstructive to the chosen strategy. This is especially problematic if such stakeholders are being asked to contribute some of their own resources to implement the strategy, or if they have legal powers of veto over some of the elements of the strategy. The lengthy process involved in the development of the Provincial Territorial Co-ordination Plan (PTCP) spanning three years of consultation with representatives of Sienese society attests to the importance of a sense of shared ownership of planning tools. In light of this intensive effort it is significant that several architects of the document expressed regret that selected issues had not been more fully discussed by relevant actors in the community before drafts were publicly debated. While these debates did result in a resolution of unanticipated conflicts, this is likely because the points of contention were thought to impose additional costs on well-represented interests. This presents the possibility that more diffuse interests in the territory may have as yet unresolved complaints about the PTCP. Legislation requiring that the PTCP be updated on a periodic basis mitigates the potential for this to dilute the effectiveness of the PTCP through time. However, tools for sustainable development require a broad consensus on the general framework if they are going to be successful in mediating conflicts that will inevitably arise from rival claims on the best reproducible use of resources. Within the context of sustainable development inclusiveness takes on much greater importance.

This is probably best expressed in the collective interpretation of "territorial capital". The central principle of discipline imposed on programming and planning by the PTCP is that the permanence and reproducibility of territorial capital may be exploited or enhanced but never dissipated for personal gain. To the extent that much of this territorial capital is embodied in assets that are privately owned, the PTCP constrains individual choice. There is nothing new in the constraint of individual choice in the pursuit of various social purposes. But the social purposes defined by the pursuit of sustainability extend the limit on acceptable behaviour to the prohibition of actions that impede the ability of future generations to realise their full potential. Lacking representation, these interests can only be expressed by current members of the community acting as stewards for the unknown composition of the community into its enduring future. Thus, the constraints on individual action in the PTCP must be viewed within the larger domain defined by the community. Again, there are useful parallels in the discussion of the industrial district model for understanding how property is to be conceived within a sustainable society.

> *"Property is to be held in trust for the community – its use subordinated to the community's maintenance. It is this recognition of the indispensability of **community** that makes yeoman democracy – a form of collective individualism – the political analogue of the co-operative competition of craft production"* (Piore and Sabel, 1984, p. 305).

Investigating how this vision coheres with reality and the strategic development options of the province is thus a central preoccupation of the review. The review will also provide insight into the particular advantages and difficulties that predominantly rural regions have in pursuing sustainable development.

Chapter 2

Territorial Patterns and Trajectories

Introduction

As a predominantly rural region with a generally favourable outlook, the Province of Siena presents a number of critical issues. First among these is the evolution of the province that has lead to the current prospect. Especially within the larger national context of significant regional dualism it is important to examine whether Siena represents a transformation of a formerly disadvantaged territory or is more indicative of the "rising tide" of north-central Italy. Comparisons with predominantly rural areas more generally will address the extent to which Siena mirrors or contrasts other rural trends. Attention then moves to a more detailed assessment of the current situation in the province. The functional borders of the territory and the extent and mode of external interaction are discussed before moving to an analysis of the geographic distribution of resources throughout the province. Factors that affect the productivity of these resources are then examined before assessing the potentials and threats for regional development.

Comparison with other regions

According to broad indicators, Siena has demonstrated exemplary performance for an Italian rural province. The overall economic achievement of the activities in the Province of Siena is summarised in data on per capita income. The most recent estimation of per capita income in the province (1999), provided by the Istituto Tagliacarne (the National Union of the Chambers of Commerce) places Siena 41st, out of 103 Italian provinces. If we take 100 to be the average in Italy, the estimation for Siena is 5.7% over the average. Since the average of Italian regions is slightly higher than that of the European Union, it is estimated that the Sienese average is 9% higher than that. In particular, in Tuscany, Siena is second only to the heart of the Florentine metropolitan area (Florence and Prato) and is hence above the level of not only the peripheral areas but also a large part of the more extensive metropolitan area.

Longitudinal data on per capita income provide insight into the path taken in arriving at this favourable position. While comparing Siena's performance to each of the other 102 Italian provinces would be intractable, grouping provinces by their level of per capita income in the initial and ending periods along with the rate of growth of this variable is more productive. Six distinctive "convergence clubs" emerge that correspond strongly with the differentiated experience of Italian provinces in the post-war period.[1] The two extremes of this classification contrast the most dynamic provinces of Milano, Bologna and Modena with the stagnation of the Mezzogiorno (Figure 1). Siena is included in the group made up mainly of predominantly rural and intermediate provinces that demonstrated stronger growth than the other grouping of such provinces. Siena avoided the marked decline in per capita income that characterised the group on average in the first years of the 1990s. In terms of the extent of income convergence over the period it is instructive to examine Siena's per capita income as a percentage of the wealthiest Italian province. In 1952, the first year for which data are available, the province's per capita income was only 43.25% of the wealthiest province, Milano. By 1995, this share had risen to 67.94% of the top province's per capita income (Bologna).

While it is evident that Siena has undergone a significant transformation in the post-war period, much of the same can be said of Italy. However, the "peripheral" status of the province within Tuscany combined with considerable difficulty in adjusting to the crisis in share-cropping in the 1950s are suggestive of a considerable

Figure 1. **Per capita income change by provincial "convergence clubs"**
1952-1995

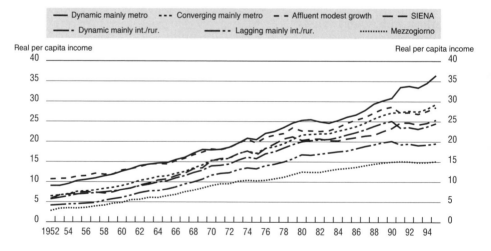

Source: Silvia Fabiani and Guido Pellegrini, 1997.

improvement in the relative status of the province that is not easily discernible from the evolution of per capita income. Examining the evolution of Siena's income rank among Italian provinces provides a clearer picture. These data demonstrate that relative status of the province has changed little over the 1952-1995 period, increasing only by 3 rungs, going from 39 to 36, or 53 to 56 in inverse rank in Figure 2 (data are limited to 92 of the 103 Italian provinces). While there is some volatility in Siena's rank throughout the study period, most notably between the mid-1970s to early 1990s, the overall trend is one of a province that has maintained a modest advantage over the average. The evolution of provincial rank in the region of Tuscany is presented in Figure 2 to provide insight regarding the relative position of Siena to its proximate neighbours. This also provides added insight into the possible interpretation that Siena benefited largely from a "rising tide". The two other predominantly rural provinces in Tuscany – Grosseto and Arezzo – provide a strong contrast. The continuous decline in rank of Grosseto cautions against a simple interpretation. Location in Tuscany was no guarantee of sustained or elevated status. However, the increasing rank of Arezzo through the period suggests that there were other progressive examples of development of predominantly rural provinces in the region. Perhaps the most striking result is the strong similarity in the rank evolution of Florence – the regional capital and centre of Tuscany – and Siena since the 1980s. These results motivate a more detailed investigation

Figure 2. **Change in Italian rank by per capita income of selected Tuscany provinces**
1952-1995

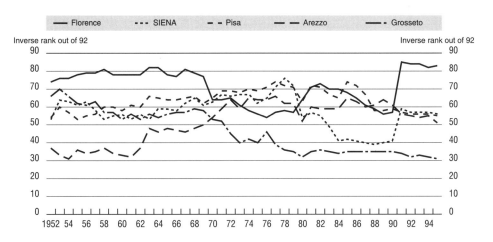

Source: Silvia Fabiani and Guido Pellegrini, 1997.

41

of both the relative status of Tuscany and a comparative analysis of the evolution of per capita income limited only to predominantly rural provinces in Italy.

Longitudinal data at the provincial level across EU countries are not available, so extending this analysis directly to a cross-national comparison is not possible. However, an analysis of data at the regional level has confirmed the ascendance of the Tuscany region in a collection of EU regions. Using the Eurostat REGIO dataset, Garmise (1994) classifies EU regions on the basis of GDP, harmonised unemployment rates and population density, and the percentage of the working population employed in agriculture, industry and services at 5 intervals between 1977 and 1990. On the basis of these attributes Tuscany begins as a member of the least favoured regional cluster in 1977 (including several southern Italian regions but also East Midlands and south-west United Kingdom), climbs into the intermediate cluster for the periods spanning 1981 to 1987 and finishes as a member of the top performing cluster in 1990. In quantitative terms, regional GDP per capita is probably the best summary measure of this performance and it is demonstrated that in 1977 Tuscany is slightly above the mean of the least favoured regions and ends in 1990 slightly below the mean of the cluster of the strongest regions (including regions such as south-east United Kingdom, Lombardy and Baden-Wurttemberg). The process of convergence demonstrated by Tuscany is a preoccupation of EU regional policy and so explanations for this performance are of considerable interest. The causative factors suggested are an economic structure based on small-firm production, supportive regional institutions that have emerged from the strong political continuity in the post-war era, and a strong civic society.

Returning to the longitudinal provincial data for Italy, it is also possible to provide some conjectures on the types of economic activities that are commonly thought to be associated with the more dynamic predominantly rural regions in the country. Figure 3 provides an illustration of the evolution of per capita income for predominantly rural Italian provinces grouped by their initial and ending income levels and the rate of growth.[2] Siena's performance closely matched the group of provinces that have had the most impressive performance, comprised of Arezzo, Belluno and Perugia. The model of development that characterises those predominantly rural provinces can be described as the combination of a strong SME sector with substantial tourism activity. These provinces have been able to improve their position relative to other Italian provinces over the 33-year period. Siena has also benefited from these same economic engines in realising a marginal increase in relative rank over the same period starting from a higher position relative to this group. But as the graph clearly demonstrates, not all predominantly rural provinces have enjoyed the same degree of success. With the exception of the Emerging group of provinces from the Mezzogiorno – beginning with very low levels of income but enjoying faster rates of growth – other provinces have either

Figure 3. **Change in per capita income for predominantly rural Italian provinces**
1952-1995

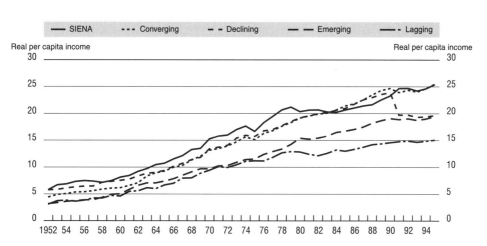

Source: Silvia Fabiani and Guido Pellegrini, 1997.

stagnated or declined. Thus, while both the Converging and Emerging groups have been able to increase their relative rank, the fall of the other provinces has outweighed this progress. The average rank of predominantly rural provinces fell from 37 (out of 92, being the highest) to 33 between 1952 and 1995. There is thus a strong motivation at the national level, and indeed throughout OECD Member countries, to arrive at a better understanding of the factors that can contribute to better performance of predominantly rural regions.

The province has also performed well with respect to employment. The statistics from Functional Labour Market Areas (LLMAs) demonstrate that the local system of Siena registered a notable growth in the rate of non-agricultural employment up to the beginning of the 1990s (Table 1). This performance outstripped growth in the national average during the 1971-1981 period, was marginally higher during the following decade when the national growth rate stagnated and fell off slightly in the 1991-1996 period when the nation recorded a modest gain. If we order all the 784 Italian local systems for the value of the employment rate, we see that Siena was 179 in 1971, 135 in 1981 and 112 in 1991, with a decline to 146 in 1996 (Table 2). This suggests that Siena is actually in a good position concerning the employment rate, thanks to its good performance during the 1971-1991 period. As will be discussed in more detail below (Box 1), the province has demonstrated employment growth performance superior to Italy.

43

Table 1. **Non-agricultural employment rate per year**

	1971	1981	1991	1996
Local system of Siena	43.6	49.4	51.0	50.4
Italy	42.0	42.9	42.9	43.1

Source: ISTAT.

Table 2. **Ranking in employment rate per year**

	1971	1981	1991	1996
Local system of Siena	179	135	112	146

Source: ISTAT.

With respect to the traditional indicators of income and employment, the province of Siena has performed admirably. However, the long-term prospects may not be as favourable if several threats to the reproducibility of the Siena model are not defused. These were outlined in the previous chapter and will be examined in more detail in this and subsequent chapters.

Functional borders of the territory and interaction

Although the northern border of the province is increasingly linked to the economic activities of the adjoining Province of Florence, Sienese society maintains a unique cultural identity within Tuscany. The annual festivals of the Palio, highlighted by a bare-back horse race around the *Piazza del Campo*, is the most concrete manifestation of this. The event, in its current format, dates back to 1656 combining a strong historical link to defiance against outside oppressors with the celebration of politics, co-operation and cunning that determines the one victor from the city's 17 neighbourhoods (*contradas*). Although the spectacle has attracted outsiders for centuries, it is regarded as an event that serves principally to reaffirm the residents' strong attachment to the territory. A more subtle manifestation of this is the high visitation rates of local residents to the various cultural attractions throughout the province. Cultural development is regarded as an essential element of Sienese identity and the museum system fills this need. As one resident put it, *"museums are much more than warehouses or hospitals for artefacts – they are critical to the unfolding cultural life of the province"*. This strong sense of local identity is an important resource for effective governance that is realised in the

Box 1. **Comparison with matched territories**

Siena is representative of a class of other rural areas in Europe that combine the seemingly contradictory attributes of reasonable access to relatively large cities[1] with a relatively low population density. Using the employment structure in agriculture, manufacturing and services as additional classification criteria, a smaller number of provinces with an even stronger similarity to Siena emerge.[2] The matched territories are listed in Table 3 along with relevant structural characteristics and recent employment performance relative to own national performance.

Table 3. **NUTS 3 level territories with a strong structural similarity to the Province of Siena**

Region name, country	% of rural population	Employment performance compared to national	Population total		Density	Employment % sector		
			Population 1995	Population 2000		Agriculture	Industry	Services
Ardennes, France	55.9	Lagging	293 100	290 900	55.6	7.3	32.8	60.0
Charente, France	59.9	Leading	341 100	339 900	57.1	10.2	32.3	57.5
Drôme, France	53.7	Lagging	428 400	436 500	66.8	7.0	29.0	64.0
Saône-et-Loire, France	60.2	Leading	552 500	546 500	63.7	7.6	32.8	59.6
Tarn, France	60.6	Lagging	341 900	343 000	59.6	9.0	26.3	64.7
Vienne, France	65.3	Leading	392 900	398 500	57.0	6.9	26.5	66.5
Isernia, Italy	65.3	Lagging	92 300	91 900	60.1	13.9	28.3	57.8
Rieti, Italy	56.9	Leading	150 100	150 600	54.8	12.3	24.0	63.7
Siena, Italy	53.9	Leading	251 200	252 000	65.9	7.8	27.8	64.3

Source: Territorial Indicators Database, TDS.

The matching exercise produces some interesting results. All of the comparison provinces are in France and Italy despite the fact that all NUTS 3 areas in European OECD countries were included in the comparison algorithm. More curious is the tendency for the algorithm to identify a number of provinces or départements that have developed a reputation for the production of world class wines or spirits: Cognac from Charente, Burgundies from Saône-et-Loire, and several rising stars from the Côtes-du-Rhône villages' appellations are from the Drôme. The tendency for clustering algorithms to generate detailed associations from a relatively simple set of structural characteristics is suggestive of their power to quickly identify productive comparison candidates.

It is notable that the recent performance of structurally similar regions demonstrates considerable divergence in their ability to generate employment relative to national performance. Possible explanations for this variation can lend considerable

45

Box 1. **Comparison with matched territories** (*cont.*)

insight to the critical factors of growth given the strong similarity in structural character-istics. The broad characteristics of structure used to match these provinces could mask significant differences at a more disaggregate level. Unfortunately, limited data avail-ability at the NUTS 3 level do not allow a rigorous test of this hypothesis. Qualitative information indicates that several of the leading regions are home to technologically dynamic sectors such as the multimedia sector connected with Futuroscope in Vienne, contract manufacturing of advanced electronics in Rieti or the expertise in plastics, imagery and mechanical engineering in Saône-et-Loire. But significant high technology activity in the Drôme has not resulted in employment performance superior to the nation.[3]

The value and density of cultural and natural amenities are characteristics that immediately come to mind in any comparison with Siena, and are not represented in the matching criteria. Siena is arguably the only province widely recognised interna-tionally as a tourist destination in the group and this is an obvious contributor to recent employment performance. To get a general impression of the attractiveness of the comparison areas to tourism the classification from the Michelin Green Guides are used (Table 4). There is a consistent association between the relative attractiveness of an area and its employment performance. In the four most attractive provinces or départements, only one area had employment performance lagging behind national performance. In contrast, three of the five at the lower half of the ranking were charac-terised by lagging employment performance.

Table 4. **The attractiveness of the matched territories to tourism**

Province/département	Number of sites worth a trip ***	Number of sites meriting a detour **	Number of interesting sites *	Employment performance
Siena, Italy	2	3	1	Leading
Tarn, France	2	0	1	Lagging
Vienne, France	1	2	0	Leading
Saône-et-Loire, France	0	3	1	Leading
Charente, France	0	1	0	Leading
Drôme, France	0	1	0	Lagging
Ardennes, France	0	0	1	Lagging
Rieti, Italy	0	0	1	Leading
Isernia, Italy	0	0	0	Lagging

Siena: *** Siena and San Gimignano; ** Montelpuciano, Pienza, Monte Oliveto Maggiore; * Chiusi;
Tarn:*** Albi, Cordes-sur-Ciel; * Castres;
Vienne: *** Futuroscope; ** Poitiers, St-Savin;
Saône-et-Loire: ** Cluny, Cormatin, Tournus; * Chalon-sur-Saône;
Charente: ** Angoulême;
Drôme: ** Grignan;
Ardennes: * Charleville;
Rieti: * Greccio.
Source: *Le Guide Vert: Italie* and *Le Guide Vert: France*, Michelin Editions des Voyages.

Box 1. **Comparison with matched territories** (*cont.*)

The wide variability in performance identified in past empirical research suggests that growth in predominantly rural regions may be more dependent on leadership capability and institutions that assist in the co-ordination of economic objectives and interests. Unfortunately, this hypothesis is the most difficult to assess in quantitative terms and thus additional insight may benefit most from the systematic selection of cases for more in-depth qualitative analysis. While beyond the scope of the current review, the potential value of this approach is demonstrated by the coincident parallel review of the Champagne-Ardenne region in France and the selection of the Ardennes département by the matching algorithm as structurally similar to Siena (OECD 2002). That review identifies three critical deficiencies in the region that need to be addressed: a weak sense of regional identity that lacks a focussed vision of development; the external orientation of many interests that often fail to co-ordinate mutual internal interests; and a civil society lacking dynamism that, among other consequences, has been unable to valorise an otherwise rich endowment of natural and cultural amenities. The reviews of Siena and Champagne-Ardenne are not directly comparable as the former examines a predominantly rural province while the latter is concerned with territorial development in an intermediate region that includes predominantly rural *départements*, including the Ardennes. Nevertheless, the detailed information available to compare a leading area and a lagging area is consonant with the hypothesis that the capacity of local government and civil society are critical to the economic performance of regions.

1. Less than two hours travel time to a city of 350 000 or a city with an international airport. See Irmen, *et al.* (2001).
2. See Isserman and Merrifield (1987) who use cluster algorithms to select counties that are statistically close to each other to construct quasi-experiments of policy initiatives.
3. Comparable data by detailed industries could go a long way in identifying possible engines of economic growth in predominantly rural areas. See Wojan and Pulver (1995).

common observation that consultation has become an instinctual component of public decision making in the province. Travel through the province will confirm its well-identifiable constituent parts (Val d'Elsa, Val di Merse, Chianti Senese, Siena and the Masse, the Crete, Val d'Orcias, Val di Chiana and Monte Amiata). But this differentiation is set against a strongly homogeneous background that has united the territories and the towns presently forming part of the province since the Middle Ages, and owing to the concentration of cultural, architectural and environmental assets which cause the Sienese territory to stand out from surrounding ones. This strong sense of identity, however, can interfere with efforts at horizontal co-operation, especially among municipalities bordering surrounding provinces, as these efforts have at times been perceived as affronts to the provincial administration.

Siena's projection into the wider economy ranges from its international standing as a city of culture and as the origin of some of the world's finest wines, to its national reputation with respect to financial services, university education and Information Society initiatives. The most striking feature of these various capabilities is the link between strong historical roots and the willingness to innovate. Siena's allure as a destination for cultural tourism has been enhanced by the creation of the Sienese Museum System in 1990, discussed further below. The history of fine wine in the province predates many of these cultural endowments, but it has only been in the last two decades that select wines from Tuscany are considered among the best in the world. This too has been based on a willingness to innovate that has produced the anomalous result that several of the best wines have one of the wine sector's least stringent classifications (IGT Toscana). The use of this classification has given their winemakers much greater flexibility in the selection of grape varietals and production techniques relative to the more stringent DOC and DOCG classifications. Other industrial sectors that have a strong export orientation include crystal, motor caravans and pharmaceuticals. It is estimated that the Colle val d'Elsa area produces 95% of Italian crystal objects thus comprising the bulk of Italy's 5% share of total world production. Great Britain, Germany, the United States, Japan and Australia alone account for 55% of the sector's exports. The highest concentration of Italian motor caravan production is located in the area around Poggibonsi and the neighbouring municipality of Barberino (in the Province of Florence), producing 80% of the vehicles made in Italy. This includes major national and international companies such as Caravan Internationals, Laika and Mobilvetta. The pharmaceutical sector has benefited from Siena's long history of research and production in the medical field. At present, research units of the highest level are active in the Sienese area as well as production units for the German based Bayer company and the California based Chiron company, working in the fields of immunological and biotechnological research. These companies have also established scientific and technological research projects in collaboration with departments at the University of Siena (Box 2).

Despite the presence of sometimes high profile export specialisations the relative levels of export activity are lower than in northern Italy. Indeed, export activity in Siena is also lower than in Tuscany as a whole. Quantitatively, the low relative export levels indicate the limited international projection of Sienese industry. Another indicator confirms this finding: the capacity to make or receive investments in or from foreign countries. Table 5 allows comparing the "propensity for internationalisation" among Italian provinces, the index rising with greater investment in or from foreign countries relative to the local industrial base. This

Box 2. **An example of excellence**

Chiron Spa was set up in 1992 through the merger between the Vaccine Department of Sclavo and one of the world's leading biotechnology companies, the Californian Chiron Corporation.

The Istituto Sieroterapico e Vaccinogeno Toscano Sclavo (Toscano Sclavo Serotherapeutical and Vaccinogene Institute), with its seat in Siena, was founded by Achille Sclavo in 1904 and acquired an international importance in 1963, when Albert Sabin, who was the inventor of the vaccine against poliomyelitis, chose exactly Sclavo as the world producer for his vaccine.

In its seats of Siena and of Rosia, the company employs approximately 800 persons, 110 of which work as researchers.

The Chiron Research Centre of Siena is in the world's lead for the study of new vaccines: it set up the first acellular against pertussis by using genetic engineering techniques.

In 2001, the budget of the Vaccine Department of Siena was increased up to ITL 25 billion only in the sector of Basic and Applied Research, therefore the personnel has been augmented: the staff (researchers, graduate students and scholarship holders) has changed from 60 to 110 persons in the last two years.

There is a close relationship between the University of Siena, which organised a Research Doctorate in Biotechnologies within the Department of Molecular Biology, and the biotechnological research companies having their seat in Siena. For example, the Department of Biological Chemistry at Torre Fiorentina, within Chiron Spa structure, offers the students the chance to carry out their vocational training within an industrial framework.

Such research frameworks that are connected to the university could be easily given a substantial boost and increase the attraction level for further parallel activities, by exploiting also the telematic network that is going to link the whole town of Siena.

In fact, the primary aim of the telematic project is to be able to place the collaboration among research centres on the Web also as an element of attraction for new structures and initiatives.

highlights clearly the relationship between local production forces and export intensity or the intensity of investment operations in or from foreign countries. Provinces in the north of Italy tend to have high positive values; the centre of Italy has intermediate values and the south has values that are decidedly below the average. The Province of Siena is in perfect line with these trends. It has a modest rate of industrialisation, modest export levels and a modest capacity to make investments in or receive investments from foreign countries.

49

Table 5. **Propensity to internationalisation of provinces of Italy**

North-west	1.39	North-east	2.47	Centre	-2.51	South and Islands	-3.64		-3.64
Torino	2.15	Bolzano	2.77	Florence	-1.56	Pescara	-2.83	Palermo	-4.13
Alessandria	3.43	Trento	-0.45	Arezzo	-1.92	L'Aquila	-5.20	Agrigento	-4.18
Asti	-2.85			Grosseto	-4.95	Chieti	-3.39	Caltanis- setta	-4.40
Cuneo	5.93	Bologna	-0.49	Livorno	-2.74	Teramo	-2.51	Catania	-4.80
Novara	-1.46	Ferrara	-1.48	Lucca	-4.90			Enna	-4.12
Vercelli	3.89	Forlì	3.15	Massa Carrara	-2.95	Campo- basso	-4.25	Messina	-4.59
		Modena	5.78	Pisa	-2.15	Isemia	-4.07	Ragusa	-4.28
Aosta	-4.58	Piacenza	5.60	Pistoia	-3.60			Siracusa	-4.59
		Parma	0.26	Siena	-3.34	Napoli	-2.13	Trapani	-3.20
Milan	2.25	Ravenna	-2.16			Avellino	-3.04		
Bergamo	0.39	Reggio Emilia	1.03	Perugia	0.33	Benevento	-4.26	Cagliari	-5.01
Brescia	1.87			Terni	-4.87	Caserta	-3.50	Nuoro	-0.78
Como	1.85	Udine	2.61			Salerno	-4.55	Oristano	-4.90
Cremona	11.02	Gorizia	-5.73	Ancona	1.31			Sassari	-4.94
Mantova	1.20	Pordenone	4.53	Ascoli Piceno	1.29	Bari	-1.64		
Pavia	-1.45	Trieste	4.81	Macerata	-3.94	Brindisi	-1.07		
Sondrio	14.98			Pesaro	0.70	Foggia	-2.56		
Varese	-1.65	Venice	-1.71			Lecce	-4.02		
		Belluno	2.25	Rome	-1.42	Taranto	-1.97		
Genova	0.57	Padova	5.46	Frosinone	-3.34				
Imperia	-5.20	Rovigo	13.78	Latina	-5.11	Potenza	-2.36		
La Spezia	-5.81	Treviso	5.09	Rieti	-5.08	Matera	-4.88		
Savona	1.20	Vicenza	0.15	Viterbo	-2.06				
		Verona	6.62			Reggio Calabria	-4.13		
						Cosenza	-3.09		
						Catanzaro	-4.23		

Source: CNEL, Italia Multinazionale, 1998.

At the national level, Siena has been identified as a leader in Information Society initiatives. The "Siena Città Cablata" (Siena – the Wired City) project is the result of close co-operation between Siena City Council, Monte dei Paschi di Siena and Telecom Italia. Work began back in 1991 and the project is now entering the fully operational phase with the promise of connecting 16 000 of the 22 000 families living within the Commune of Siena. The main technological benefit will come from bi-directional broadband that will make possible numerous interactive services and high-speed Internet connection. Some of the capabilities that have already been realised include a services centre providing access to council services of the Commune of Siena and distribution and use of Siena Card: a smart card that gives unified access to a whole range of personal and administrative services. The card serves as an ID-access key to all the Net-linked administrative, health and financial services: council administration, hospital services, other local health authority services, council finance offices, education office. Enlisting the capabilities of the University of Siena, the newly-created Multimedia Academy, numerous specialised companies both in Siena and internationally, Siena Città Cablata will lay the foundation for a range of innovative services, enhancing consumer choice, citizen involvement and productive capability. Perhaps the most novel initiatives are those envisioning applications of "new economy" capabilities in art cities.

Transportation policy at both the regional and national levels has largely bypassed the province, contributing both to the preservation of an idyllic landscape and to additional costs of limited accessibility. The possible causative effects of infrastructure policy on the development trajectory are clearly debatable but the undeniable fact is that the Province of Siena is not centrally integrated in Italian transportation networks. On the one hand, this has created quite considerable logistics problems (it has certainly slowed down industrial growth processes), but on the other hand it has contributed to maintaining one of the most beautiful and integral agricultural landscapes in Italy. At the present time, the major transport routes that serve the Province of Siena form an "H" (Figure 4). The eastern North-South Axis is constituted by the Rome-Florence infrastructural corridor (motorway and two railway lines, express and "slow"), and the western North-South Axis by the Siena-Grosseto section of the "Due Mari" highway (southwards from Siena) and the Siena-Florence highway (known as the "Autopalio") running northwards. The East-West Axis joining these two (intersecting the eastern North-South Axis at the "Val di Chiana" motorway tollgate) consists of the Siena-Bettolle section of the "Due Mari" highway, which connects Grosseto with Fano.

The railway system consists mainly of minor lines with relatively long travel times. On the Siena-Empoli-Florence line, there are 19 couples of trains per day, although only 11 are through trains, as at Empoli the line is linked to the Florence-Pisa line; therefore, on 8 rail links per day one has to change trains. The travelling

Figure 4.   **Siena road network**

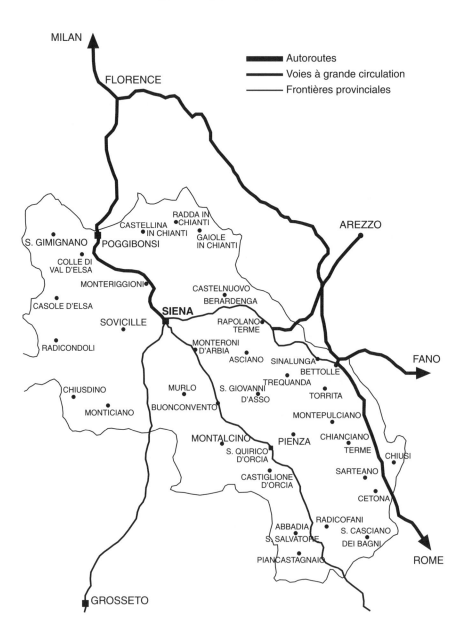

times vary from 1 hour and 30 minutes to 1 hour and 50 minutes. On the Siena-Asciano-Chiusi-Chianciano Terme line, there are 22 couples of trains per day. The travelling time is approximately 1 hour and 30 minutes. This is a very important line as it connects Siena to the main Italian rail link between the south and the north. The network is completed by the Siena-Grosseto line with 8 couples of trains per day and an average travelling time of 1 hour and 30 minutes. The most important railway line, which marginally touches the Province of Siena, is the Florence-Rome line that is one of the leading lines in Italy. The station of Chiusi-Chianciano Terme is the only station of the Florence-Rome line within the Province of Siena. Every day, 10 couples of intercity trains going from north to south and approximately 21 couples of other trains (fast, regional, express trains, etc.) stop at the station of Chiusi. At present, the "Eurostar" fast service affects Chiusi station only marginally; from the north there is only one specific train departing from Florence, from the south there are three links: in the morning departing from Chiusi and leading to Milan, as a stage of the Rome-Perugia train and one on the Naples-Milan line.

Concerning intermodal logistics and goods traffic, construction of an intermodal centre at Chiusi station is planned, as well as two small goods stations (at Isola d'Arbia and Poggibonsi/Barberino Val d'Elsa). There is also a small airport in the province (Ampugnano), used solely for a limited amount of cargo transport. It has no facilities for passenger transport, and does not plan to develop any. It is to be stressed that the apparently fragile transport system in the Province of Siena today represents a positive balance between logistics requirements and the need not to violate a territory of rare beauty with infrastructures having a strong impact on the landscape, while in any case they would be under-used because of the low density of the centres. In this sense the provincial transport policies are well oriented towards strengthening public transport (for example, a considerable amount of commuter traffic is generated by the Municipality of Siena) rather than towards increasing the infrastructures.

Geographic distribution of resources

Settlement patterns

The Province of Siena lies on the periphery of the main urban and metropolitan systems. On a map of the urban and metropolitan systems in Italy, the Siena area appears to be a transitional one between the peripheral extensions of the Florentine multi-metropolitan system (Florence, Prato and Pistoia), to the north, and an area of scattered, fragmented settlements, to the south as illustrated in Figure 5.

53

Figure 5. **Functional Italian settlement pattern**

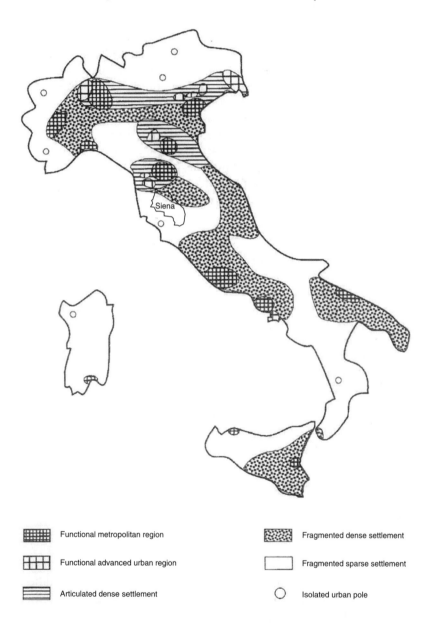

Functional metropolitan region		Fragmented dense settlement	
Functional advanced urban region		Fragmented sparse settlement	
Articulated dense settlement		Isolated urban pole	

The Tuscan region presents from the point of view of settlements a clear distinction between the northern part and the central-southern part, to which the Sienese territory belongs. The densely populated settlements are concentrated in the northern part, starting from the Florentine metropolitan area (Florence, Prato and Pistoia). These settlements then spread out westwards towards the sea over a large territory, from Lucca, Empoli and Pisa to Leghorn. Towards the south and east the settlements become more scattered and are of a linear type. A linear settlement can be seen south-west of Florence to Arezzo and a linear settlement south of Empoli towards Siena. In actual fact, the southern linear settlement only slightly penetrates the Sienese Province and mainly concerns only the northernmost territory called the Upper Val d'Elsa, in which the urban conglomerations of Poggibonsi and Colle stand out. South of the Upper Val d'Elsa you find the relatively isolated urban site of Siena, and the structure of settlement becomes decidedly more sparse, surrounded by a predominantly hilly countryside, with furrows spreading out in various directions following the valleys of the rivers.

Two further significant elements in the formation of the sparsely urbanised countryside should be noted. Between the linear directions from Empoli to Poggibonsi and from Florence to Arezzo, one can find the hills of Chianti, an area that belongs partly to the Province of Florence and partly to that of Siena. South of the Sienese Province there is the mountainous area of Mount Amiata, which also partly falls within the Province of Grosseto. How the settlements become increasingly more scattered can clearly be seen in Figure 6, which shows the distribution of urban centres and nuclei in the Province of Siena.

The Province of Siena covers an area of 3 821 km^2, which is larger than the average Italian province, of less than 3 000 km^2. The population today is about 252 000 inhabitants. In 1951 it was slightly over 277 000 inhabitants and gradually dropped off until the beginning of the 1970s (255 000). That Siena lies on the periphery of the Tuscan urban/metropolitan area is reflected in the difference in the density of population: 66 inhabitants per km^2 compared to 153. The Italian average is even greater: 191 inhabitants per km^2. The dispersion of the population in small settlements throughout the province is also suggested by the small share of population living in the City of Siena, the provincial capital. Only 27.3% of the province's inhabitants live in the city. The corresponding average for the whole of Tuscany is 55.4, and the Italian average is 42.9. It is important to note that the Sienese territory does not correspond to other models of settlement that typify northern Italy or Tuscany. In the former case the average size of the capital towns of the province do not account for a high share of the provincial population since they are surrounded by other fairly large urban centres, within networks of settlements that are particularly dense and distributed throughout the territory. In the Tuscan case, there are no very large cities and the capital cities of the province

Figure 6. **Urban centres and settlement areas in the Province of Siena**

account for a relatively high share of the provincial population. This contrasts with the settlement pattern in Siena where low population density is mated to a small capital city.

Within the limits of the scarce density of settlement, the extent of urbanisation, and more recently some incipient phenomena of urban decentralisation, can be assessed by examining population trends in the inhabited centres (not the perimeters of boroughs) (Table 6). From 1951 to 1971, the main urban centres in the province took in a large number of inhabitants: Siena grew from 40 000 to 57 000 inhabitants; in the Upper Val d'Elsa, Poggibonsi and Colle grew from 14 000 to 32 000. This phenomenon was also reflected on the same level in the south-west, for example in the centres of Torrita-Sinelunga (from nearly 4 000 to almost 8 000)

Table 6. **Population trends in municipalities in the Province of Siena**

	Population 1991	Population 1971	Population 1951	Percentage change 1991-1951	Percentage change 1991-1971	Percentage change 1971-1951
Provincial total	251 349	255 201	277 437	-9.40	-1.5	-8.0
Concentrated population	209 222	195 681	140 598	48.8	6.9	39.2
% concentrated	83.24	76.68	50.68			
% dispersed	16.76	23.32	49.32			
Centre Commune						
Siena	51 086	56 801	40 121	27.3	-10.1	41.6
Poggibonsi	21 263	21 024	7 236	193.9	1.1	190.6
Colle V. d'E.	13 021	10 730	6 627	96.5	21.4	61.9
Abbadia	7 067	8 257	5 956	18.7	-14.4	38.6
Chiusi	6 572	6 068	4 463	47.3	8.3	36.0
Chianciano	6 287	5 406	2 758	128.0	16.3	96.0
Sinalunga	5 869	4 897	1 976	197.0	19.9	147.8
Torrita	4 978	3 868	1 817	174.0	28.7	112.9
Total c.1 8	116 143	117 051	70 954	63.7	-0.8	65.0
% provincial population	46.21	45.87	25.57			
Montepulciano	3 955	4 277	3 288	20.3	-7.5	30.1
Monteroni	3 830	2 252	835	358.7	70.1	169.1
S. Gimignano	3 762	4 010	3 616	4.0	-6.2	10.9
Sarteano	3 705	2 699	1 994	85.8	37.3	35.4
Asciano	3 627	3 335	2 258	60.6	8.8	47.7
Piancastagnaio	3 212	3 336	3 260	-1.5	-3.7	2.3
Rapolano	2 941	2 516	1 578	86.4	16.9	59.4
Buonconvento	2 584	1 981	1 434	80.2	30.4	38.2
Sinalunga	2 315	1 941	1 169	98.0	19.3	66.0
Sovicille	2 295	850	280	719.6	170.0	203.6
S. Quirico	2 120	1 749	1 187	78.6	21.2	47.4
Montalcino	2 091	2 357	2 766	-24.4	-11.3	-14.8
Total c.II 13	36 437	31 303	23 665	54.0	16.4	32.3
% population > 2000	60.70	58.13	34.10			

Table 6. **Population trends in municipalities in the Province of Siena** (cont.)

		Population 1991	Population 1971	Population 1951	Percentage change 1991-1951	Percentage change 1991-1971	Percentage change 1971-1951
Staggia	Poggibonsi	1 822	1 078	968	88.2	69.0	11.4
Rosia	Sovicille	1 747	1 157	808	116.2	51.0	43.2
Castellina Scalo	Montereggioni	1 428	1 126	516	176.7	26.8	118.2
Stazione Montelp.	Montelpulciano	1 411	1 160	555	154.2	21.6	109.0
Serre	Rapolano	1 410	1 403	922	52.9	0.5	52.2
Belverde	Montereggioni	1 404	601	38	3 594.7	133.6	1 481.6
Pienza	Pienza	1 363	1 493	1 327	2.7	-8.7	12.5
Acquaviva	Montepulciano	1 356	1 290	1 028	31.9	5.1	25.5
Castelnuovo B.	Castelnuovo B.	1 350	981	1 023	32.0	37.6	-4.1
Centona	Cetona	1 341	1 272	1 508	-11.1	5.4	-15.7
Arbia	Asciano	1 305	393	336	288.4	232.1	17.0
Taverne d'Arbia	Siena	1 288	535	422	205.2	140.8	26.8
Castellina	Castellina	1 170	1 116	784	49.2	4.8	42.4
Torrenieri	Montalcino	1 154	1 137	1 100	4.9	1.5	3.4
Bellavista	Poggibonsi	1 123	151	85	1 221.2	643.7	77.7
Abbadia	Montepulciano	1 070	802	694	54.2	33.4	15.6
S. Martino- Tognaz	Montereggioni	1 053	473	30	3 410.0	122.6	1 476.7
Radda	Radda	1 013	554	556	82.2	82.9	-0.4
Total c.III	18	23 808	16 722	12 700	87.5	42.4	31.7
Ponte a Tressa	Monteroni	975	495	450	116.7	97.0	10.0
S. Albino	Montepulciano	971	481	116	737.1	101.9	31 466.0
Quercegrossa	Castelnuovo B.	937	292	137	583.9	220.9	113.1
Casole	Casole	911	903	930	-2.0	0.9	-2.9
Gaiole	Gaiole	899	747	702	28.1	20.4	6.4
Monticiano	Monticiano	811	984	1 001	-19.0	-17.6	-1.7
Guazzino	Sinalunga	775	778	117	562.4	-0.4	565.0

Source: Documents of the Administration of Province of Siena.

or Chianciano-Chiusi (from 7 000 to 11 500), and so on, even in smaller centres. In short, there was a certain regularity in the growth of agglomerations. In the following twenty years (1971-1991), along with the contrary tendency towards migration beyond the confines of the province, this phenomenon of centralisation slowed down noticeably. The urban centre of Siena even lost inhabitants. In actual fact, the phenomena of centralisation continued, but was interwoven with suburbanisation and partly masked by a clear drop in the birth rate. Hence, in the 1990s these phenomena could not be considered from the point of view of single urban centres. Since the urban effect began to go beyond the confines of the municipalities, it is useful to look at a wider aggregation of the territory, represented by the Local Economic Systems (LES)[3] in Figure 7. Population growth within these functional areas is examined in the next section.

Figure 7. **Local Economic Systems in the Province of Siena**

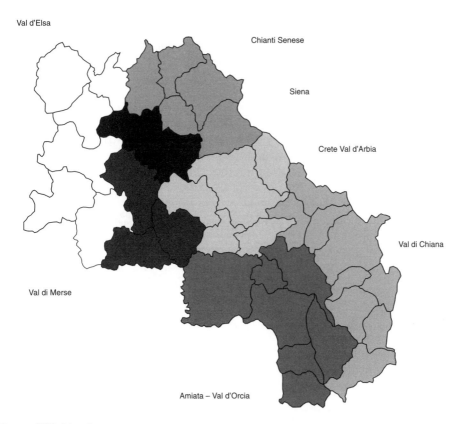

Source: SMP elaboration.

Population: *migration and natural balance*

As an alternative to the model of industrialisation that affected the northern part of Tuscany, the substantial environmental, historical, cultural and landscape resources presented considerable opportunity. One of the fundamental movers has been high-quality Italian and foreign tourism interested in the artistic and landscape values. At the same time, the Sienese territory has attracted many outsiders, who have restored abandoned farmhouses and in some instances entire villages to use them as holiday houses or to start agri-tourist activities. This positive, albeit modest, impact on in-migration combined with much greater economic opportunities have reversed the earlier pattern of outmigration in the 1970s. The stability of the population has been maintained however by a natural balance that has become increasingly more negative. In addition, the apparent stability at the provincial level is the result of considerable variation across Local Economic Systems (Table 7). The Val d'Elsa, affected by the relationship with the nearby metropolitan area, has continued to increase in population. The Municipality of Siena continues to suffer from a drop in population, but is, in fact, the driving force behind the growth in Chianti, in the Val di Merse and in the Crete, since the fast developing centres here are nothing but an extension of the Sienese urban system. All the other areas have witnessed a drop in population, mainly caused by the effect of natural balance.

The low fertility rate raises considerable uncertainty regarding the province's ability to stabilise the increasing share of elderly in its population. In this instance, the potential difficulty is not caused by the ruralness of the province *per se* but appears to be a phenomenon that characterises all of central and many

Table 7. **Population by homogeneous areas, Province of Siena**
1985-1998

	1985	1991	1993	1995	1996	1997	1998	Percentage change 1985 to 1998
Val d'Orcia e Amiata	26 505	25 591	25 463	25 227	25 099	24 964	24 879	−6.1
Crete senesi e Val d'Arbia	22 804	23 093	23 201	23 347	23 413	23 411	23 442	2.8
Val d'Elsa	60 733	61 094	61 776	62 646	63 345	63 828	64 263	5.8
Chianti	12 307	12 766	13 200	13 510	13 695	13 774	13 873	12.7
Val di Merse	12 408	12 799	13 002	13 160	13 195	13 264	13 458	8.5
Val di Chiana	58 808	58 441	58 480	58 215	58 105	57 983	57 170	−1.9
Siena	60 192	56 956	56 518	55 090	54 931	54 668	54 435	−9.6
Province of Siena	253 757	250 740	251 640	251 195	251 783	251 892	252 069	−0.7

Source: Administration of Province of Siena, Statistic Report.

parts of northern Italy. Although the socio-economic factors contributing to this phenomenon are complex, its localisation in contiguous parts of Tuscany, Emilio-Romagnia, Lombardy and Liguria are suggestive of a strong cultural factor. These regions have the lowest rate of reproduction in all of Europe with fertility indices (number of children per woman) ranging from only 0.8 to 1.2 (Grasland, n.d.). While most areas of Western Europe fail to reach a fertility index greater than 2 required of a positive natural balance, the very low rate in central Italy will accelerate the concentration of population in the elderly segment of the age distribution. Indeed, comparative data (Table 8) confirm that this process has already resulted in the Province of Siena having the highest ratio of population over 65 to total population in all of Italy. And while the causes do not necessarily have a rural origin, the effects of this process on rural areas may be more pronounced. First, the urban/rural nature of the Sienese

Table 8. **Age structure in Italian regions**
1998

1998	% 0-14	% 15-64	Ageing index (> 65/total population)
Piedmont	11.9	68	20.1
Valle d'Aosta	12.6	69.1	18.5
Liguria	10.3	65.1	24.4
Lombardy	13.0	70.0	17.2
North-west	12.4	68.9	18.8
Trentino Alto Adige	15.9	67.9	16.5
Veneto	13.3	69.4	17.5
Friuli Venezia Giulia	11.1	67.9	21.0
Emilia Romagna	11.1	67.2	21.9
North-east	12.4	68.3	19.5
Marche	12.9	66.2	21.1
Siena	11.0	64.3	24.7
Tuscany	11.5	66.8	21.7
Umbria	12.3	65.8	22.0
Lazio	14.2	69.1	16.8
Centre	13.0	67.8	19.5
Campania	19.5	67.1	13.4
Abruzzo	14.6	66.0	19.5
Molise	14.9	64.8	20.1
Puglia	17.5	67.7	14.7
Basilicata	16.6	65.9	17.3
Calabria	17.7	66.1	16.0
South	18.0	66.9	15.0
Sicily	18.3	65.8	15.8
Sardegna	14.8	70.0	15.0
Isole	17.4	66.8	15.6
Italy	14.5	67.8	17.7

Source: ISTAT.

61

territory with widespread existence of smaller centres means that local service provision will be hampered by a lack of technical economies of scale. This poses widespread problems to the upkeep of the preservation of the land and its cultural heritage, which directly or indirectly supports all the Sienese economy. Second, it signifies that there are no powerful forces in the transformation of the structure of the population through migration.

The eventual countervailing effects of positive migration flows on negative natural balance are illustrated in Figure 8. Until 1971 the natural balance was positive but was insufficient to compensate for the negative migration flow leading to population declines. From 1971 to 1996 natural balance became increasingly negative but during this period was counterbalanced by a positive flow of migration that has stabilised the resident population numbers after 1991.

The effect of these two components on population decline and growth are best illustrated in Figure 9.

A graph of the fertility rate by age for the Region of Tuscany provides some hints as to the socio-economic factors underlying the fall in the birth rate (Figure 10). The graph presents the number of births for every 1 000 women by the

Figure 8. **Contributions to population growth and decline in the Province of Siena**
1951-1996

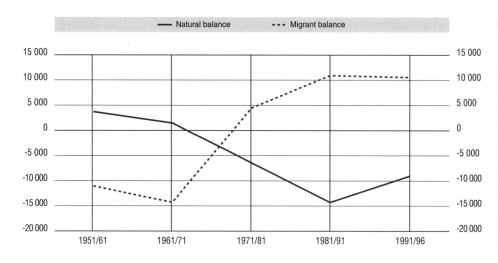

Source: SMP elaboration of ISTAT data.

Figure 9.   **Population trends of Siena**
1951-1996

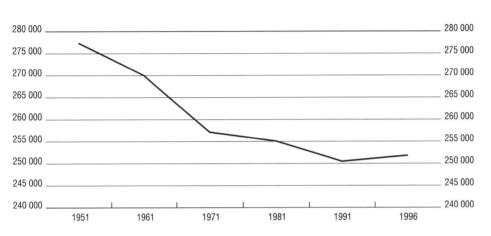

Source: SMP elaboration of ISTAT data.

age of reproduction (from < 16 to 50). The examined period is from 1952 to 1993. From 1975 to the end of the period, the share of births by women 25 or younger fell from more than three-fifths to less than one-third. This is a clear indication of the general trend to devote a much larger share of these traditional child-bearing years to greater investments in education. The impact of this on the fertility rate is great however, as the decision for deferral in the earlier years is not compensated by significant increases in fertility in older cohorts. Instead there is a reduction in births in most age groups with the only consistent enlargement found in the oldest age cohorts from 40 to 50, albeit starting from very small bases. The overall result is a birth rate that has fallen by 40% in less than 20 years.

As is evident in the comparative Italian data above, a generation marked by a continual decline in the birth rate is already expressed in the current age structure that is skewed to the more elderly age groups. For the Province of Siena the share of the population 14 or below, 15 to 64 and 65 or older are 11.0%, 64.3%, 24.7%, respectively. Again examining statistics based on the Local Economic Systems, we see that the Municipality of Siena makes a substantial contribution to the large proportion of elderly in the age structure in which the 0-14 age group makes up only 9.2%, while those over 65 years of age constitute 26.4% of the population (Table 9). The youngest structure in the province, while still within the average level in Tuscany, is that in Val d'Elsa, as it has more industries. The data concerning the ageing of the population have, therefore, to be added to those on the low density

Figure 10. **Fecundity rate trends in Tuscany**
1952-1993

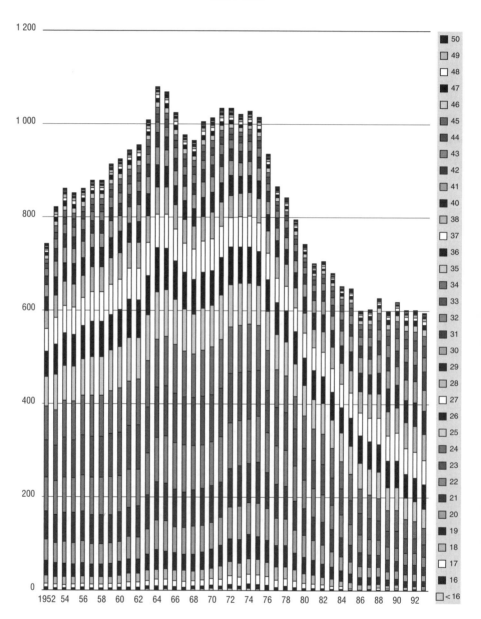

Source: SMP elaboration of ISTAT data.

Table 9.   **Age structure, dependency ratio, fertility and gender balance,
Province of Siena**
1999

	% population 0-14	% population > 65	> 65/ >14	% fertile women	Female ratio (100 = male/ female equal)
Val d'Orcia e Amiata	10.2	27.4	268.6	41.3	106.9
Crete Senesi e Val d'Arbia	11.1	24.6	222.2	43.9	101.3
Val d'Elsa	12.1	21.4	176.4	45.7	101.3
Chianti	12.1	23.5	194.6	45.8	100.0
Val di Merse	10.7	26.7	248.8	42.6	103.1
Val di Chiana	11.0	25.3	229.9	42.7	108.0
Siena	9.2	26.4	286.4	40.4	115.5
Province of Siena	10.9	24.7	226.7	43.1	106.3

Source: Administration of Province of Siena, Statistic Report.

of population and the fragmented settlement pattern characterising much of the province. This will exacerbate the negative effects of the phenomenon that may be mitigated in urban/metropolitan areas by higher rates of international and domestic immigration and greater economies of scale in service provision.

An emerging issue in the history of the province is the growing number of non-EU immigrants that introduce new challenges of social cohesion along with new opportunities of greater diversity. The migratory flows are driven by the possibility of employment in jobs that are difficult to fill with resident employment. This situation has more recently been exacerbated by labour shortages more generally. Statistics on the informal economy in the province compiled by IRPET (Istituto Regionale per la Programmazione Economica della Toscana – Regional Economic Planning Institute), estimate that 13% of all workers were irregular and 3.8% were irregular immigrant workers in 1997. These data suggest a greater dependence on this source of labour than for the Region of Tuscany as a whole as shown in Table 10.

Much of this employment is concentrated in the construction sector, hotels and restaurants and services for households (Table 11). These same sectors are likely to find it increasingly difficult to meet labour demands in a period of relative labour scarcity.

In addition to meeting current labour needs these migratory flows are also seen as contributing to the re-balancing of the age structure. Unfortunately, the

Table 10.   **Worker status for the Province of Siena and Region of Tuscany, 1997**

Per cent

	Siena	Tuscany
Regular workers	73.4	76.1
Irregular workers	12.7	11.8
Double workers	9.7	8.4
Not declared	0.4	0.5
Non-resident foreigner	3.8	3.3
Total	100.0	100.0

Note: With regular employment contract.
Source: Irpet, 2000.

Table 11.   **Irregular and non-resident foreign worker employment by sector, Province of Siena and Region of Tuscany, 1997**

Per cent

	Siena		Tuscany	
	Irregular workers	Non-resident foreigners	Irregular workers	Non-resident foreigners
Agriculture	23.7	2.4	17.3	2.9
Heavy industry	16.1	0.0	10.6	0.0
Metal and mechanical	13.2	1.9	12.9	1.2
Agrofood	11.8	0.0	13.1	0.0
Construction	17.2	11.7	20.0	9.0
Trade	15.8	5.5	13.5	3.8
Hotels and restaurants	8.5	7.8	9.2	9.6
Transports and communications	8.6	0.9	8.2	1.3
Services for enterprises	9.9	1.1	12.9	1.2
Services for households	11.4	9.4	12.9	8.7
Public services	0.0	0.0	0.0	0.0
Total	12.7	3.8	11.8	3.3

Source: Irpet, 2000.

capacity of migration to moderate the effects of population ageing is limited and accompanied by several complicating issues (OECD, 2000b). The anticipated improvement in population dynamics, given the typically higher rate of fertility of immigrants relative to residents, is considerably weakened by additions to the middle of the age distribution. Given the implementation and ethical difficulties attached to controlling the age-structure of migratory flows, immigration is a highly imperfect instrument for addressing population ageing. In addition, the history of North American and European migration shows that immigrants have a better chance of integrating into the host society if the native population is experiencing a natural increase. Fertility and immigration are complementary, not substitutable. Simulations made to date demonstrate the impossibility of a migration solution, and the analysis of migration processes reinforces this assessment (OECD, 2000b). Thus, even if national immigration policy were directed to long-term demographic objectives, it could not solve the problem.

Education and human resources

Consistent with per capita incomes close to the national average, educational attainment in the province is similar to that of the national population. According to the ISTAT statistics for 1991, 79.4% of the population finished at least primary school in relation to 83.1% in Tuscany and 80.1% in Italy, whereas the number of graduates was 4%; therefore more than Tuscany and Italy which both stand at 3.6% (Table 12).

Given that the 2001 Census was still being carried out at the time of writing, it may be useful to examine the present level of participation in secondary school courses. Note that until 2000 schooling was obligatory only up to 14 years of age; that coincided with the completion of the first degree of secondary school. At present a school reform is being carried out which raises obligatory school attendance to the age of 16. Despite this, the level of second degree secondary schooling in Siena is extremely high, 97.08%, higher than the average for Tuscany and all the other "provinces" (administrative unit based on a major town) in the region. The level of abandonment does not even reach 3%. Most of the students are enrolled in technical or professional schools (61.44%), similar to the figure for Tuscany, even if the breakdown is different, due mainly to the high levels of industrialisation in the

Table 12. **Level of education – percentage of the resident population, Province of Siena**
1991

	Primary school	First degree of secondary school	Second degree of secondary school	Graduated from university
Siena	34.6	23.6	17.2	4.0
Tuscany	34.8	27.2	17.5	3.6
Italy	30.7	28.9	17.1	3.6

Source: ISTAT.

Table 13. **Second degree of secondary school, distribution of enrolled students, Province of Siena and Region of Tuscany**
1997-98

	Professional schools	Technical institutes	Primary school teacher	Classical scientific lycee	Art school
Siena	14.63	46.81	9.61	26.26	2.69
Tuscany	21.25	39.53	7.07	26.91	3.59

Source: *www.regione.toscana.it*

other areas of Tuscany (Table 13). The level of enrolment at state schools is extremely high, 97.38%; above that of the average for Tuscany, 95.48%.

Retaining the most highly skilled workers in the province has been a continual struggle, since they are often attracted to the richer set of employment opportunities available in large urban areas. These problems have been exacerbated by the small size of firms producing significant problems for the absorption of highly skilled workers as new entrants into the job market. Part of the problem is one of co-ordination in which potential employees do not have good knowledge of the particular skills required and employers do not have knowledge of the range of skills available and how they might be most productively utilised. The University of Siena Liaison Office is providing an important co-ordination function in this area by connecting current students with companies investigating the advantages of employment of university graduates. The program has resulted in a 40% placement rate of stages who eventually become employees. In contrast to many predominantly rural areas, there are a large number of students that receive their qualifications here accompanied by a strong attachment to place. In 1999, 18 204 students enrolled in 8 faculties (Table 14).

Table 14. **Student enrolment by major field of study, University of Siena**
1999

Courses	Students
Literature and philosophy	3 017
Political science	2 091
Law	3 784
Medicine	1 442
Pharmacology	819
Mathematics, physics and natural science	1 299
Economics	3 444
Engineering	730

Source: *www.regione.toscana.it*

Between 1995 and 1998, 1 868 students graduated. This figure breaks down into the various degree courses as follows:

Table 15. **Graduates by major field of study, University of Siena**
1995-1998

Course	Graduated
Literature and philosophy	295
Political science	156
Law	297
Medicine	159
Pharmacology	49
Mathematics, physics and natural science	123
Economics	663
Engineering	18

Source: www.regione.toscana.it

Service provision and infrastructure

While rich educational experiences at the secondary level are available in the city of Siena and a few of the larger towns, their provision throughout the province is not assured. The crisis in the urban influence on local territories described above has a considerable effect on the services, such as schools and the health service, distributed around the territory. All territorial areas in the province have been affected by such problems, mainly due to the long-term changes in population. A complex network of public and private transport combined with a great variety of choices facilitates adapting to this problem in an urban/metropolitan context. The case of Siena is a different matter because the historical extension of the service, presumably motivated by the objective to spread out the control of the territory over a wide area, has fallen below the minimum efficient scale of production. The census carried out by the National Institute of Statistics in 1991 shows that the local demand for services was satisfied, within each municipality, as far as primary schools are concerned. Only one municipality at that time did not have a junior high school, for children aged 11-14. But in moving from the junior to the senior high-school level at the age of 14, there is an abrupt transition from territorial diffusion to that of a selective and hierarchical structuralisation of the territory.

The municipalities having a senior high dropped to 10 out of 36 with considerable variety of schools offered by each district (from a vast range available in Siena, Poggibonsi/Colle and Montepulciano, to a wholly specialised school of hoteliers in Chianciano). The territory seen in the quantitative and qualitative demand for "senior high schools" was very clearly structured (Table 16).

69

Table 16.   **Distribution and utilisation of public service establishments for municipalities in the Province of Siena**

1993

Municipalities	Hospitals	Beds	Ambulatory	Spaces in infant schools	Pupils	Primary school rooms	Primary school pupils	1st level secondary school rooms	1st level secondary school pupils	2nd level secondary school rooms	2nd level secondary school pupils
Casole d'Elsa			3	2	47	10	124	4	62		
Colle Val d'Elsa	1	75	1	17	419	48	744	24	510	57	1 370
Poggibonsi	1	114		21	527	61	1 083	43	758	60	1 309
Radicondoli				1	14	5	37	3	26	5	84
San Geminiano	1	35	1	5	128	20	229	10	156		
Asciano				6	147	19	241	6	129		
Boconvento			1	3	68	10	153	6	100		
Monteroni			1	8	148	15	256	8	142		
Rapola			3	5	108	16	189	6	108		
S. Giovanni d'Asso			1	1	16	3	14				
Cetona			1	3	54	9	90	7	53		
Chianciano			1	6	126	17	297	12	209	11	287
Chiusi			1	8	191	23	338	18	234	40	594
Montepulsiano	1	251	1	15	311	33	533	20	354	80	1 767
Sarteano			1	4	92	10	162	6	106		
S. Casciano			1	3	58	11	64	3	46		
Sinalunga			2	13	279	44	485	17	308		
Torrita			1	7	165	22	300	13	199		
Trequanda			1	2	34	5	49	3	40		
Abbadia S. Salvatore	1	59		5	109	16	285	9	188	14	172
Castiglione d'Orcia			1	3	43	10	88	5	66	14	172
Montalcino			2	6	109	15	187	6	95	4	67
Piancastagnaio			1	6	134	11	162	9	134	5	111
Pienza			1	2	38	5	72	3	66		
Radicofani			1	2	38	6	64	3	25		
S. Quirico d'Orcia				3	70	6	96	4	57		
Chiusdino			1	2	35	5	62	3	30		
Monticiano			1	1	24	5	49	3	35		
Murlo			1	2	41	5	48	3	33		
Sovicille			1	8	181	18	261	8	148		
Castellina in Chianti				2	49	9	84	4	60		
Castelnuovo Berardenga			1	5	103	13	209	6	98		
Gaiole in Chianti				2	44	9	67	3	45		
Radda in chianti			2	1	30	5	75	3	38		
Siena	2	1 641		45	1 147	117	1 883	76	1 524	265	52 033

Source: National Italian Municipality Association (ANCI) and Province Administration of Siena.

- The Val d'Elsa gravitated around Poggibonsi/Colle and to a lesser extent Radicondoli. The influence of this centre extended beyond the province at least as far as Certaldo and Barberino.

- The Sienese, the Chianti, the Crete (excluding perhaps Trequanda), and Montalcino gravitated to Siena alone as, in any case, there were no other centres (except for a very small one in Montalcino).

- The rest of the territory (basically Chiana and Amiata) had centres in Montepulciano, Chianciano, Chiusi, Abbazia and Piancastagnaio), but the hub was Montepulciano, thanks to the variety of subjects taught.

At least four of these centres are either at risk (Abbadia and Piancastagnaio) or are already below the minimum threshold of numbers (Radicondoli and Montalcino). These risks are also reflected in the lower levels. In the junior high schools (in 35 municipalities out of 36), 15 boroughs fell below the level of 66 pupils enrolled (22 pupils per year, with only one class for each of the three years) in the 1994/95 school year. The tendency towards a fall in the birth rate weakens the prospects of any great demand in the future for the lower grade levels. It is clear that it is very difficult to compensate for the lack of an urban effect on the territory regarding the delivery of primary and secondary education.

In another sector of fundamental social services, health services provided by hospitals, the situation can immediately be seen as hierarchical (Table 16). By far, Siena has the greatest number of hospital beds (1 641), followed by Montepulciano (thus confirming it as a centre of services within the polycentrism of the Val di Chiana) and by small centres in the Val d'Elsa (Poggibonsi, Colle, S. Gimignano, 224 beds in all in 1995). The hospital system is therefore fairly close to becoming centralised and expensive (something that afflicts the whole health system in every part of Italy). At the other end of the health care spectrum, pharmacies are found in all the municipalities of the province, and represent the most accessible sources of medical care. In 20 municipalities in the province there is only one chemist and in seven others there are two. Therefore, the survival of this essential service is at risk in much of the province. The growing need of every outlet to provide a wide range of specialist products contributes to this crisis as costs of providing variety increase as the level of demand falls below a certain threshold. Thus the growth in the variety of available products is an imminent problem for the whole of the health service's capillary distribution of cures within the territory.

The promotion of producer, consumer and social co-operatives has provided a viable alternative for structuring various activities. The experience of social service co-operatives in the province could potentially provide alternative models for service delivery applied in the more sparsely populated areas. The existing co-operatives provide childcare or services for the elderly. However, their formation was not perceived as a response to a public service gap. Rather, their functioning and role is often perceived as complementary to existing public services. The example of child care is instructive of how mothers self-organised the provision of this service to meet the specific requirements of their own children. As such, social cooperatives represent both a new model of development and the welfare state where citizens are seen as people who can do effective things rather than merely as consumers or demanders of services. Reservations about the applicability of social cooperatives to more sparsely populated areas emerged from the observation that these co-operatives to date are under-represented in these areas.

Investments in transportation infrastructure have been largely incremental. The one exception has been planning for development of a commercial airport, but this proposal is currently tabled. However, the apparently fragile transport system in the Province of Siena represents the interdependence between logistics requirements and the need not to violate a territory of rare beauty with infrastructures having a strong impact on the landscape. The PRUSST programmes (Urban Renewal and Sustainable Development Programmes discussed in more detail in Chapter 3), are very recent instruments (disciplined at national level by DM No. 195 of 10 August 1998) which act at territorial scale through an integrated ensemble of projects proposed jointly by administrations of various levels, public and mixed companies, and private parties. As an instrument to implement the land-use planning disciplines in the recently adopted Plan of Territorial Co-ordination, the interdependent concerns regarding transportation access and preserving the landscape could be addressed in the investment programme. Although the programme will co-ordinate more than ITL 1.8 billion (approximately EUR 930 000) between public and private initiatives, the great majority of infrastructure investment is in the form of improvements to existing road and rail. The only proposed new construction is a roadway of 8 km.

Agriculture

The differentiated/high value added agricultural products that the province is renowned for contribute to an idyllic rural landscape. But cultivation in much of the agricultural land area is dependent on EU subsidies for economic viability. The Utilised Agricultural Area (SAU) in the Province of Siena covers 56.3% of the total area[4] (347 439). The last agricultural Census (1991) shows that 15 099 agricultural companies work a total land area of 347 439 hectares (Table 17). Forests account for 36.7% of the total area. In comparison to the 1982 and 1970 Census data, there have been no changes in the number of companies, although there has been a slight reduction in the total area. Analysis of the total land surface area shows a reduced number of farms and surface areas within the middle classes (5-30 hectares) and a

Table 17.   **Companies and relative land area in the Province of Siena**
Hectares

	1991	%	1982	%	Change 1991/1982	Percentage change 1991/1982
Number of companies	15 099		15 094		5	0.00
Total SAU	195 446	56.3	196 165	56.0	−720	−0.37
Of which:						
Sowable land	139 184	40.1	138 822	39.7	362	0.26
Permanent cultivations	31 596	9.1	34 041	9.7	−2 445	−7.18
Permanent grassland and pastures	24 666	7.1	23 302	6.7	1 364	5.85
Woods	127 371	36.7	129 836	37.1	−2 465	−1.90
Other land areas	23 885	6.9	24 051	6.9	−166	−0.69
Total area	347 439	100.0	350 053	100.0	−2 614	−0.75

Source: Istat Census Data Processed by S.M.P.

corresponding increase at the extreme ends of the scale (less than one hectare and more than 50 hectares) (Table 18). This means that from a structural point of view, agriculture in Siena has gone through a polarisation process, with the number of large-scale farms and extremely small-scale farms increasing to the detriment of medium-size ones. Compared to other provinces within the Tuscany region, agriculture in Siena is dominated by medium/large scale companies.[5] The most important productions are extensive crops (cereals, oil-protein crops) and high added value products, such as wine and olive oil. In the 1991 Census approximately 71% of total SAU was cultivated seed land with initial estimates from the 2001 Census demonstrating a nearly identical share with a small decline in the total SAU. Sixteen per cent of the total SAU is permanent cultivation (mainly vineyards – 9% – and olive groves). Market garden and fruit crops are not common; about 0.3% of the provincial SAU percentage is devoted to market garden produce and fruit orchards cover over 585 hectares.

It is possible to outline the main characteristics of the different agricultural areas in the territory of Siena. The Val d'Orcia area and that around Siena itself emphasise production of extensive cereal crops, animal grazing and animal farming (mostly cattle and pigs). The Val di Chiana is characterised by an entrepreneurial agriculture, producing both cereals and more industrial crops (sunflower, sugar beet and tobacco). This area also includes intensive and wide-ranging animal farms. Vineyards total about 17 000 hectares and are concentrated in the Chianti area where more than one-third of available SAU is dedicated to vineyards, as compared to a provincial average of 9%. The Chianti area is characterised by land not well suited to intensive agriculture and has long specialised in quality

Table 18. **Division of farms by number and total surface area**

By number

Farm size by total surface (ha)	Farms 1990	Farms 1982	Farms 1970	Percentage change 1982 to 1990	Percentage change 1970 to 1990	Percentage change 1970 to 1982
No land	19	43	52	−55.8	−63.5	−17.3
< 1	3 683	3 304	2 467	11.5	49.3	33.9
1-2	2 305	2 302	2 155	0.1	7.0	6.8
2-3	1 399	1 424	1 416	−1.8	−1.2	0.6
3-5	1 744	1 807	1 907	−3.5	−8.5	−5.2
5-10	1 933	2 089	2 618	−7.5	−26.2	−20.2
10-20	1 395	1 455	2 136	−4.1	−34.7	−31.9
20-30	634	707	829	−10.3	−23.5	−14.7
30-50	665	680	716	2.2	−7.1	−5.0
50-100	626	591	587	5.9	6.6	0.7
>100	696	694	641	0.3	8.6	8.3
Total	15 099	15 096	15 524	0.0	−2.7	−2.8

By total surface area

Farm size by total surface (ha)	Surface total 1990	Surface total 1982	Surface total 1970	Percentage change 1982 to 1990	Percentage change 1970 to 1990	Percentage change 1970 to 1982
No land	0	0.0	0.0			
< 1	1 725.5	1 639.3	1 276.6	5.3	35.2	28.4
1-2	3 131.3	3 096.2	2 893.5	1.1	8.2	7.0
2-3	3 307.9	3 333.0	3 312.7	−0.8	−0.1	0.6
3-5	6 531.9	6 740.6	7 087.9	−3.1	−7.8	−4.9
5-10	13 265.4	14 392.6	18 127.4	−7.8	−26.8	−20.6
10-20	19 219.2	20 055.9	29 384.0	−4.2	−34.6	−31.7
20-30	15 347.9	17 092.5	19 930.0	−10.2	−23.0	−14.2
30-50	25 711.3	26 020.6	27 069.9	6.3	−5.0	−3.9
50-100	43 160.1	40 603.0	39 985.8	−0.5	7.9	1.5
>100	216 037.8	217 079.0	205 078.8	−0.7	5.3	5.9
Total	347 438.5	350 052.8	354 147.8	−0.7	−1.9	−1.2

Source: SMP processing of ISTAT data.

wine vineyards, in the production of internationally famous DOC and DOCG wine, and olive oil production. Montalcino, with 13% of the provincial total dedicated to DOC wines, has confirmed its vocation for high quality wines. Val d'Elsa alternates wine and oil with cereals and forage. This area also has animal farming.

The Gross Domestic Product (GDP) in the primary sector in 1996 was ITL 391.2 billion and represented 5% of the overall provincial GDP. Siena stands third in Tuscany behind Grosseto (6.8%) and Pistoia (5.9%). in 1999, Saleable Production (SP) in agriculture and forestry was ITL 516 billion. The entire agricultural system is based on a significant vocation for certain products (cereals, wine and animal farming). Animal products total 22.5% of SP; woody plants crops (wine and oil) 39% and herbaceous crops (cereals, wheat, corn and vegetables) 35%.[6] In 1999, herbaceous crops, mainly cereals and sunflowers, decreased both in terms of cultivated areas and turnovers. Siena accounts for 8% of Tuscany's agro-food industries, which are mainly partnership and sole-proprietor companies. They are small and medium-sized businesses, a common feature of the entire regional food sector. Co-operatives play an important role in the agro-food sector of Siena. In 1997 the value added of agro-industry in Siena was about ITL 377 billion and accounted for 8% of the total value added of industry.

Despite the fact that the number of employees employed in agriculture is higher than the regional figures (7.8% compared with 4.8%), employment in agriculture and the food industry is nevertheless declining in line with recent trends. The problem of an ageing workforce and agricultural management also has an impact on the Province of Siena. Once again, however, the dynamism of the agricultural sector in this area encourages many young people to become involved and the percentage of young people employed in agriculture is highest in Siena for the Tuscany region as shown in Table 19.

Table 19. **Working population in agriculture, age group 19-34**
1991

Age group 19-34	Siena	Tuscany
Total population	9 624	4 600
Population working in agriculture	2 215	6 965
% population working in agriculture	23.0	15.1

Source: Istat Census 1991.

Cultural resources

The Province of Siena is home to three UNESCO World Heritage Sites that assure high visibility accompanied by greater responsibility for maintaining historical integrity. The criteria used to select these sites confirms that San Gimignano, and the town centres of Siena and Pienza provide far more than opportunities for "spectating", but rather require a significant interpretative component. Unfortunately, it appears that the promotional value of confirmed *"masterpieces of human creative genius"* directed at local sites has outpaced the ability of the parties to the Convention at the national level to devise legislation that facilitates its sustainable management and protection. Both Article 5 and Article 17 of the Convention provide recommendations regarding *"effective and active measures [to ensure] protection"*

75

and how this might be funded through public and private foundations and donations. Some of these recommendations are examined in more detail in Chapter 5.

Some of the cultural resources are so prized, the main challenge is finding ways to disperse tourists to other less well known cultural assets through the system of Siena museums. To testify to the unitary nature of Sienese history, and also to facilitate the use of the museums by citizens and tourists, the Provincial Administration of Siena, as early as 1990, promoted the formation of the Sienese Museum System, in collaboration with several municipalities and cultural institutions. At present the Sienese Museum System includes 17 museums.[7] The museum system policy provides a good example of efforts to increase the experiential value of the province to tourists while also relieving the carrying capacity problem ("the Venice effect") of the most popular destinations. It does this by providing a mechanism for redirecting tourists to less popular areas that rely more on cultural heritage. Each museum in the network provides links to other museums in the network. The idea is to assemble a sort of organised serendipity so that in the course of discovery in one museum one is directed to the other sites. For example, a tourist's interest in terracotta, or mining or the Tuscan countryside introduced in one of the main museums can be investigated in depth at these topical museums off the beaten track. The system is seen as a first step in guiding interested tourists to a Siena itinerary or "path", but the need for greater co-ordination and better information delivery is understood. Current thinking is focused on developing reception centres and improving Internet access as a window on the territory reaching the most remote locations in the province.

Strengths affecting the productivity of factors

The main concern regarding the productivity of factors in the province is lost opportunities due to a lack of co-ordination. While large urban areas are sufficiently concentrated and diversified to assure the eventual realisation of many productive relationships, areas such as Siena are more dependent on the purposive identification of these relationships. Indeed, this would appear to be the central challenge facing predominantly rural areas in responding to competitive pressures that are increasingly reliant on the novel combination of productive factors. But whereas rural areas are disadvantaged by much thinner factor markets and spatial dispersion that lessens serendipitous interaction, they do have the potential advantage of better knowledge of the interests and capabilities of various economic actors. Given the long history of associative relations in the province, this lack of co-ordination is often expressed as a frustration regarding the ability to combine currently fragmented activities. The considerable untapped potential noted by many actors in the province is evidence of this knowledge that is also expressed in the provisional Strategic Plan where co-ordination is a principal objective.

As discussed above, the co-ordination of skilled labour supply to meet existing or potential demands of local firms is a central preoccupation of the University Liaison that is accomplished by placing students as stages or interns in local firms. This is probably the clearest example of the need for co-ordination in smaller labour markets that would otherwise be self-organising in larger urban agglomerations. In order to improve the uptake of technologies into SMEs, the University Liaison is particularly active in reinforcing the connection between the academic and business sectors; a connection that is traditionally weak in Italy. The Liaison Office[8] modelling itself after the well-established MIT Industrial Liaison Programme[9] (Box 3) should be mentioned as a best practice in Italy. The Liaison Office is currently developing several agreements with the private sector to start research programmes based on the actual needs of local companies. Closely related to the Liaison Office is the CUSTOM[10] Centre, an inter-university research institute specialising in the management of scientific and technological research systems. The centre, bringing together researchers from the three universities of Siena, Urbino and Chieti, is becoming a point of reference for both SMEs and local institutions in what concerns the supply of information and services for new technologies and markets. Moreover, a co-operative initiative between the Municipality of Siena and Telecom (the first telecommunications company in Italy) was launched at the end of 2000 to create a "virtual district", a test-bench for innovative forms of co-operation through the Web among local entrepreneurs. All of these initiatives are recent but representative of a dynamism that is not easily found in rural areas.

The uptake of new technologies has also extended to the more traditional sectors of the economy. Particularly active is the tourism sector. According to a recent survey,[11] 68% of the agri-tourism operators of the province make use of an Internet site and more than half of those that still do not have one have declared plans to create one. Best practices are found among those initiatives aimed at promoting through the Net the province's typical local products, associating them with the already well-established tourist reputation. The Web sites of the province and of the municipality[12] are quoted as best practices by the Italian authorities responsible for the National Action Plan for the Information Society. They represent one of the earliest experiences in the country of Internet-based, public-private partnerships operating in the field of territorial marketing. In practical terms, the public Web sites host links to private producers of certified quality, thereby "guaranteeing" the quality of their products and authenticity.

The major impediment to capital investment in Siena is not availability of financial capital but the knowledge and competency of the numerous small and medium-sized firms for developing persuasive business plans. Thus, capital availability for smaller businesses is characteristically described as constrained, comprising a common complaint in all developed economies. There are a number of initiatives to try to alleviate this bottleneck for the uptake of capital throughout the

---

Box 3. The MIT Industrial Liaison Programme

The MIT Industrial Liaison Programme (ILP), based on the concept of university-industry liaisons founded in 1948, acts as a valuable link between the industry and academic sectors. The primary goal of the ILP is to establish an interactive exchange between both sectors, which results in a mutually beneficial relationship. Through this exclusive interaction with MIT, companies have an advantage in anticipating trends in and accessing cutting-edge technology developments. MIT faculty, researchers and students have greater research-funding opportunities via ILP companies and can potentially apply their research as consultants or future employees of member companies. Through the active interaction between the sectors, research developments have the opportunity to be quickly applied to the industry, contributing to this industry's rapid advancement. The ILP's membership includes companies such as Fiat SpA, Microsoft, Inc., Nokia and Tokyo Electric Power Co., Inc.

The key element to ILP membership is access to new and emerging technology developments in MIT activities. Companies have the opportunity to meet with MIT faculty members and research scientists to discuss novel technologies and monitor advances. They can also meet with those directly involved with research of their interest and/or fund the research of faculty and students in specific areas. An additional aspect to this programme is the Industrial Liaison Officer (ILO). Companies are assigned an ILO who is responsible for addressing their unique interests and needs. S/he acts as the contact person for company activities at MIT and represents their interests to MIT staff. The ILO engages in planning and information meetings with a specially designated company representative in order to maintain an on-going assessment of their interests and needs. The ILO links companies with MIT experts most pertinent to their needs and engages MIT staff in company projects when appropriate.

The ILP also aims to address the education of company employees. It organises one-day seminars for a maximum of 20 company employees where they examine emerging technologies and discuss new management approaches and strategic planning. Researchers and/or faculty members engaged in research pertinent to companies can arrange a half or full day visit to companies which could include a seminar conducted by them concerning their research. MIT also has special educational programmes that range from week courses to Masters programmes in engineering and management.

---

province in the form of consultancy services provided by mixed public-private organisations such as the EUROBIC (Business Innovation Centres) and development finance institutions. In addition, the large number of approved Territorial Pacts in the province (e.g., VATO, VATO Verde and Siena Verde) have also contributed to the availability of capital as loan applications of approved projects are expedited. But this generates a similar small business complaint that the Pacts put a high administrative burden on the smallest firms. Although these complaints may have some merit, any possibility of a true capital gap – that may be a genuine rural concern given the greater mobility of financial capital – is highly improbable in Siena. The continual demonstration of a strong commitment to the economic success of the province by one of the five largest Italian banks that is headquartered there ensures an adequate conventional supply of credit. However, if the very small firm is regarded as an essential component to a viable ecology of firms dependent on an entrepreneurial culture, then micro-enterprise lending schemes may be an effective way to provide credit at low administrative cost with the social collateral absent in a conventional loan.

Indications with respect to ICT also suggest that the full contribution to productivity is not being realised due to under-utilisation rather than limited supply. The lag between the adoption of new information technologies and their significant contribution to productivity is in fact a common characteristic rooted in the immediate deficiencies of both transferable and tacit skills. At the organisational level, the penetration of e-mail and Internet connection has been wide, and, as discussed above, many firms maintain Web sites. However, traditional post is still the main means of correspondence for many firms, and e-commerce is often regarded as a distant potential rather than a strategy to be implemented. Forecasts for the full utilisation of these technologies are not all that encouraging as the timid initial response is often described as a generational problem rather than one of acquiring new skills. The fact that the supply of many productive resources in Siena is not a binding constraint provides a useful demonstration for development policy in areas of more limited resources that these assets often enable rather than propel economic growth. It also suggests that improving the human resource base may have considerable leverage in increasing the returns to the substantial on-going investment in wires and cables.

Excluding industrial development on the northern and eastern borders of the province, the concentration and localisation of industry is too weak to support industrial districts. The largest concentration of manufacturing employment outside these areas is in the municipality of Siena (especially Sovicille), with a number of important, highly qualified companies. In terms of quantity, however, the industrial sector is extremely small in comparison with employment levels in the capital of the province, where jobs are mainly in the service sector. Districts are found in Sinalunga, which lies to the east of the province, bordering on and forming a continuous residential belt with the Province of Arezzo. The "district" definition is based for the most part on the furniture industry. The Val d' Elsa is adjacent to the southernmost layer of the Florence-Pistoia industrial area. This agglomeration forms part of the urbanised agglomeration that connects the north of Siena to the Florence-Prato-Pistoia metropolitan area. The Elsa Valley zone is qualified as a "district"; in particular, a furniture district, but also contains a concentration of motor caravan and glass and ceramics firms. A general picture of industrial employment in the Province of Siena is given in Table 20.

Table 20. **Manufacturing employment by municipality, Province of Siena**
1996

Municipalities	Manufacturing employment
Abbadia San Salvatore	403
Asciano	531
Buonconvento	144
Casole d' Elsa	839
Castellina in Chianti	304
Castenuovo Berardenga	162
Castiglione d' Orcia	149
Cetona	72
Chianciano Terme	151
Chiusdino	64
Chiusi	632
Colle di Val d' Elsa	2 456
Gaiole in Chianti	277
Montalcino	320
Montepulciano	882
Monteriggioni	1 286
Monteroni d' Arbia	386
Monticiano	20
Murlo	42
Piancastagnaio	772
Pienza	159
Poggibonsi	2 962
Radda in Chianti	157
Radicofani	228
Radicondoli	14
Rapalano Terme	485
San Casciano dei Bagni	48
San Gimignano	1 258
San Giovanni d' Asso	59
San Quirico d' Orcia	256
Sartano	96
Siena	2 602
Sinalunga	1 573
Sovicille	536
Torrita di Siena	1 020
Trequanda	160

Source: ISTAT Intermediate Census of Industry and Services.

The breakdown of employees into size classes is very similar to that of Tuscany, even if it tends slightly towards the smaller classes, and differs from the national average, confirming that the companies that operate in this area tend to be either small or very small (Table 21).

It is the export specialisation in the caravan and crystal industries in Poggibonsi that provides greater evidence of external economies contributing to competitiveness. A specialisation index[13] that compares Siena with Tuscany demonstrates the

Table 21.   **Employment size classes of manufacturing establishment**
1996

Sizes of classes	1-49 employees	50-249 employees	Over 250 employees
		%	
Siena	75.1	15.5	9.4
Tuscany	74.5	15.3	10.3
Italy	59.4	22.4	18.3

Source: ISTAT Intermediate Census of Industry and Services.

extent of this specialisation (Table 22). Although the manufacturing industry has a value much lower than 1 (0.7), suggesting that share of the population employed in manufacturing is significantly less than that for Tuscany, a number of sectors are characterised by large values; *i.e.*, pharmaceuticals, non-metallic mineral production industry (glass and ceramics), and the furniture industry. More dramatic are the shares of production in detailed industries that are located in Siena: 95% of the Italian crystal industry output are produced in the province and 80% of the motor caravan vehicles in Italy are produced in the area around Poggibonsi and the neighbouring municipality of Barberino (in the Province of Florence).

In agriculture, producer consortia contribute to highly favourable demand conditions aggressively promoting differentiated quality products such as wine, olive oil and other typical products. And although these producers are often dispersed across significant expanses of the Sienese countryside, the consortia

Table 22.   **Relative specialisation of Siena, Tuscany and Italy by manufacturing sectors**
1996

Sectors	Siena/Tuscany	Tuscany/Italy	Siena/Italy
Manufacture of food products	1.3	0.9	1.2
Manufacture of wood and wood products	1.5	1.3	2.0
Manufacture of chemicals	1.2	1.1	1.3
Pharmaceutical	2.4	1.6	3.9
Manufacture of other non-metallic mineral products	2.1	1.8	3.6
Glass and glass products	3.3	2.3	7.5
Ceramic goods other than for construction purposes	2.9	2.2	6.2
Manufacture of machinery and equipment	1.1	0.8	0.8
Manufacture of furniture	1.8	1.5	2.7
Total manufacturing	0.7	1.4	1.0
Construction	1.0	1.2	1.2

Source: SMP elaboration of ISTAT data.

facilitate many of the functions contributing to the marketing and innovative capacity of members that are often identified with more localised industrial districts. Attending trade fairs is a common strategy for extending long-channel markets that would otherwise be beyond the means of many smaller producers. In addition, several consortia have been able to capitalise on the notoriety of a single product such as wine to increase the appeal of other products from the area such as olive oil, speciality meats and cheeses. If the promise of e-commerce is realised the consortia will become increasingly important in providing the economies of scale needed to justify costs associated with secure electronic payment, provide sufficient volume to meet variability in demand, and provide the diversity of offer that will appeal to a wider consumer base. The experience of *Consorzio del Marchio Storico Chianti Classico* that has created a shop on line selling different types of Chianti wines, olive oil and other products such as honey and vinegar has demonstrated these benefits of association. This consortium also provides one of the best examples of increased innovative capacity through its Chianti Classico 2000 Project that supported intensive research for improving the quality of the grapevines and cultivation practices that would have been beyond the capability of any single producer (see Chapter 6).

The potential demand situation for typical products locally is also quite favourable given the large influx of tourists, but it is widely believed that better co-ordination is required to fully exploit these opportunities. The sale of merchandise that is not produced in the province that substitutes for authentic typical and artisanal Sienese products is a seemingly intractable problem. The Bersani Law that severely limits the ability to regulate the form of economic activity in commercial districts embodies the economic logic of merchants satisfying consumer demand. Of course, this same economic logic relies on assumptions of access to information and minimal search costs that are not likely to hold for one-time sales to tourists. Given the prohibition on instruments that would regulate economic activity, the other alternative is to reduce the informational constraints and search costs for tourists finding the types of authentic products that truly represent the territory and thus should be more highly valued. Although there was a general expression of "supporting" those merchants that selected the high-value added approach, explicit strategies on how to do this have not been formulated. Defining agreed-upon standards of authenticity of products sold as representative of Siena would allow merchants to make a more rationale decision regarding their marketing strategy as either high-value added or high-volume mass tourism oriented. Informational constraints of visitors could be reduced by providing a seal or label for merchants meeting the standard of authenticity and providing public promotion of where to buy authentic products. Finally, transforming the one-time encounter between visitor and merchant to a potentially recurring interaction could be facilitated by establishing a Web presence for certified merchants where visitors would be able to order additional merchandise if it met or exceeded their expectations on returning home.

Territorial potentials and threats

All told, the major challenges in realising greater potential of the territory are for better co-ordination of assets and abilities that respect natural and cultural carrying capacity. The critical policy concerns are not limited to the stimulation of growth but must assess the desirability of various paths of growth and find ways to point the economy in the preferred direction. Experience in the province has demonstrated that the large tourist flows to some areas have resulted in negative consequences of various forms of growth. This experience has informed the tourist development strategies of other areas "off the beaten path" and holds important lessons for other areas wishing to pursue sustainable tourism strategies long before limits to their carrying capacity are reached. In this respect, Montalcino provides a number of useful examples of appealing to the sectors of the tourism market that are in line with the long-term development objectives of the municipality. In keeping with the quality orientation of many of the town's tourists that were attracted by the reputation of Brunello di Montalcino wine, events have focused on quality experience rather than large attendance. The jazz festival in town is held in a venue for 200 to 300 people in contrast to the thousands that attend the neighbouring festival in Umbria. The storefronts of this hill town are noticeably devoid of advertisements for film processing or displays of souvenirs. Rather, one is drawn into the shops on the basis of the quality and authenticity of the goods displayed for sale. As the first municipality in Italy to apply for certification of its environmental management system under ISO 14000 the town also hopes to discipline its policies and programs with an adherence to explicit environmental principles that will appeal to a growing number of tourists. The critical requirement for co-ordination in all of these examples has been the agreement of local actors as to the norms and conventions of appropriate activity that has been aided by the community's small size.

Siena's challenge of ensuring the sustainable valorisation of its amenities parallels a much more common rural problem: potential visitors must be made aware of the full complement of possible experiences offered by the region. In the more typical case, the challenge is to amass the various attractions of a territory into a critical mass needed to make the area a compelling tourist destination. These development challenges were outlined in the two previous Territorial Reviews in the rural regions of Teruel (Spain) and Tzoumerka (Greece). The basic element of the strategy is to appeal to the growing demand for experiential tourism – visitors that seek a substantive connection to the people, culture and environment at the vacation destination – by promoting the authentic character of landscapes, environmentally protected areas, cultural heritage and traditional vocations. While it is clear that the Province of Siena has surpassed the critical mass needed to provide a compelling tourist destination, there is a need to better inform future visitors of the significant experiential possibilities that extend far beyond some prized photo opportunities and the traditional allure of art cities. Important intermediaries in this effort are the tour operators that have already been identified by some of the tourism associations in the province as the critical players in altering the profiles of visitors. Providing tour operators with better information on the full range of experiences available serves both the operators' interest in adding value to clients' visits and the province's interest in sustainable tourism. For visitors co-ordinating their own excursions, more accessible information on the Internet that would also allow for bookings, reservations and the construction of feasible itineraries would go a long way in realising the ultimate objective of a tourism system where visitors are able to construct totally individualised touristic paths.

Both unused capacities in the spa tourism sector and the potential for tourism flows directed to the mountain communities present more typical problems of tourism development. Over-capacity in the spa tourism sector has resulted from the inability of many of the spas to develop a new model of tourism to replace the therapeutic model that had benefited from the inclusion of "thermal spa treatments" in the national health plan. The national government substantially reduced the reimbursement for these treatments in 1989 that resulted in a 50% reduction in occupancy. What is required is a transformation from "spa tourism" into more comprehensive health tourism. While some of the smaller spas have been able to diversify their offerings, Chianciano – the centre of the therapeutic spa offer – has been unable to make this transformation. The tourist market for health tourism is a growing one internationally, but the trend is for integrated health resorts offering a wide range of facilities and services. The substantial investment of both public and private sector actors for realising such a transformation and the necessity for there being a co-ordinated and integrated vision of the strategy is parallel to the objective of Territorial Pacts, matching social purpose with private initiative. Another tourism sector that is enjoying rapid growth is ecotourism and this trend is in line with the desire to disperse tourism flows, on a carefully controlled basis, to the mountain areas located in the southern areas of the province. Other significant protected areas that would form the attraction for ecotourism are also found in the west-central part of the province. Ecotourism has the advantages of attracting good quality tourist markets and, if developed carefully, can help justify and pay for conservation of the natural environment, especially the protected areas. The province has already put together a programme for developing ecotourism that is described in Chapter 5 and that should be pursued according to schedule.

The large amount of resources flowing from the Fondazione dei Monte dei Paschi begs the question of the effectiveness of the substantial grants economy in fostering the development of the province. The question is rhetorical owing to the difficulty of evaluation, the impossibility of considering counterfactuals and the inability to impose a metric of evaluation on an autonomous philanthropic organisation. However, the question does define a topic for discussion that can only benefit the province if it is periodically revisited. Perhaps the most salient indicator that the yearly distribution of approximately ITL 200 billion (roughly EUR 100 million) has not had perverse effects in the form of growing dependency is the demonstrated success in securing European Union and national funding for a large number of competitive grants, loans and co-financing arrangements. Given the significant demonstrated ability for uptake of these various funding sources, it would appear that the availability of foundation resources are not crowding out other sources of funding for public entrepreneurship. Another point of agreement is that the current regulations guiding the activities of the foundation since its creation in 1995 have resulted in a much more critical assessment of grant making than had been true of the philanthropic activities of the bank in the past. The contentious issue presently and into the future is whether those grant proposals that hold the most promise for the conservation and development of Sienese society are the ones that are awarded funds. The significant representation on the foundation board from municipalities in Siena, the provincial administration and the voluntary and religious sectors should help to align the interests of the wider community with the funding decisions of the foundation. However, the limits of representation could be best overcome by proactively improving its communication with the population in the Province of Siena.

This concern with transparency and the value of mobilising the widest range of information and capabilities of citizens also conditions the seeming satisfaction with past success of corporatist forms of consultation and representation that may prove less effective in pursuing sustainable development. Given the understanding that democratically elected governments have the duty to make decisions on public policy, both citizens and policy makers are exploring new ways to interact throughout OECD Member countries (OECD, 2001c). This pursuit is driven by the realisation that sustainable development becomes merely a platitude if it does not seriously embark upon defining the appropriate ends of policy. This in turn places greater emphasis on citizen involvement in decision making. It requires governments to provide ample opportunity for information, consultation and participation by citizens in developing policy options prior to decision making and to give reasons for their policy choices once a decision has been taken. There are a large number of benefits that emerge from this greater openness and access that could be facilitated through the various e-government initiatives, essentially augmenting the corporatist forms that have proven so successful to now.

1. *Transparency*: providing citizens with more information on, and access to, government and its decision-making processes makes a significant contribution to greater openness within the administration.

85

2. *Accountability*: greater information and access, in turn, opens up decision making to direct public scrutiny by individual citizens and indirectly via media and oversight institutions – all of whom will hold governments to account for their decisions and actions.

3. *Legitimacy*: introducing new rules for policy making which ensure a greater degree of citizen involvement lends greater credibility to the process of government decision making – even in instances where some citizens do not agree with its results.

4. *Quality*: greater citizen participation brings a wider range of information, perspectives, priorities and solutions to bear on a given policy issue and thereby contributes to raising the standards for decisions reached.

5. *Effectiveness*: more information, consultation and participation in policy making ensures better implementation by raising the level of awareness of, and compliance with, policy provisions – especially among target groups who have helped to define them. (OECD, 2001*c*, p. 74)

In this evolving area of citizen-government relations it is important that prescriptions for greater access and transparency are not perceived as deficiencies of current administration but rather as a means to realise the full potential of their communities. This is easily seen in Siena where considerable success in the traditional performance indicators such as income growth or employment creation provides strong evidence of government success. But this same success provokes a more critical examination of the objectives of development policy. Incremental improvement in the traditional indicators is a laudable goal as it enlarges important means for citizens that can contribute to full and enriching lives. But enlarging these means does not necessarily guarantee this. To know if the pattern of development is contributing to full and enriching lives of citizens, governments must ask them. To pursue a pattern of development with this result, governments must engage citizens.

Notes

1. *i)* Dynamic Mainly Metro: Milano, Bologna, Modena.
   ii) Converging Mainly Metro: Bergamo, Brescia, Como, Mantova, Bolzano, Trento, Padova, Treviso, Venezia, Verona, Vicenza, Gorizia, Udine, Spezia, Parma, Piacenza, Ravenna, Reggio-Emilia, Firenze, Ancona, Roma.
   iii) Affluent Modest Growth: Novara, Torino, Vercelli, Varese, Trieste, Genova, Savona.
   iv) Dynamic Mainly Intermediate/Rural: Alessandria, Asti, Cuneo, Cremona, Pavia, Belluno, Rovigo, Imperia, Ferrara, Forli, Arezzo, Livorno, Lucca, Pisa, Pistoia, **Siena**, Perugia, Ascoli, Macerata, Pesaro, Pescara
   v) Lagging Mainly Intermediate/Rural: Grosseto, Massa, Terni, Frosinone, Latina, Rieti, Viterbo, Campobasso, Chieti, Aquila, Teramo, Bari, Taranto, Ragusa, Cagliari, Sassari
   vi) Mezzogiorno : Avellino, Benevento, Caserta, Napoli, Salerno, Brindisi, Foggia, Lecce, Matera, Potenza, Catanzaro, Cosenza, Reggio-Calabria, Agrigento, Caltanissetta, Catania, Enna, Messina, Palermo, Siracusa, Trapani, Nuoro

2. Converging: Arezzo, Perugia, Belluno;
   Declining: Rieti, Sondrio, Viterbo, Grosseto;
   Emerging: Potenza, Aquila, Campobasso, Ascoli, Sassari;
   Lagging: Nuoro, Matera, Foggia, Enna.

3. SEL (Sistemi Economici Locali – Local Economic Systems) are territorial divisions. They were defined on the basis of the shiftings between homes and working places. The 1991 Population Census defined 784 gravitation areas which were used by ISTAT as important references to define some socio-economic indicators. In Tuscany, IRPET (Regional Institute for Economic Planning) and Regional Administration were the first to use these units of territorial analysis. SEL were considered not only as analytical bases but also as informal references for regional and local planning. This utilisation, although SEL were not real planning units, was useful to unify some policies between municipalities.

4. Istat Census data for 1991. Final figures from the 2001 last agriculture Census are still not available. It is significant that in 1998 there were 5 995 active agricultural companies enrolled in the Registry of Chamber of Commerce of the Province of Siena.

5. Twelve point five per cent of total companies have a SAU higher than 20 hectares, owning 77% of total area and cultivating 79% of total SAU.

6. The last 3.4% are services.

7. Museum of Archaeology and Sacred Art – Palazzo Corboli (Asciano); Museum of Mezzadria nel "900 (Buonconvento); Archaeological and Collegiata Museum (Casole d'Elsa); Countryside Thematic Museum (Castelnuovo Berardenga); Services Centre and Civic Museum of the Prehistory of Monte Cetona (Cetona); Civil Archaeological Museum of the Waters (Chianciano); Epigraphic and Lapidary Museum (Chiusi; there is also a National Archaeological Museum in the town); Civic and Sacred Art Museum (Colle Val

d'Elsa); Civic and Sacred Art Museum (Montalcino); Civil Museum and Crociani Picture Gallery (Montepulciano); Museum of the Poor Theatre and of Tuscan Popular Entertainment (Montichiello-Pienza); Spicery of Santa Fina (San Gimignano); Archaeological Museum (Sarteano); Documentation Centre on Granges and exhibitions of workshops of contemporary art (Serre di Rapolano – Rapolano Terme); Museums of the Accademia dei Fisiocritici (Siena); Civic Museum (Siena); Woods Museum (Orgia – Sovicille).

8. See *www.unisi.it/liason*

9. See *http://ilp.mit.edu/ocr*

10. See *www.unisi.it/custom/*

11. See the *Rapporto* 2000 *sull'Economia Senese*, Istituto Guglielmo Tagliacarne.

12. See *www.provincia.siena.it* and *www.comune.siena.it*

13. The specialisation index is calculated by the following formula:
    (ss / pops) / (sit / popit)
    where:
    ss = employees by sector in Siena
    sit = employees by sector in Italy
    pops = resident population in Siena
    popit = resident population in Italy

Chapter 3

Governance for Sustainable Rural Development in Siena

Sustainable rural development as a strategic goal in the Province of Siena

The Province of Siena is an important case study in sustainable rural development for OECD Member countries. Despite possessing idyllic rural landscapes, artistic and cultural assets, a well-developed local economy, a strong network of voluntary associations and various initiatives to maintain a high quality of life, the province struggles with sustainable development.

The variety of actions at different levels of government and in different sectors makes the Siena case study particularly valuable for other OECD Member countries, which all committed themselves at the 1992 Rio Conference on Environment and Development. Yet, as a recent OECD report points out, *"action to meet these commitments remains slow"* (OECD, 2001i). Different approaches towards sustainable development also show that it is difficult to define sustainable development *a priori*.

Nevertheless, there seems to be common agreement that sustainable development policies should encompass more than the environment. Indeed, sustainable development involves integrating economic, social and environmental goals in a balanced way. Thus, territorial planning, economic programming and strategic management are proving to be important tools, as are partnerships and alliances formed across levels of government and across the private, public and voluntary sector. Finally, the long-term change involved requires leadership to identify common goals and engage all stakeholders in the process.

The context

The Bassanini reforms as a new starting point

The Bassanini reforms of 1998 (named after Minister Franco Bassanini elected in the Province of Siena) came in response to Italy's political, social and financial crisis and concomitant pressure from the Maastricht criteria to reduce public debt.

What became clear was a need to decentralise power and financial means to the regions, provinces and municipalities. The Bassannini reforms did just that.

The reforms led to (among other things) a three-stage decentralisation. First, the central government transferred all non-core functions to regional and local governments, keeping for itself – as called for in the law – justice, defence, European and foreign policies, territorial security, social protection, foreign trade, protection of cultural, historic and artistic heritage, economic policies, telecommunications, transport, public education, and research. Second, each region was authorised to determine how to exercise its state-transferred responsibilities. As a result, the region could pass on additional responsibilities to the local level. This "decentralised decentralisation process" led to regional variation in local level authority. Unlike many other Italian regions, which have been hesitant to transfer parts of their newly acquired portfolio to local levels, the region of Tuscany has taken the process of decentralisation quite far. The third and final step in the decentralisation process transferred the necessary human resources, finances and other equipment to the regions, provinces and municipalities so that they could carry out their new responsibilities.

Obviously, this comprehensive reform package provides opportunities as well as challenges to the Province of Siena. While the province has a long tradition of co-operation between the public and private sectors, the decentralisation adds a vertical dimension to provincial governance. In short, the province emerges as a new institutional player with a strategic role. In concrete terms, the province now has strong political accountability via direct election of the president of the province, and a new responsibility for territorial, economic and environmental planning. In particular, the province:

- collects and co-ordinates proposals submitted by the municipalities for the region's economic, territorial and environmental programming;
- contributes to the definition of the regional development programme and other regional plans in accordance with regional laws;
- draws up and adopts, with reference to the forecasts and to the objectives of the regional development plan, its own multi-annual programmes (both general and sectoral), and promotes the co-ordination of the municipalities' programming activity;
- draws up and adopts the Provincial Territorial Co-ordination Plan (PTCP) whilst considering the tasks of municipalities as well as the regional plans and legislation;
- forecasts the general trends for the province;
- implements managerial reforms in human resources, budgeting and accounting in the provincial administration;

- introduces e-government to the provincial administration; and

- integrates former central government staff into the provincial administration.

These new governance issues add to the challenges described below.

Some relevant actors: voluntary organisations and proactive leaders

Even though decentralisation strengthened the provincial government, by itself it cannot fully exploit all the opportunities created. Good local governance requires more than good local government. Other stakeholders – municipalities, voluntary organisations, and businesses – must also play a role in improving the quality of life and overall welfare in the Province of Siena. Among those is the Monte dei Paschi Bank, which has traditionally had a key financing role in the province.

Monte dei Paschi, the oldest operating bank in the world and one of Italy's five largest banking groups, has maintained its headquarters in the Province of Siena for centuries. The relationship between Monte dei Paschi and the province has benefited both. The bank's successful development is tied to the province. Likewise, the economic prosperity of the province is largely due to the financial support of the bank. Thus, Monte dei Paschi plays an important role in the public, private and voluntary sectors in the Province of Siena (Figure 11).

With the banking group's recent split, this development role has been taken on by a new, not-for-profit Monte dei Paschi Foundation. The foundation is completely autonomous from the bank and concentrates its funding activities on science, education, art, health and cultural heritage. Any organisation or individual citizen in the Province of Siena may seek funding from the foundation. Projects are selected for funding based on criteria established by the foundation. Clearly, the composition of the governing board (*Deputazione Generale*) is an important mechanism for integrating the foundation into the network of stakeholders in the province (Figure 11). Although the voluntary sector was not represented on the board of Monte dei Paschi Bank, the statutes of the new foundation call for the Province of Siena – in agreement with the *Consulta Provinciale del Volontariato di Siena* – to select one representative of the voluntary sector to serve on the foundation's board. The Siena Chamber of Commerce selects one member, from among eight proposed by the municipalities, to represent the business community.

The foundation is, in fact, a powerful instrument of social, territorial and even political cohesion. First, all social, economic and political interests in the province are represented on the governing board. Representatives of the opposition parties have even been appointed in recent years. Furthermore, the foundation's bylaws specify that its funds may only go to projects within the geographical boundaries of the province. These funds may be allocated to public entities, the service sector and the university. Nevertheless, there is a need for greater transparency

Figure 11. **Governing board of the foundation Monte dei Paschi**

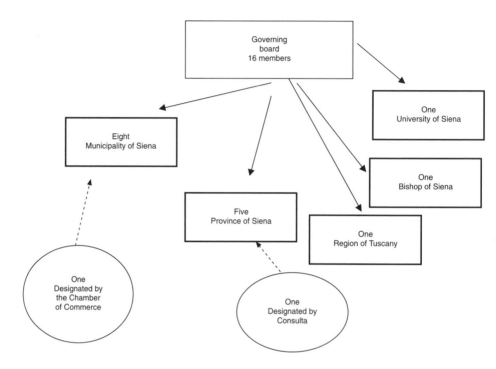

Note: Consulta is the umbrella organisation of the voluntary sector in the Province of Siena.
Source: Province of Siena.

regarding appointments of managerial positions in the foundation. On the whole, the information policies of the previous banking group were quite restrictive. It is hoped that the new foundation will not only set up a more accessible press office, but will also be more proactive in improving communications with the Sienese.

As mentioned above, Tuscany in general, and the Province of Siena in particular, historically boast a high level of social capital. In 1997, 50% of the Sienese population belonged to one or more of the province's voluntary organisations (Salvini, 1999). The percentage of the population belonging to a voluntary organisation is much lower in the rest of Italy (35%).

That said, only 10% of Sienese organisation members were active in their organisations in 1997 (Salvini, 1999). This relationship between membership in voluntary organisations and active engagement is atypical in southern European societies, which tend to be characterised by a "narrow civil society" – low member-

Table 23. **Membership, volunteering and the "activism index" in selected countries**
1990

	Category of civil society	Population as members (%) (1)	Members as volunteers (%) (2)	Activism index (1) x (2) %
United States	Active	72	64	46.1
Canada	Active	65	67	43.5
Sweden	Broad	85	46	39.1
Norway	Broad	81	45	36.5
Netherlands	Broad	85	42	35.7
Germany	Other	67	45	30.2
Belgium	Other	57	49	27.9
Ireland	Other	49	54	26.5
Denmark	Broad	81	32	25.9
Italy	Narrow	35	68	23.8
France	Narrow	39	60	23.4
Great Britain	Other	53	41	21.7
Spain	Narrow	23	52	12.0

Source: Adapted from Table 26.1 in Van den Broek and Dekker (1998), based on World Values Survey, 1990.

ship but high levels of activity by those who are members. The profile of voluntarism in the Province of Siena reflects the "broad civil society" characteristic of Scandinavian countries, where there is high membership but low levels of volunteering activity by members (see the analysis of the 1990 World Values Survey by Van den Broek and Dekker, 1998).

At present, there are 204 voluntary organisations listed in the provincial registry. They cover diverse areas, such as culture, health, civil protection, social services and blood donation. Obviously, many voluntary organisations work in the same areas, and they often have the same problems and interests with regard to public agencies. In order to facilitate co-ordination between the voluntary organisations and to provide an effective interface with the provincial administration, an umbrella organisation – the *Consulta Provinciale del Volontariato di Siena* (Consulta) – was founded at the provincial level in 1997. It represents 186 associations and has the following objectives:

- To express its opinion regarding the provincial administration's proposals in the area of voluntarism.

- To influence public opinion and public agencies in the province on issues of the service sector.

- To co-ordinate the interests of its member organisations and to bring common problems to the attention of provincial and municipal authorities.

- To make proposals promoting the voluntary sector and social policies to provincial and municipal authorities.

These are not easy tasks, given the myriad voluntary organisations in the Province of Siena. Moreover, Consulta's position would be much stronger if it disposed of an appropriate budget to support its core activities.

Participatory planning tools for coherent economic territorial governance

Territorial pacts: a network of public-private partnerships in Siena

Design process

Territorial pacts are a relatively new participatory planning tool in Italy. Their objective is to strengthen economic development via a bottom-up approach rather than the traditional top-down implementation of national economic development policies. They are specifically designed to build trust among various entities in the territory and to stimulate and co-ordinate investment by private enterprises and local administrations. Through the pacts, public and private sector investments are made in business development (industry, agro-industry, services and tourism) and infrastructure. At present, there are nearly 100 territorial pacts in Italy. The Provinces of Siena, Terni and Perugia had already signed a protocol of intention in 1994, expressing a will for joint action programmes in rural development, before the concept of participatory planning (so-called *programmazione negoziata*) was "invented" in Italy. Indeed, territorial pacts already existed in the Province of Siena before the legal instrument was even created. Thus, the design of territorial pacts can be considered as a real bottom-up development.

The various players in the Province of Siena welcomed the national government's initiative introducing territorial pacts as an experimental planning tool

---

Box 4.   **Territorial pacts**

Territorial pacts are an instrument for territorial development policies. They consist of the agreement among public and private actors to undertake interventions which can have a different nature (infrastructures or private investments), in a co-ordinated manner, in order to promote local development.

The pact takes place in an area defined at a sub-regional level, and concerns industry, agro-food, services, tourism, agriculture and fisheries.

Pacts may be promoted by local entities, social actors, or by other actors, public and private, and must be an expression of local partnership. The Italian regions and provinces, as well as financial institutions may also be parties to the pacts.

in 1996. The definition and use of territorial pacts was specifically motivated by the conviction that

- a variety of stakeholders who agree on common goals should define rural development; and

- all stakeholders in the respective economic areas should contribute to reaching the common goals.

Indeed, territorial pacts assign each partner a specific role in order to make the economic environment more conducive to business investment. For example, public agencies ensure that permits, licences and other authorisations necessary for conducting business are issued in a timely manner; trade unions reach special agreements regarding the flexibility of labour (*e.g.*, by committing themselves to a higher number of hours per week); employers commit to clear working regulations; banks give advantageous credits to investors based on agreements with the national Ministry of Finance; and companies bring in private capital and create jobs.

There are three territorial pacts in the Province of Siena at present; the "VATO 2000" Pact (VATO is the acronym of four historical regions: Valdichiana, Amiata, Trasimeno and Orvietano) came first, followed by "VATO Verde" (meaning Green VATO) and "Green Siena". (See a discussion of VATO Verde and Green Siena in Chapter 6.)

The implementation of territorial pacts in the Province of Siena

- Implementation of VATO 2000

VATO 2000 was signed in 1999 by 44 municipalities from the VATO regions, the Chambers of Commerce of Arezzo, Perugia, Siena and Terni, as well as representatives from trade unions, banks and other professional associations. The territorial pact covers 3 336 km that is home to some 210 000 inhabitants. Not only does the area have low population density (79 people per km^2), it also suffers from depopulation. When VATO 2000 went into effect, the unemployment rate in the area (about 10%) was rather high. And while the pact covers territory classified as an area of industrial decline in terms of Objective 2 of the EU, it also covers areas in need of economic diversification in terms of Objective 5*b* of the EU. As a result, VATO 2000 covers quite an economically diverse geographic area.

The promoters of VATO 2000 agreed that the redevelopment of an economically disadvantaged area had to be based on seven strategic goals:

- Upgrade the production system of the area and promote environmentally friendly tourism.

- Encourage entrepreneurial activities and the creation of jobs.

95

- Foster co-operation between public and private players to improve endogenous growth.

- Create complementary products for the area's main economic activities.

- Integrate tourism, culture and the environment to take maximum advantage of the cultural, historical and environmental heritage.

- Create infrastructure that meets the demands of the area's business community.

- Integrate the territorial pact's objectives with regional planning policies.

In light of the diversified economy, implementing these objectives implied activities in several sectors, including tourism, industry (mainly wood, metal, construction and textiles), services, and agro-industry. It also meant putting in place infrastructure for tourism as well as for industrial activities. The following figures give some idea of the political and economic significance of VATO 2000.

- One hundred and ninety-eight approved projects, including 109 in the private sector and 30 pertaining to infrastructure.

- Investments totalling more than ITL 366 billion – ITL 300 billion for private-sector projects and ITL 66 billion for public-sector infrastructure.

- Credits amounting to ITL 90 billion.

- Eight hundred and fifty-three new jobs to be created directly in the private sector and another 1 460 as a result of spin-offs.

Assessment

Even though VATO 2000 and the other two pacts are relatively new in the official sense, they already show a number of tangible and intangible results. This may be due in part to the fact that the pacts have been in existence for some time as informal networks. It may also be the result of successful project management. For example, a Tuscany credit institute, which supervises the VATO 2000 on behalf of the Treasury in Rome, confirmed the high quality of the project management with regard to the validity and credibility of the projects selected and the high degree of cohesion between infrastructure and private-sector investments.

VATO 2000 has already had some positive economic effects. It has stimulated additional investment at a time when investment in Italy was generally low. Regarding the labour market, the various projects undertaken within VATO 2000 have already created 550 jobs. VATO 2000 proponents claim that the number of indirect spin-offs may be 4 to 5 times higher. Although there is no way to assess the claim in advance, even the "rule-of-thumb" employment multiplier of 2 suggests a substantial employment creation impact.

At this stage, the three pacts face very different problems with respect to the labour market than they did when introduced. As there is now full employment in the area covered by the two VATO pacts, it has become increasingly difficult to attract highly qualified labour. VATO 2000 has already partly responded to this new challenge by organising three training programmes to upgrade skills in the local labour market. However, attracting enough low-skilled workers is also proving problematic. The managers of the pacts thought that it was appropriate to consider implementing special agreements to attract low-skilled immigrants to the area.

The territorial pacts have also contributed to the public and private governance of the areas covered. As a recent VATO Verde report points out, there has been

- a learning process among the various stakeholders on common problems in the respective areas;

- improved mutual understanding;

- a better dialogue between employers and trade unions; and

- the development of communications with civil society – this includes listening more carefully to its representatives.

Furthermore, the territorial pact managers pointed out that the pacts have enabled rural development *"based on a democratic consensus"* instead of decisions made by autonomous, private stakeholders.

Accomplishments aside, the pacts have run into some obstacles. Some small and medium-sized businesses have criticised the pacts' administrative costs, even though the reporting requirements for private companies seem to be fairly light – invoices showing that that the money was properly spent and evidence that the promised number of jobs have been created. The Treasury in Rome also has reporting requirements for the territorial pacts, but they are not onerous either. Territorial pact reports must be generated on a quarterly basis, indicating the investments made and the direct and indirect impacts on employment. Another issue is whether investments made and jobs created are sufficient measures for evaluating territorial pacts. Since the strategic goals of all three pacts have not been operationalised, goal achievement cannot be assessed.

Another obstacle to the smooth functioning of the three territorial pacts is the way in which Rome handles this participatory planning instrument. The managers of the three pacts found that supervision by the Treasury remains quite centralised and bureaucratic. For example, when changes occur in the environmental conditions and investment projects need to be adapted accordingly, the projects as a whole need to be reconfirmed by the Treasury. In short, there is very little local autonomy. Territorial pact partners also need more commitment from Rome concerning the medium- and long-term future of the pacts. Investment is unlikely

97 |

Box 5. Administrative simplification in territorial pacts in the Province of Caltanissetta in Sicily

Local policies reached through territorial pacts have reduced processing time for business permits from two or three years to 60 days, due mainly to "one-stop shops". An official representing one of the partners (often the municipality) is appointed to ensure that the authorised delay is respected. The officer has the authority to sanction investment projects even if not all of the administrative procedures have been completed within the timeframe agreed.

Source: OECD (2001*g*).

---

to be continuous if territorial pacts are only used as a policy instrument to deal with specific economic crises.

The future of territorial agreements is somewhat up in the air. There is a shared concern among the proponents of the three pacts in the Province of Siena that the new government in Rome may favour tax incentives for enterprises instead of territorial pacts. In this respect, the Sienese experience with territorial pacts may be useful to evaluate the use of participatory planning in economic development policies.

Territorial Plans of Provincial Co-ordination as an integrated planning tool

Design process

As far as territorial planning is concerned, the region of Tuscany has a complex planning system that consists of a hierarchy of plans for different local levels:

- Regional Territorial Policy Plan;
- Territorial Plan of Provincial Co-ordination (PTCP): the province acts as programme co-ordinator between the region's territorial policies and town planning; and
- Municipal General Master Plan.

According to a recent regional framework law on regional planning, other important elements of regional and provincial planning are:

- Co-ordination among public institutions, as well as the participation of economic and social players in the planning process through consultation or concerted action;
- Regular performance monitoring and evaluation of plans, as agreed with various stakeholders, through concerted action.

The PTCP gives the provinces in Tuscany a key co-ordinating role in territorial planning. By doing so, it provides them with the means to carry out their new territorial planning responsibility, which the region of Tuscany had previously transferred to them. The Province of Siena was one of the few local governments in Tuscany to respond proactively to the regional law.

The process of drafting the PTCP was innovative in two respects. First, in Italy, the drafting of land-use plans is usually contracted out to an architect, who draws up the plan based on technical expertise. In Siena, it was obvious that the PTCP would have to go beyond traditional plans for land use and would also have to consider environmental aspects. In other words, the task was to reorganise existing knowledge about territorial planning. Therefore, the provincial administration made a conscious decision to set up a working group that would bring in outside expertise, such as experts from academia. Indeed, the working group represented a variety of experts in areas such as administrative issues, soil protection, fauna, urbanism and landscape. It was also agreed that the working group would be made up of peers and have no leader.

Second, the working group incorporated a consultation process with various stakeholders in the planning process. This consultation process proved to be very beneficial in gaining the necessary consensus for Siena's PTCP. Altogether, the consultation process was carried out in three phases:

- A first planning conference was organised on 4 October 1997. The provincial government stated its intention to draft a PTCP and set forth its general objectives. This was followed by a two-month consultation period, during which the region of Tuscany, mountain communities, municipalities, cultural and environmental associations, as well as individual citizens, had the opportunity to provide input to the draft.

- The second planning conference took place on 26 November 1998. At this time, the first draft of the PTCP was presented to the public. During a four-month period, various stakeholders had a chance to react to the draft PTCP. Indeed, the working group received more than 100 sets of comments.

- The second draft was presented to the public on 12 April 1999. This time, the consultation period was extended to four months. During this period, the working group received 400 comments and followed up on about 200. The final version of the PTCP was approved on 20 October 2000 by the government majority, as well as the opposition in the provincial council.

While some associations approached the working group on their own initiative, the working group invited the following types of organised interest groups to the consultation process:

- *Municipalities and mountain communities*. These were obvious stakeholders since the PTCP primarily concerns municipalities. One issue during the consulta-

99

tion phase was the timeframe for updating municipal plans. Municipalities that did not even have old master plans were particularly concerned that they would not have enough time to undertake a municipal plan based on the PTCP. For municipalities with more planning experience, it was simply a matter of updating their old master plans. A more controversial issue was limiting urbanisation. The PTCP determined that only 100 urban centres out of some 500 aggregates with more than 50 inhabitants would be allowed to grow.

- *Region of Tuscany*. It proved to be necessary to streamline some regional regulations in order to avoid inconsistencies with the PTCP.

- *Agricultural associations*. Farmers were rather critical of the PTCP, as they considered that protecting the landscape and soil would result in additional costs for them.

Contents of Siena's PTCP

The PTCP enumerates six strategic priorities for territorial governance:

- limit urban sprawl to ensure basic services in the future;
- manage the countryside not only as a cultural resource, but also as a factor of production;
- identify the mix of economic activities that contribute to the overall economic welfare of each of the 36 municipalities and the seven economic systems in the Province of Siena discussed in Chapter 2;
- better integrate the Province of Siena's cultural and environmental assets, so as to reduce the effects of congestion brought about by mass tourism in specific areas of the province;
- modernise the existing network of roads whilst ensuring the integrity of the landscape; and
- make existing urban areas sustainable through extending and enforcing the protection of ecosystems and assessing environmental risk.

Implementation process

According to regional law, the PTCP must be reviewed every two years, with the first review in 2002. However, written guidelines for the evaluation procedure are not yet ready. Nevertheless, the provincial government has some ideas about the issues upon which the evaluation should focus. First, the PTCP's impact on the environment in the Province of Siena should be evaluated. This also includes an assessment of whether the expenditure levels have been appropriate to reach specific goals. Second, the evaluation should assess behavioural effects of the PTCP on the master plans of the municipalities in the province.

Assessment

Before assessing the preparation process of the PCPT, it is important to stress that this is the first plan that the provincial government formulated. Before the Bassanini reforms, Italian provinces had no planning competencies. In spite of this lack of experience, the working group managed to carry out the planning process in a timely and efficient manner. As a result, the PTCP could be finalised within three years.

Forming the PTCP working group can be considered good practice. Instead of relying solely on the technical expertise of architects, the Province of Siena's decision to call upon a variety of experiences and professional knowledge in drafting the PTCP proved to be valuable. Furthermore, the consultation process proved to be a beneficial exercise not just in the context of the PTCP, but also because it laid the foundation for a new type of communication between the Province of Siena and the municipalities. The latter were used to perceiving themselves as part of a vertical chain of command, whereas the consultation process turned them into interlocutors. Not only did the consultation process improve vertical intergovernmental relationships, it also improved horizontal communication between municipalities. While it would be going too far to claim that the PTCP's consultation process had overcome Italian "municipal individualism" – the so-called *campanilismo* – it did pave the way for horizontal municipal co-operation within the Programme for Urban Regeneration and Sustainable Territorial Development.

According to the working group, the consultation process went well on the whole, with a very high level of participation. Nevertheless, there are indications that the consultation was not yet a genuine dialogue among all stakeholders interested in the PTCP. As the working group admitted, it was difficult to consult with agricultural associations. This was partially due to the fact that there is no public agency responsible for landscape protection in Italy. However, another reason was that the consultation seemed to involve more lobbying than identification of common interests. Also, the consultation process did not fully include every party: some environmental associations complained that they had not been consulted at all. Even the working group has acknowledged that not all stakeholders are aware of the PTCP yet.

Finally, even though the working group has consciously based the drafting of the PTCP with a view to sustainable development in keeping with Agenda 21, the PTCP is quite limited in scope. For example, the Sienese population has not been analysed in terms of demographics, nor have the different population segments been studied from a sociological standpoint.

The "Sienese Land" PRUSST as a complex infrastructure planning instrument

Design process

The PRUSST (Programme for Urban Regeneration and Sustainable Territorial Development) belongs to the latest generation of complex planning instruments promoted by the national government. In short, the PRUSST is a financing tool for urban redevelopment with a strong focus on infrastructure projects. PRUSST typically mixes public and private funds and is used to pursue predefined objectives.

The "Sienese Land" PRUSST was created in response to a 1998 call for tenders by the Ministry of Public Works in Rome. It had three particular characteristics:

- It involved a large number of local authorities – 30 municipalities plus the province. The City of Siena was selected to manage Sienese Land PRUSST.

- Many private players (117 companies), ranging from large pharmaceutical companies to hotels, also took part in the call for tenders. The private companies brought in capital of ITL 936 billion, 51% of the total PRUSST funding.

- The PRUSST was based on the province's PTCP and considered a way to implement the PTCP.

Three main objectives motivated the PRUSST application:

- To promote sustainable development in the Province of Siena by implementing the PTCP. One way to do so was to improve physical access to, and within, the Province of Siena.

- To foster public-private partnerships in the province.

- To establish networks between small and medium-sized municipalities in order to increase their competitiveness.

Contents of the Sienese Land PRUSST

The PRUSST is a phased action plan with 210 actions to be carried out over eight years. The actions are divided into four categories:

1. In the first phase, the main network of roads connecting the Province of Siena to external provinces is to be improved. This involves 16 large-scale actions with an estimated total cost of ITL 475 billion. As a result, 26% of the total financial volume of the Sienese Land PRUSST will be spent during the first phase.

2. In the second phase, the province's minor roads are to be improved. This includes actions to slow down the traffic in urban centres as well as on ring roads, thereby keeping the main traffic out of urban centres. All told, these 26 actions amount to ITL 175 billion.

3. In the third phase (48 actions costing ITL 250 billion), more diversified actions are to be carried out, involving:

   • The restoration of town centres or individual buildings of historical or artistic value.

   • The expansion of services for tourists.

   • Urban redevelopment in areas of industrial decline.

   • The provision of infrastructure for investment sites.

4. And finally, private companies are committed to invest ITL 963 billion to finance 117 actions, such as:

   • Establishing new industries or handcrafts.

   • Restoring buildings for commercial use; *i.e.*, hotels or agro-tourism sites.

   • Extending thermal structures.

   • Establishing new facilities for public amenities and sport.

The range of actions to be carried out within the Sienese Land PRUSST marks a commitment to modernise the existing systems of roads – and construct new roads. This fully corresponds to the sustainable development strategy codified in the PTCP.

Assessment

Without a doubt, the previous drafting of the PTCP made it easier to draw up the PRUSST. Indeed, the provincial government believes that the PRUSST would not have been the same without the PTCP. First, the provincial government acquired valuable experience with complex planning tools when drafting the PTCP. Second, the previous consultation between the Province of Siena and the municipalities built up trust on both sides. Therefore, all the local stakeholders agreed that the Sienese Land PRUSST should be widely implemented in order to increase the chances of a positive answer from Rome.

Implementation of the Sienese Land PRUSST is still at a very early stage. A steering group has only been in place as of May 2001, and their first task is to develop a project management framework. Even though none of the projects are underway yet, the PRUSST has already produced positive results in terms of building social capital during the planning process. According to representatives of the provincial administration, the PRUSST has further strengthened co-operation between public actors on the local level. It has also fostered co-operation between public and private actors in the Province of Siena. And it should be mentioned that an instrument intended for an urban context has been successfully adapted to such a vast and complex area as the Province of Siena.

Nevertheless, the real challenge lies in implementation. Several steps can help contribute to success.

- *Clear accountability structures*. The myriad projects and actors, as well as the long timeframe, make it critical to codify whom is responsible for what.

- *Performance incentives*. The timely completion of projects should be rewarded, delays should be penalised.

- *Phased funding*. Funds should be released only after milestones are accomplished, with the last instalment paid only after successful completion of the project.

- *Co-ordination of project teams*. The large number of teams make co-ordination critical to avoid gaps, overlaps, and inefficiencies.

- *Definition of milestones*. This allows the tracking, evaluating, and rewarding/ penalising of progress.

- *Mid-course corrections*. Redesigning project plans may be necessary as external or internal changes occur.

Even if the project management succeeds in implementing the vast number of projects as planned, there will be high co-ordination costs. The question of whether the PRUSST was the appropriate planning tool to be used in the Siena case is raised. The high co-ordination costs seem to be more justified when the PRUSST is used to develop new infrastructure rather than improve existing infrastructure. Obviously, the PRUSST was a readily available opportunity to obtain resources from the central government and to finance the PTCP. Yet, other sources of funding may have also been available. Moreover, local partnerships are not always the most cost-effective solution as they exclude potentially more competitive external bidders from the public call for tenders.

The biggest question is whether the Sienese Land PRUSST deals effectively with the weaknesses of public infrastructure in the Province of Siena. The strategic choice to improve existing roads rather than building new roads is compatible with the PTCP but it may dissatisfy some business groups. Therefore, it becomes more and more obvious that trade-offs have to be made.

The strategic planning process in the Province of Siena

Strategic plans as a new instrument in territorial governance

Strategic plans seem to be *passé* in the private sector; however, they have become a powerful tool in governance reforms. New issues, such as sustainable development and social exclusion, require a new scope of co-ordination. Leaders must debate, persuade and negotiate agreements with different stakeholders.

Once long-term visions are agreed upon and formalised in a strategic plan, they may be used as an instrument for planning and controlling action, performance and change. This usually involves defining operational goals and performance targets. It also calls for reporting systems and accountability frameworks to monitor goal achievement by the various stakeholders.

Nevertheless, strategies are not always based on written documents that formalise long-term visions. Circumstances may change quickly, and leaders may find it necessary to address unforeseen strategic issues in the short- and medium-term. In practice, issue management and strategic change involving a vision of the future may occur separately. Issue management is appropriate for solving problems in the short- and medium-term. Visionary strategic planning allows governments to improve public governance over time and public service organisations to increase the efficiency and quality of services. In short, when it works, strategic management is a way of engaging stakeholders; obtaining their commitment; guiding the local community and specific organisations into the future; framing efforts at restructuring and redesigning for better programme and organisational performance; and forming partnerships and joint ventures with other organisations.

Having said that, the process of designing a strategic plan may be more important than the document itself. However, the real challenge is not the design of a strategic plan, but its implementation. The key question is how to motivate various stakeholders to act in a strategic way. This requires educating individuals and organisations to bring about:

• the ability to act in partnership with other stakeholders;

• competence in project management;

• negotiating skills;

• alignment of the ideas of key actors with those of the community; and

• the ability to learn and provide criticism.

In other words, local authorities are not necessarily strategic in their orientation simply because they have a strategic plan. Many local authorities have had good experience in running workshops where multiple stakeholders practice role changes and role reversals, in order to more clearly understand each other's perspectives. This kind of training should begin at the same time the commitment is made to a strategic planning process and should initially involve those who will lead the process. Eventually, it should include all provincial staff, including not only administrative staff but also elected officials. This requires real cultural change, particularly on the part of elected officials, who are often convinced that

105

the electoral mandate gives them the sufficient right to manage their office without reference to other stakeholders.

Obviously, the Province of Siena alone cannot provide all of the necessary training in public strategic management, although it clearly has a role in such training. It is essential that national civil service colleges and other training institutions specialising in public management and governance be given significant roles in the training. Ideally, the Province of Siena should work with higher education institutions in the region to design and run training programmes on a regular basis, often in collaboration with other local authorities and public agencies. This way, staff will receive high quality, up-to-date training in management, which is often far removed from their original area of expertise. Moreover, staff should undertake these programmes with counterparts from other departments of local authority government, public bodies, non-governmental organisations, and, in some cases, with officials from community organisations and the private sector. Consequently, such training programmes would act not only as a way to enhance the knowledge base and competence levels of the staff in the organisation, but they could also provide a rich platform for developing new networks between organisations.

Incentives for strategic management may also stem from inter-municipal benchmarking, as for example in the USA and Germany. Comparing the local development and performance of municipal services from a town like Siena highlights shortcomings that the local government needs to address and opportunities that it should consider pursuing. The awareness that "we are performing worse than the neighbouring village" can be a very powerful motivator.

The motives for drawing up a strategic development plan in the Province of Siena

It is important to note that strategic planning is new not only in the Province of Siena but also in Italy. While local authorities in Italy have a long tradition of urban planning, they have little experience with designing and implementing strategic plans. Nevertheless, there are a small number of places in Italy, such as Florence and Torino, that are currently experimenting with strategic planning. However, the strategic plan in the Province of Siena is the first exercise of this kind at the province level. Unlike other recent planning instruments, which were readily applied in the Province of Siena, the strategic plan has no legal basis. This is very significant, since public governance and public management reforms in Italy still tend to be implemented by law. In this respect, the strategic plan in the Province of Siena is a real bottom-up initiative. Given the lack of experience with strategic planning in Italy, the provincial government had to look abroad, notably to the Spanish cities of Barcelona and Valencia.

Box 6. **Strategic planning in the City of Barcelona**

The "Barcelona model" of strategic planning is characterised by a strong culture of consultation and co-operation with various stakeholders in the city, political planning and quality management in public services. In 1988, strategic planning began, taking advantage of the dynamic changes needed by the 1992 Barcelona Olympics. The strategic plan was initiated by the city council, which also encouraged the establishment of a General Council for the Economic and Social Strategic Plan of Barcelona. At that time, the council consisted of 181 public, private and voluntary organisations and citizens. Signed in 1990, the first strategic plan had as its vision to transform Barcelona into *"an entrepreneurial European city, with influence in the macro-region where it is situated, with a modern quality of life, socially balanced and strongly rooted in Mediterranean culture"*.

The purpose of the second strategic plan (1994) was to transition from a quantitative development model to a qualitative model. The plan consisted of the new vision *"to integrate the Barcelona area into an international economy with the aim to guarantee its growth in terms of economic and social progress as well as quality of life"*. It included five strategic objectives and 68 action plans with qualitative and quantitative performance indicators.

The objective of the current, third strategic plan (1999-2005) is to respond to the new challenges imposed by the *"information and knowledge society of the 21st century"*. Therefore, the mission of all stakeholders in the metropolitan region of Barcelona is to *"consolidate its position as one of the most important metropolitan regions in the European city network and to contribute with the purpose of connecting that network to the broader network of cities of the world through its own particularities and identity"*. The mission is defined in five strategic guidelines and 25 objectives. As was the first plan, the successive plans were approved by the General Council, which now has more than 200 corporate and individual members.

Source: www.bcn2000.es/english/menu.html

The purpose of the strategic plan is to guide decision making, and, in particular, to improve structural economic weaknesses in the Province of Siena. The second draft of the Guidelines for the Strategic Development Plan enumerates several challenges.

- The further diversification of the local economies requires a bottom-up approach towards economic development – one that is based on experiences and conditions at the local level.

- Even though the Province of Siena has a variety of economic motors, it also has a number of weak points. The draft guidelines for the Strategic Devel-

107

opment plan suggest that economic statistics indicate a slower growth rate in the provincial economy than in other comparable economic systems, although the document does not explain which other systems.

- It is necessary to intervene in a timely manner before the province's social and economic bases are damaged. It is very important to sustain the area's social capital, particularly the networks between organised interest groups and local authorities, which have been very beneficial to economic development in the past.

- Due to the recent decentralisation in Italy, local authorities have to face the challenge of multi-level governance and respect the principle of subsidiarity. The transition from government towards governance also implies significant changes in the way in which policy making operates at local levels.

Even though the Provincial Territorial Co-ordination Plan already contains some strategic elements, there is increasing awareness that the plan is too limited. It leaves out important sectors, such as tourism. Thus, a broader plan – that includes all of the province's major economic sectors – must be drafted. The idea is that the future Strategic Development Plan will be the foundation for more specific sectoral plans.

At the time of the OECD review visit, a consulting firm had finalised the second draft of the Guidelines for the Strategic Development Plan. While the first version was quite theoretical, the second focused somewhat more on what the contents of a future Strategic Development Plan should be. The first part (Chapters 1-3) enumerates the challenges to the Province of Siena in general terms. Chapter 4 describes the purposes of strategic planning at the local level. Chapter 5 discusses Italy's new approach to long-term planning (the so-called *nuova programmazione*), which is characterised by consultation with all local stakeholders, and analyses the relationships between various existing plans at regional, provincial and municipal levels. Chapter 7 points out that it is still unclear what should be the scope of future Local Development Plans based on the provincial Strategic Development Plan. The last part sets out some broad possibilities for the Province of Siena.

Altogether, the draft document identifies eight critical issues for sustainable economic development in the Province of Siena:

1. *Physical accessibility of the Province of Siena.* This section explains the important role the Urban Renewal and Sustainable Development Programme (PRUSST) plays in improving external access to the province. It also describes a number of experiences with inter-provincial co-operation aimed at improving the physical accessibility of southern Tuscany.

2. *Non-physical aspects of the territory's accessibility.* The guidelines recommend the creation of a province-wide communication infrastructure, based on a

broadband network with full access in all parts of the province. Such infrastructure appears to be vital to the development of a knowledge economy that will reinforce individual and organisational learning.

3. *Strengthening of the manufacturing sector.* The diversified structure of the manufacturing sector in the Province of Siena is a major challenge to sustainable economic development. While vertically integrated industries such as glass and bio-medical pharmaceuticals are concentrated in industrial districts in the Val d'Elsa and Val di Chiana, other industrial sectors such as mechanics are distributed throughout the province. This creates a need to:

- reinforce or create value-adding supply chains;

- support spin-offs from leading companies;

- maintain a permanent process of innovation by bringing research and production systems together;

- facilitate access to modern information and communication technologies (ICTs);

- sustain the improvement of services in companies working in the new economy;

- support existing partnerships and the development of new partnerships;

- handle problems of financing; and

- support the formation of new companies and the growth of small and medium-sized companies.

4. *Logistics.* The movement of goods and persons – logistics – is also considered to be of great importance for the economic development of the province. It, as well as the location of plants, must be taken into account when considering options for the future configuration of economic production in the province.

5. *Modernisation of the institutional system towards institutional co-operation.* The ability of public agencies in the Province of Siena to respond to the needs of businesses is influenced by companies' investment decisions. Therefore, modernising public management at the local level is an urgent requirement for the economic development strategy. While "one-stop shops" are an important instrument to facilitate "doing business" in the province – they offer increased speed and quality of information to enquiring companies – they are not enough. It is also necessary to encourage the co-production of services between municipalities, in order to exploit economies of scale and to ensure that a more comprehensive set of services, including information services, are available to the business sector.

109

6. *Tourism and cultural goods.* In spite of the high quality of services available to tourists in the Province of Siena, there is room for improvement in some areas. Congestion in specific areas especially needs to be dealt with, partly by diversifying the tourism sector. This could be done, for example, by investing in local areas where the tourism potential has not yet been fully exploited. There is also an obvious need to better integrate the tourism sector into the cultural and heritage sectors and the environment. Developing an integrated tourism promotion strategy that emphasises characteristics specific to the Province of Siena – typical local foods, wines and crafts, its famous landscape and stunning environment – could be one way of achieving this.

7. *Agro-food sector.* Food products are not only an important part of the provincial economy, they also help determine the way the province presents itself to the outside world. Public initiatives must focus on improving the competitiveness of the production system, designing ways to protect the image and reputation of typical local products, integrating this sector into the tourism sector and the environment, and accelerating the transformation of companies in sectors that still use antiquated technology or environment-unfriendly production methods.

8. *Financial system.* The structural problems of a provincial economy based on small and medium-sized businesses and a craft-production system cannot be ignored. There is a particular need to reflect on how the banking and credit system might better support the growth of small and medium-sized companies. This entails not only examining the role of specialised credit institutions, but also exploring opportunities for innovative financing mechanisms, such as the use of risk capital.

Next steps: *designing the consultation process with multiple stakeholders*

As the above scheme points out, the Italian understanding of negotiated planning only involves concerted action and not public consultation. Concerted action includes both negotiations between public and private players and eventually leads to public-private partnerships as well as horizontal and vertical co-ordination of public actions between public agencies. This means that in Italy the legal framework does not encourage consultation with citizens. Nevertheless, the City of Barcelona's experience with strategic planning and other best practice cases in OECD countries shows that a genuine and wide consultation with citizens is an important element of strategic planning.

When an OECD team of experts visited the Province of Siena in June 2000, the provincial administration had no details regarding the design of the concerted-action

Figure 12. **The mechanism of co-operation in collective action: forms and instruments of integrated territorial planning**

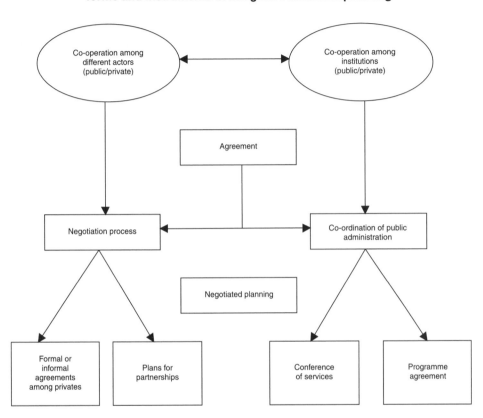

Source: Province of Siena.

process, nor the implementation of the strategy, including resource allocation, and project and change management.

Assessment

The provincial government has shown courage in embarking on a strategic planning process. Although the PTCP provided some experience in strategic planning, designing a strategic economic development plan is still a daunting challenge. Therefore, it was reasonable to contract out the initial preparation phases of the process to a consulting company. But as the province moves to implement the draft guidelines, with a view to an actual Strategic Development Plan, it will be important to learn from other OECD countries' experiences with strategic planning at the local level. The City of Barcelona is an especially valuable example, showing the need to make a strategic plan "air-tight" if it is to be used for fund-raising in the private and public sectors. It is essential that the Strategic Development Plan be based on sound medium-term financial planning. Also, the plan's chances of implementation significantly increase if its objectives, priorities and performance indicators are concrete.

Even though there is no best way to structure a business plan, most business plans for local governments – and indeed for private-sector organisations – share a number of characteristics and elements. Typically, business plans for public agencies consist of the following elements:

1. Mission statement defining the fundamental vision of the locality.
2. Context of the locality in terms of its strengths, weaknesses, opportunities and threats.
3. Portfolio of desired activities.
4. Priority groups in the population in terms of social groups, special needs groups, target segments, etc.
5. Hierarchy of objectives (from desired quality-of-life to service levels and logistical and support activities).
6. Priorities for the plan period.
7. Financial plan forecasting the income and expenditure of the public agencies over 3-5 years and supplemented by contingency plans analysing potential risks.
8. Performance indicators including targets for the plan period in terms of quality-of-life, service quality, cost-effectiveness and efficiency.

When we compare this "standard" format of a strategic plan with the elements of the future Strategic Development Plan for the Province of Siena as stipulated in the draft guidelines, it is striking to note that neither priority groups from the provincial population nor performance indicators are stated. Furthermore, in spite of some feedback loops, evaluation is not included in the scheme either.

In the Province of Siena, rural sustainable development policies and initiatives are defined and implemented within an environment of devolved authority and responsibility. As a result, a multitude of players are involved in sustainable development. This specific local governance context implies a shared discussion of territorial strategic change as well as a co-planning approach for strategic management. Therefore, it becomes all the more important to involve multiple stakeholders in strategy development and the content of strategic plans: each partner is able to bring to the table different understandings of available opportunities, risk assessments, creative abilities for problem solving, and types of resources needed to carry out the agreed actions. Moreover, stakeholders who do not actively participate in the choice of strategy are unlikely to participate wholeheart-edly in its implementation. Indeed, they may be hostile to and even impede the chosen strategy. The political arena is one in which some stakeholders can mobil-ise opposition, effectively blocking key elements of change. They could, for exam-ple, use their contacts in the media and in the social networks (which each political party is able to influence).

Strategic change invariably involves both gains and losses. It therefore neces-sitates trade-offs in which stakeholders agree to accept the losses they suffer because of the compensating gains they receive. If stakeholders are not involved throughout the strategy development and planning process, it is diffi-cult for them to get an adequate feel for which aspects are acceptable to each partner, which are "non-negotiable" and what "terms of trade" are needed for each stakeholder to be satisfied. Many local authorities develop their mission statement with the active involvement of local stakeholders. This gives citizens, members of the local council, representatives of voluntary organisations and other NGOs as well as representatives of business and trade unions the chance to map all possible alternatives and agree to medium- and long-term goals for their city. The Bertelsmann Foundation in Germany has developed "best practice guide-lines" on how to identify local visions in a participative way.

Box 7. **Compass – A project of the Bertelsmann Foundation to develop strategic management at the local level**

In Germany, more and more local governments recognise the need to make long-term and sustainable development plans. All the local authorities involved in the Bertelsmann Foundation's Compass Project in Germany (Arnsberg, Celle, Coesfeld, Dortmund, Herford and the district of Osnabrueck) have started their strategic planning by defining an overall vision and goals for specific sectors via public workshops. Citizens, elected officials and administrative employees took part in the process. The local authorities then used the results of the workshops to set priorities. In a second step, operational targets were developed for each of the goals. The targets may be objective (*e.g.*, the unemployment rate) or subjective (*e.g.*, the satisfaction of citizens with the quality of life). The vision, sectoral goals and targets all provided the basis for developing a scorecard for strategic management.

Source: *www.bertelsmann-stiftung.de*

113

In the Province of Siena, this kind of exercise was, to some extent, done through the consultation process used in preparing the PTCP. Thus, by the initiation of the strategic planning process, a certain degree of social consensus on the Province of Siena's vision could be assumed. However, consultation and commitment should not be limited to the preparation of strategic plans – they should also be factors throughout the implementation process of the strategic plan (and all other plans as well). Moreover, there has been a significant omission in the consultation process to date and in the proposals for future consultation. The process and proposals largely ignore the importance of engaging citizens and the institutions of civil society. As the experience of other local authorities in OECD countries teaches, plans risk becoming meaningless technocratic instruments, even if enacted in law, unless all relevant stakeholders support them. (Indeed, although Italian administration places great emphasis on giving legal status to public sector initiatives, legal status in itself provides no guarantee of implementation.)

In particular, medium and long-term plans that extend beyond the current political administration's term of office are unlikely to generate commitment from new political leadership. This may be less of a problem in the Province of Siena, which enjoys remarkable political stability, with centre-left majorities dominating over a long period of time. However, stable political administrations do not translate into stable political decision making – in a locality where everybody knows everybody else, elected officials are confronted almost daily with pressures to give in to the wishes and complaints of local residents. As a result, strategic goals may be jeopardised. Therefore, the provincial administration must ensure an inclusive and effective dialogue with all major stakeholders, including individual citizens and institutions representing various groups of citizens. The challenge for the Province of Siena will be to gain the attention and interest of the community at large for the Strategic Development Plan, rather than simply consulting with "the usual suspects". Obviously, less articulate segments of the population may be unmotivated to attend and speak at public hearings. As a result, it will be necessary to conduct market research, through surveys and/or focus groups, in order to identify the needs and perceptions of different segments of the population of the province.

Effective consultation processes are a necessary condition, but they are not enough to engage organised interest groups and individual citizens in an effective dialogue. Experience with consultation processes on the local level, found in other OECD countries, shows that local authorities quickly lose the commitment of the stakeholders they have been consulting unless they follow up in a timely manner. Citizens and organisations require evidence that their input is taken seriously and that actions have been taken to meet their needs. Of course, it is not possible to implement every suggestion made in consultation processes; in such instances it is important to communicate what is and is not feasible and why.

Apart from consultation, it is also important to combine the strategic planning as a top-down approach with bottom-up community initiatives. Such a mixed approach is more "messy" because the public authorities will not always feel in control of the process. While community initiatives will not always fit in well with the strategic plan, they will draw the attention of public agencies to emerging issues that require concerted action. The reverse is also true: the strategic plan may provide guidance to community initiatives and make sure that street-level activities do not jeopardise the long-term vision of the locality. Finally, this combined top-down/bottom-up approach ensures that the local community has some ownership in strategic management. It seems likely that the Province of Siena is especially fertile ground for a more active engagement from the bottom, given the historic neighbourhoods of the city of Siena as well as the surrounding small local authorities which each have separate and distinct neighbourhoods. However, it may be necessary to "unfreeze" the hidden potential of citizen and group engagement and ideas through targeted public relations efforts to raise awareness throughout the province.

Finally, strategic management requires appropriate information and management control systems. This applies in particular to quality management and financial management systems, since strategic management involves setting priorities and balancing quality and cost. In the City of Barcelona, the introduction of strategic management went hand in hand with the development of quality management systems in all public agencies. It is important to stress that the "Barcelona, Quality City" programme, which was launched in 1994 by the Strategic Plan Barcelona 2000 association, strongly focused on stakeholder involvement. The City of Barcelona, and a group of companies, NGOs and individuals set up the "Barcelona Quality Network" to monitor the quality of municipal services. In 1996, the Barcelona City Council also conducted a survey to assess local quality of life. As the provincial government only recently initiated the move to modern budgeting methods, there is a need to speed up managerial reforms. Results-oriented management will also require more ICT support than is presently available in the provincial government. Specifically, basic ICT training must be provided to all provincial employees. In addition, management control experts must also be recruited.

The acid test for strategic management is whether it has achieved cultural change. Key cultural change in Siena will involve local politicians who must display an ability to protect the long-term objectives set out in the strategic plan, whilst juggling on a daily basis the satisfaction of short-term interests and responding to crisis situations. The experience of other OECD countries shows that it is unrealistic to persuade politicians to concentrate on the "what" while the administration is allowed to keep the "how" as its exclusive domain. Rather, current governance think-tanks suggest that every stakeholder has a right to be involved in collective decision making in areas in which they have relevant expertise. Experience with complex strategic management systems in OECD countries has also shown that local politicians need training and development, perhaps with qualifications awarded, in order to move from a role of decision making to one of moderating or steering. This may be the greatest challenge facing the Province of Siena, where the president of the province and the mayors of the municipalities have recently been directly elected for the first time.

Recommendations

Enhancing the strategic planning process

Strategic planning is a powerful tool in governance reform. The emphasis, however, should not be solely on the production of a written document. Rather, the planning process and the implementation are of most importance. And in order to ensure their success it is critical to develop a participatory process that includes all relevant parties – something that is currently lacking in Siena's efforts. Absent meaningful involvement of all parties, plans risk great opposition as well as the likelihood of becoming meaningless. To enhance the strategic planning process, the following recommendations are made.

- Educate officials, individuals and organisations to motivate and enable their effective participation in the process.

- Broaden participation in the planning and implementation process to include a wide range of stakeholders. Moving from "concerted action" to "public consultation" will make the strategic planning effort in Siena more in line with best practices in other OECD countries and help ensure its effectiveness.

- To enlist broader participation, it will be necessary to conduct market research to identify the needs and perceptions of different population segments.

- To maintain that participation and commitment, it will be necessary for officials to follow up on consultations in a timely manner. That is not to say that every desire will be granted. It is, however, important to communicate back what is and is not feasible and why.

- Make the plan's objectives, priorities, performance indicators and evaluation mechanisms as concrete as possible.

- Combine strategic planning as a top-down approach with bottom-up community initiatives to help ensure that the two efforts inform and enhance one another and increase local ownership of the strategic effort.

- Incorporate the necessary information and management systems alongside the strategic effort. Quality management, financial management and ICT systems (and training) are particularly needed to set priorities and balance quality and cost.

Strengthening the PTCP

Despite some success, there are indications that the PTCP consultation did not establish a genuine dialogue among all stakeholders. The following recommendations are made to help remedy that situation.

- Ensure that every relevant party is made aware of the process and invited to participate.
- Focus participation on identification of common interests rather than lobbying.
- Broaden the scope of the process to include analysis of the demographic and sociological characteristics of the population.

Implementing the PRUSST

Still in its early stages, the PRUSST has already produced positive results in terms of building social capital during the planning process. Nevertheless, the real challenges lie in implementation. Several steps can help contribute to success.

- Create clear accountability structures that codify whom is responsible for what.
- Establish performance incentives to reward timely completion and penalise delays.
- Define project milestones, measure progress against those milestones, and release funds only after milestones are accomplished, with the final instalment paid only after successful completion of the project.
- Co-ordinate the various project teams to avoid gaps, overlaps, and inefficiencies.

Chapter 4

Access to Public Services and Infrastructures

The challenge of infrastructure and service provision in Siena

Public infrastructures and public services have an important role to play in the sustainable development of Siena. They reduce isolation, promote social cohesion and improve the territory's competitiveness. And in spite of Siena's small, scattered settlements and population scarcity, which make service provision a challenging task, even small municipalities (with contributions from the voluntary sector) have thus far been financially able to provide a wide range of services. Nonetheless, demographic changes taking place in the province, as discussed in Chapter 2, make it necessary to reconsider the current model of service provision. That said, Siena is ahead of the curve in one respect. Unlike many rural areas that often invest in "heavy infrastructure" while postponing investments in information technologies, Siena is focusing on ICT provision rather than transport infrastructure.

The chapter begins by briefly examining how the administrative decentralisation in Italy has changed the institutional framework for service delivery and produced a number of relevant managerial reforms. This is followed by a review of different OECD Member country approaches to increase the efficiency of service delivery, stressing those options that appear most appropriate for Siena. The chapter concludes with an assessment of the ICT development options pursued by the province, a look at the potential of e-service delivery, and recommendations.

Service provision changes brought about by the Bassanini reforms

The far-reaching process of administrative decentralisation has given real power to mayors of municipalities. Now elected directly, mayors are directly accountable to citizens for a wide range of municipal public services. This accountability has been reinforced by a new local taxation regime that allows municipalities to collect local taxes and user fees. For example, in 1997, 58% of the income of Tuscany's municipalities came from local taxes and user fees; transfers from the national government amounted to only 27%. It is expected that these national grants will decrease further.

In addition to changing the institutional framework for service delivery, the Bassanini reforms changed a number of managerial practices, rendering local services more efficient and citizen-oriented.

First, important changes have been achieved in municipal oversight. Whereas until 1990, the regions, through a mix of state and regional control boards (*comitati regionali di controlo*), exerted a rigid ex-ante control over all local administrative acts, there are now only a few external legal and financial *ex-ante* controls. Since 1990, mayors of municipalities with more than 15 000 inhabitants and presidents of provinces may appoint a city manager (*direttore generale*) under a fixed-term contract. The manager is to be in charge of the overall management of the local authority. In particular, the manager is responsible for implementing the executive management plan. Since 1997, it has also become possible to appoint a secretary general (*segretario generale*) who is responsible for the legal oversight of municipal acts. This person is also nominated by the mayor or president of the province for a fixed-term period. In 1999, the Province of Siena appointed a single person to the position of secretary general and executive director. Like all other Italian local authorities, the province has had an accounting board (*collegio dei revisori*) since 1990 that is responsible for internal financial control.

Second, the Bassanini reforms also resulted in a more efficient and flexible use of human resources in the civil service. In addition to eliminating the special status conferred by administrative law to most civil servants, the reforms also changed the classification system, reducing eight classification levels to four and instituting performance evaluations and performance-related pay.

Third, the Bassanini reforms shifted the management control at the local level. In the Province of Siena, the development of a management control system is still at an embryonic stage. Another challenge for the province lies in the effective implementation of ICT systems within the provincial administration. Until now, there has been little staff training. However, training programmes in co-operation with the region of Tuscany are being considered. The province agreed with the engineering faculty of the University of Siena to offer specialised ICT courses. The first post-graduate programme of its kind in Italy, the training is co-financed by Monte dei Paschi, the Marconi Mobile company and the Province of Siena.

Public infrastructures and service provision in Siena

The Region of Tuscany has 10 provinces, 287 municipalities and 18 consortia of local authorities in mountain areas (also known as mountain communities). The population of many of those municipalities is small, as is the population density of the province. In spite of that, the Province of Siena faces the problem of urban sprawl. The combined effects of sprawl and low population density raise major challenges to the efficient delivery of services at the local level. For example, demographic analyses in the PTPC show that municipalities in rural areas can no longer provide compulsory school education. Even as far as private services are concerned, the offer in rural areas is insufficient and their condition is poor.

Table 24. **The effects of low population density on public and private services in the Province of Siena**

Municipality	Number of compulsory education programmes	Number of pharmacies	Number of banks	Number of post offices
Chiusdino	0	1	1	4
Monticiano	0	1	1	3
Murlo	0	2	2	2
Sovicille	2-3	3	4	3
Chianti				
Castellina in Chianti	1	1	3	1
Castenuovo erardenga	1-2	2	4	5
Gaiole in Chianti	0-1	1	3	3
Radda in Chianti	0-1	1	2	1
Siena	25-26	16	29	8

Source: Piano Territoriale di Coordinamento della Provincia di Siena, 2000:8 (only part of the original table referring to the historical region of Val di Merse has been reproduced).

According to Italian "league tables", the Province of Siena ranks 72nd in the country in terms of public infrastructure provision. As the table below shows, the province has few airports and limited railway infrastructure. Electrical plants, ports and business services are also seriously lacking. Only in telecommunications does the province nearly match the Region of Tuscany or the centre of Italy.

Table 25. **Indicators of the provision of infrastructure**
Italy = 100

Province and region	Street and highway	Railway	Natural gas	Electrical plants	Water and sewage	Telecom- munica- tions	Harbours	Airports	Services for com- panies	Total
Siena	88.9	46.7	81.1	59.0	95.6	97.6	61.6	37.2	67.0	72.3
Tuscany	109.8	108.9	92.5	84.9	96.9	100.9	134.6	46.2	88.6	95.7
Centre	105.3	105.6	107.2	94.5	101.5	105.4	104.4	67.2	135.5	102.9

Source: Osservatorio Economico Provinciale 2000:16.

Nevertheless, the figures should not be overestimated. As an official from the Ministry of Public Administration pointed out, in spite of rather poor infrastructure, the well-developed social capital in the Province of Siena has been an important pull-factor for investments. Surprisingly, the lack of infrastructure is not due to a lack of capital, but rather to the conscious decision of the provincial administration to prioritise environmental protection over new infrastructure projects. The resulting isolation preserves the integrity of a beautiful landscape – one of the major assets of the territory. The decision to limit infrastructure will also be incorporated in the long-term development vision for the province as reflected in the Draft Strategic Plan. As a result, much has been paid to incremental improvements, rather than large additions, to the rail and road network.

When it comes to ICT provision, however, the story is quite different. The level of ICTs within the province is quite high compared with other rural provinces, though that reflects the high density of ICTs in the Municipality of Siena, one of the most wired cities in Italy. This will soon have an impact in the rest of the province, as discussed later in this chapter; an ambitious project was recently initiated with the aim of bringing broadband infrastructure to all areas of the province.

Major trends in service provision in rural areas in OECD Member countries

Many rural areas in OECD countries face difficulties in providing services to their citizens. During the 1980s and 1990s, many OECD countries experienced fiscal crises that increased budgetary pressure on local authorities. The pressure came in several forms: fluctuating tax income, rising demand for municipal services and the transfer of service responsibilities from higher levels of government. As a result, local authorities in many rural areas were to curtail services. Nevertheless, many rural municipalities managed to keep up or even improve the level and quality of local services by following one or more of the following approaches.

Merging small local authorities

This approach has several objectives: combine resources; reduce unit costs; strengthen policy capacity at the local level; increase the efficiency and responsiveness of service delivery; improve the prioritisation and quality of local services; and improve local governance.

In the United Kingdom and Germany, territorial reforms were carried out in the 1970s that significantly reduced the number of local authorities. Consequently, the United Kingdom now has the largest per authority average population in the OECD. More recently, the central governments of New Zealand and Greece carried out far-reaching reforms that significantly reduced the number of local authorities. In Canada, the Province of Ontario was particularly proactive in exerting pressure on local authorities to merge into larger units.

Increasing the size of local authorities by consolidating and removing entities is not, however, always the best policy choice. The shift from small-size municipalities to a single consolidated can impose high costs on communities. For example, too much time and energy tend to be wasted on "territorial wars" and local identity can be lost. As a result, there is growing awareness that no optimal solution exists to accommodate the wide range of local services. While a merger may improve the scale of production of technical services such as garbage disposal and therefore help reduce fixed costs, it may increase the unit costs of other services such as residential care for the elderly by, among other things, driving up transport costs.

Contracting-out to the private sector

Fiscal constraints in some OECD countries have forced many small-sized municipalities to contract with the private sector for the provision of almost all local services. Unfortunately, many of those municipalities lack the expertise needed to monitor the contracts. This raises important questions concerning the accountability and efficiency of devolved service delivery. Such expertise can of course be acquired, for example, by hiring contract management specialists or management consultants. Another possibility is to share these specialists with other local authorities or public agencies.

Joint provision of local services with other municipalities

The joint provision of services entails formal agreements through which two or more authorities pool resources and constitute a partnership to deliver services. The two prerequisites are flexibility and the ability to relinquish former levels of control over operations. Small municipalities in rural areas seem quite suitable partners for this kind of intergovernmental agreement. Such joint action allows the maximisation of benefits (through cost savings), higher quality and a greater availability of services. However, as the case of the Uribe-Kosta Services Partnership – a Spanish *mancomunidad* in Metropolitan Bilbao – illustrates, inter-municipal partnerships often run into problems such as a lack of accountability due to inappropriate "corporate governance" mechanisms.

These two examples from Spain (Box 8) show that appropriate governance of municipal partnerships is essential. Indeed, executive managers of municipal partnerships should be recruited on the basis of professional skills rather than political affiliations. Furthermore, executive managers should be employed for a fixed-term only, should have their performance evaluated and should be terminated in case of ongoing poor economic performance of the consortium.

123|

Box 8. **Mancomunidades and consortia as forms of inter-municipal partnership in Spain**

As an example of *mancomunidad*, the Uribe-Kosta Sevices Partnership (UKSP) provides a wide range of services, including waste management, social services, consumer information and protection of the Basque language. Because of the wide variety and the very nature of services provided by the UKSP, there has been a loss of accountability. On the one hand, elected political leaders have a vested interest in supplying affordable social and cultural services to their electorate. They therefore tend to fix the price of politically important services below the estimated average cost. As a result, higher levels of government end up funding part of the running costs. On the other hand, the UKSP managers end up having less autonomy since municipal councillors have strong incentives to micromanage the UKSP. The spectrum and non-technical nature of the services provided, enables them to interfere with operational management. *Mancomunidades* also raise financial and legal accountability problems, as members tend to avoid paying their fees. Because of the recurrent lack of financial commitment from municipal members in *mancomunidades*, the Province of Biscay passed a special law in order to punish free-riding behaviour.

The Greater Bilbao Water Partnership is a promising example of effective management. Consortia are typically (although not always) single-purpose associations between municipalities and higher levels of government, with occasional involvement of the private sector. Most consortia are run by a professional manager accountable to the politically appointed members of the consortium's governing body. Because of the technical nature of the service provided by consortia, politicians have fewer incentives to micro-manage the partnership. The Greater Bilbao Water Partnership represents a vertical intergovernmental partnership with a highly decentralised control structure. The 19 founding municipalities and the 24 municipalities that later have voting powers to make strategic decisions as well as executive powers to monitor the performance of the GBWP managers. The managers provide the governing board with timely financial information as well as information on outputs.

Source: Font, Gutierrez Suarez and Parrado Diez, 2000.

Co-producing social services with user groups and voluntary organisations

One major change in the local administration of welfare in OECD Member countries is the requirement that many recipients of social services must now take part in the production of those services. This is partly the result of self-organisation among service users who were dissatisfied with the nature of services they were receiving as well as with their lack of control over them. Central governments have also adopted new community care policies with a strong focus on user involvement. For example, in the United Kingdom, the aim of the 1990 National Health Service and Community Care Act was to change the system in favour of "consumer" rather than "producer" interests by requiring local authorities (in consultation with health authorities, housing authorities, other relevant agencies, community care service users representatives and their caregivers and independent sector providers) to prepare and publish plans for providing community care services.

Many governments in OECD Member countries are now providing community-based social services as opposed to institutional care. This new approach is driven by both financial and community governance considerations. Residential care provided by family, friends or neighbours is more cost-effective than institutional care in private hospitals or care homes. And locally-based social services, in contrast to remote hospitals and care homes, help integrate socially disadvantaged groups into the community and thereby reduce social exclusion.

E-*government*

The "digitalisation" of our society is a fact. New technologies are redefining not only business, but also government and the nature of public life. The on-going technological changes may offer invaluable opportunities to overcome structural disadvantages in rural areas. Such opportunities are far-reaching, encompassing the fields of education, healthcare, territorial marketing and e-government. If such opportunities for technological change are seized, all these fields will benefit from new, faster and cheaper means of communication.

The OECD recently highlighted possible advantages as well as major risks of ICTs in rural areas.[1] On the one hand, peripheral areas can benefit from the Information Society since ICT diminishes the constraints linked to time and distance. On the one hand, it is clear that remoteness, low population density and certain cultural factors make ICT development more difficult in non-urban areas. One aspect of ICT – e-government – holds promise for rural areas by not only improving access for individuals who live far from service centres or who lack physical mobility, but also by offering the possibility of entirely new services (such as e-health).

Unfortunately, not all citizens can be expected to quickly adopt ICTs. For example, socially disadvantaged groups will likely find it more difficult to access ICT and to use e-government properly. The digital divide problem in rural areas should not be underestimated. Investment in training and education should be increased in order to make citizens ICT-literate. Furthermore, traditional and new forms of service and information delivery should co-exist in the short- and medium-term to allow time for transition. Another challenge for e-government lies in improving communication between different parts of government. For example,

125|

e-users should not be repeatedly asked by different service providers for the same information. To mitigate this, many OECD countries are encouraging "one-stop shops" that concentrate services of one public agency with different geographically distant departments, or of several public agencies. Such facilities eliminate the need for travelling from one department to another, and because one-stop shops give staff better access to information, they enable better service to customers.

Not surprisingly, citizens tend to shy away from this new "customer relations management approach" when they find more than one "one-stop shop" on the same High Street. Indeed, because ICT systems are often developed separately by different public service agencies, one-stop shops are not always able to provide adequate service – to be, in fact, "one-stop". Finally, implementing e-government services can be quite costly and out of range for many small and rural municipalities. One way for municipalities to deal with this challenge is to share the cost of infrastructure, training and management with other local service providers such as school systems, hospitals and even businesses.

ICTs may also be used as a governance tool to enable citizens to solve their own problems and thus become active members of their own community. The "digital town" project in the French district of Parthenay is considered a European best practice. It implements a new role for local government as community developer.

Box 9. **The digital town project: promoting citizenship**

Parthenay is a small rural community in western France (population of 11 000 *intra muros*). The digital town e-government project started in 1996 resulted from organisational reforms in the municipal administration that increased managerial flexibility and accountability. The aim of the project was to increase the involvement of individual citizens in public issues and therefore expand the role of civil society. It involved establishing a local Intranet system, hosted by the municipality, where citizens may create home pages free of charge. It also took steps to narrow the digital divide, by

- creating digital spaces where free ICT related training is provided to citizens;
- providing all citizens with free Internet access; and
- partnering with computer manufacturers to help citizens purchase computers at a lower cost.

Mayor Michel Herve claimed that the ICT investments led to 100 new jobs in 20 companies. Critics, however, claimed that the investments were too expensive and that the economic effects were too limited. After 22 years in office, Mr. Herve lost his next bid for re-election.

Source: www.fonction-publique.gouv.fr/lareform/modernisation/accueil.htm.

Multifunctional service shops

This relatively new network approach goes beyond the traditional one-stop shop by integrating public and private services into one common spot. In this approach, a bank, the post office, a social security branch office, an employment branch office and a gas company might all serve customers from a common location – the "service shop" – while maintaining their own separate locations – "back offices" – many kilometres away. Specially trained front-line managers, highly competent in communication skills and able to cope with various needs of citizens, should staff the service shop. In the event that specialised knowledge and training is required to deal with a specific enquiry (*e.g.*, a social services inquiry), a videoconference between the citizen and a "technical" employee working in the back office could be arranged. The potential of multifunctional service shops is greatest in rural areas as evidenced by two service shops established in 1995 and 1997 in the German state Saxony-Anhalt.

This kind of arrangement has several advantages. It brings services closer to customers and facilitates citizen access to public agencies. It also allows for the distribution of different services to be bundled while their production originates from the service provider or remains under the jurisdiction of the respective administrative body. Multifunctional service shops can thus help citizens avoid going on a "pilgrimage tour" from one service provider to the next. At the same time, they allow citizens who prefer personal contact to have it rather than dealing with anonymous service providers over the phone or computer. Finally, they help reduce running costs by eliminating the need for duplicate customer service offices and personnel.

Multifunctional service shops require both public-private partnerships as well as an effective co-operation between local, regional and central government. Unlike many other rural areas, which lack the financial and technical capacity for such an undertaking, the Province of Siena possesses the administrative and technological know-how needed to successfully implement a multifunctional service shop. They also require adequate investment in ICT and in staff training.

Some feasible options for improving service delivery in Siena

Joining up local government in the Province of Siena

In Italy, one-stop shops are an obvious way to join local governments. Two preconditions have already been met: the transfer of administrative functions from central government to regions and local authorities and the administrative simplification within the framework of the Bassanini laws.

There are today two types of one-stop shops in Italy. The first is an information office for the public – accessible electronically, providing diverse information

127|

on municipal and provincial life, tourism, culture, and social issues. These information offices must be set up by every public administration in Italy. The second, business one-stop shops, serve all kinds of productive activities (trade, industry, agriculture, crafts, etc.). Their objective is to simplify the administrative procedures required for setting up, expanding, or restructuring productive activities. They also provide information and advice to private companies. They can be set up individually or jointly by several municipalities.

As far as the implementation of one-stop shops in the Province of Siena is concerned, there seems to be a digital divide between the City of Siena and the other small municipalities in the province. In information offices, there are no links between the municipalities nor with the City of Siena or the province. This lack of links is due to a problem of co-ordination among 36 extremely small communities.

Business one-stop shops in the province seem further along. Indeed, the Municipality of Siena was one of the first in Italy to establish one. Furthermore, in August 2001, the province, the Siena Chamber of Commerce and the 36 municipalities signed an agreement to network 36 business one-stop shops. The Municipality of Siena will provide assistance and co-ordination for procedural matters, and the Province of Siena will be responsible for technical and connecting aspects.

The main obstacles for this process are found first in the small size of the communities and their lack of appropriate personnel and skills, and second in their strong individualistic culture. *Campanilismo*, a common Italian phenomenon at local level implying that each local authority promotes and protects its own interests, is particularly strong in Tuscany. This is not surprising, given that small municipalities like Castellina used to be states in the Middle Ages.

Activating civil society in rural areas as co-producers

Unlike other Italian regions, Tuscany has a long tradition of co-producing public services, especially in the Province of Siena. The former hospital Santa Maria della Scala, which was run by civil associations in the 13th century, gives historical evidence of a very active civil society. Even at present, activism in the province is higher than in the rest of Italy. According to a survey by ABACUS in 1999, 6% of Italians performed volunteer work on a frequent basis. In Siena, some 10% of individuals over the age of 14 volunteered for more than one activity per month. Because volunteers in the province tend to be well-educated professionals, they offer a high level of social capital and enable small, rural municipalities to maintain a high-level of public service provision. For example, the Siena chapter of the Italian National Alpine Association (*Club Alpino*) built additional trails for the existing network of municipal and provincial trails. And the Siena chapter of the National Environmental Association (*Legambiente*) carries out environmental projects in local schools in order to improve environmental consciousness among the Siena youth.

Box 10.   **Sienese examples of co-production of public services with civil society**

The municipality of Montalcino was able to keep basic sanitary services after the relocation of its local hospital thanks to voluntary support from the Catholic voluntary association Misericordia. As a result, the hospital continues to provide care for the elderly and first aid services, including emergency surgery.

The province's Department of the Environment helped train 300 volunteers to act as environmental officers in natural reserves. In addition to funding training courses, the provincial administration also paid for the officers' uniforms as well as their travel expenses to the natural sites. The environmental officers' task is to co-operate with provincial police to ensure that tourists and hikers respect the regulations of the natural reserves.

Source: OECD.

In spite of these positive examples, there is still a need to increase the role of the voluntary sector. In order to encourage voluntary organisations to become more involved in the provision of public services, several problems need to be addressed. First, professionals do not always know how to deal with volunteers and the latter claim they are not always treated professionally. Second, accountability is often lacking, especially when things go wrong. For example, voluntary organisations often provide infrastructure such as hiking trails, but follow-up maintenance goes undone. This is both a governance problem and a financial problem. Local authorities and voluntary organisations need to clarify from the very beginning which partner is responsible for maintenance and other ongoing costs. Third, public funding for co-production with the voluntary sector is inadequate. Local authorities have an important role to play in addressing these problems. However, other local stakeholders – businesses, the media (local newspapers, citizen TV, etc.) and the voluntary sector itself should also be involved.

Enabling the Information Society: the potential of e-service delivery

The province faces a challenge: bringing in technological innovation without creating an internal digital divide.[2] New technologies are needed to improve the overall competitiveness of the province. Yet, the province's economically disadvantaged regions and populations will have great difficulty taking advantage of those new technologies and may, in fact, fall further behind as a result.

On the opposite end of the spectrum from the disadvantaged, stands the City of Siena. The municipality, with its remarkable technological infrastructure, is considered a pioneer in e-government in Italy. Indeed, the Italian government selected it as a "best case studies" for the first EU Quality Conference for Public Administrations in the spring of 2000. E-government became a reality in Siena in 1997, when the project known as "keys of the city" or Siena Card was launched. This ambitious project aims to provide citizens and tourists with better access to shops and a variety of municipal services (schools, fines, local taxes, parking, museums, etc.) 24 hours a day and 7 days a week. A "smart card", the Siena Card, contains a user's personal data and fiscal code. It is a sort of electronic wallet, allowing users to identify themselves as well as book and pay for public and private services. To date, 66% of Siena residents have a Siena Card.

The Siena Card project is financed by the banking group Monte dei Paschi and other private sources. Monte dei Paschi is a shareholder of the Society for Banking Services, which is in charge of the production of the card. The project required substantial organisational reforms (for example, greater co-operation between various public authorities and decentralisation of public services). It was also necessary to set up a service centre to link the municipal Intranet with other public agencies such as the local health unit, the hospital, banks and other private companies. All these agencies agreed to provide the necessary data to allow a seamless distribution of services and financial flows.

In addition to the Siena Card, the city has created other new services: a Web portal that allows Internet users to easily access various municipal departments, an electronic telematic commerce service that small and medium-sized enterprises to market their products and investors to explore the economic and tourist potential of Siena; and an Internet television project that enables citizens to access municipal services via their televisions. This last project may prove quite useful in narrowing the digital divide, as more people are familiar with the TV than the computer. It will also make antennas and satellites obsolete (they are actually forbidden in the old City of Siena for aesthetic reasons). Furthermore, citizens will be able to see a larger number of TV channels, including a civic channel managed by the city in co-operation with the University of Siena and other European partners.

These services are not only an important investment in Siena's future, they are also a source of city income. The special municipal regulation of 1996 allows the City of Siena to be an Internet provider, and at the time of writing, it was the only local authority in Italy which had integrated its e-government activities with e-commerce programmes – allowing it to act as an e-commerce promoter for local businesses.

The Province of Siena is adopting an "endogenous" ICT development model based on a broadband infrastructure that is to be installed within the main municipality and throughout the province. The project, being done in conjunction with Telecom Italia, will benefit from the strong financial support of Monte dei Paschi Bank. Initial investment should amount to ITL 150 billion. The stated objective of this public operation is to ensure that high quality telecommunications infrastructure reaches remote or "marginal" areas. The idea is to prevent the emergence of a digital divide in rural areas, which would likely occur if market forces were left to their own devices.

The plan is certainly innovative and ambitious, particularly in comparison to other rural areas in the country where there is little broadband infrastructure. However, the economic feasibility and suitability of current proposals are in doubt. Regarding its economic feasibility, a crucial factor will be the willingness of the local government and bank to finance the operation. Broadband infrastructure is expensive to build and operate, particularly in rural areas. Funding aside, implementing a highly modern telecommunications infrastructure throughout the entire province will not be possible or necessarily useful. A careful territorial analysis is needed to accurately identify the areas likely to make better use of technologies, and that therefore warrant investment.

Infrastructure, of course, is only one factor in readiness for the Information Society. Other factors are needed to create the proper conditions for the territory to make the best use of ICTs. For example, education and training are critical if people are to use the new technologies. Without improvement in computer literacy and language skills, those who could benefit the most from ICTs risk exclusion, and investment in infrastructure development will not produce effective results.

Recommendations

Making the most of ICTs

Investments in ICTs are a necessary, and expensive, but insufficient condition for rural development in the Information Age. Making the most of them in the Province of Siena will require the co-ordinated efforts of all public and private stakeholders in creating a comprehensive and evolving strategy that seeks coherence between ICT development objectives and existing strategic plans. Isolated actions will not suffice. Despite the province's overall advanced planning capacity, it lacks a clear and widely shared strategy for bringing the province into the Information Age. Therefore, the following recommendations are made.

- Identify and bring together all of the relevant stakeholders – public and private – to build a consensus, define a common vision and develop an action plan.

131

Box 11. ICTs in rural areas: successful initiatives

Matawinie (Quebec, Canada): Matawinie, one of Quebec's 96 regional county municipalities, covers a territory of 10 600 km^2 and has a population of approximately 45 000. Matawinie's Community Futures Development Corporation (CFDC) – a public not-for-profit corporation – was founded in 1992. There are 250 CFDCs throughout Canada as the result of co-ordinated initiatives by federal, provincial and local authorities to develop rural regions. The most significant ICT initiative funded by the CFDCs is the network of Community Access Centres (CACs). Each municipality of Matawinie has a CAC. The CACs serve as easily accessible public access centres in schools, community libraries and municipal buildings. They increase computer literacy by introducing basic computer skills and Internet applications to the general public and firms.

The Western Isles (the Highlands and Islands of Scotland): The Western Isles include an area of 3 000 km^2 and a population of 32 000. Despite the area's recent decline of traditional activities (*i.e.*, fishing and weaving), it has introduced new economic activity based on telework. Under the co-ordination of the Local Enterprise Company, the Western Isles and the European LEADER, the telework initiative – Western Isles Information and Communications Technology Service – was launched in 1994. By utilising telecommunications, which allow people to work from home via the Internet and other services, this project provides employment and revenue without requiring urban migration.

Ennis Information Age Town (Shannon Region of Ireland): Ennis is a town with a population of 18 000 located in the rural area of the Shannon Region. It has been designated as the Information Age Town of Ireland and acts as a living laboratory and showcase for Eircom (formerly Telecom Eirann, Ireland's sole telecom operator until deregulation). The Information Age Town project is organised as a private venture and thus, receives funding from Eircom, a private company. It is under the joint direction of Eircom, which owns 51%, and the local task force, which owns 49% of it in trust for the community. The town is characterised by new and emerging technologies. There is a digital broadband fibre optic ring circling the town and a digital exchange capacity of 3 000 ISDN lines. It is undergoing trials for ADSL and will soon test new technologies such as mobile access to the Internet.

Source: See OECD (2001d) *Information and Communication Technologies and their Implications for the Development of Rural Areas.*

- As part of that effort, survey citizens to determine their needs and preferences.

- Ensure that effective monitoring, evaluation and reporting systems are put in place in order to correct problems in implementation and disseminate best practices.

- Use financial resources made available by Monte dei Paschi to support strategically inter-related programmes, not isolated initiatives.

- Resources should be devoted to experimental projects using the Internet to mitigate social exclusion and provide basic services in remote areas. To this extent, tele-medicine and tele-education should be developed as part of the existing provincial strategies, building upon the variety of successful experiments conducted in several OECD countries. Finally, more resources should be made available to collect and analyse data on the extent to which the territory is digitalised and to monitor its evolution.

Delivering local services efficiently

Even though very small municipalities have been able to provide a full range of local services, this costly municipal autarky will no longer be possible in the future. Demographic changes will reduce local demand for some services (primary and secondary education), and increase demand for others (health and social services). Consequently, municipalities will have to work together to produce these services efficiently. Because of strong local identities, municipal mergers are not a realistic option. Likewise, contracting-out public services is also limited by the lack of expertise needed to ensure an effective monitoring of the service quality provided by private companies. It is possible, however, for municipalities to work together to jointly produce services. The following recommendations are made to help facilitate that joint production.

- Establish governance structures that ensure transparency and accountability.

- The strong municipal culture may hinder the realisation of one-stop shops even though their small size provides a strong economic rationale for joint provision. Resistance to co-operate could be overcome by bringing in external actors, such as private operators. This makes the relatively new approach of *multifunctional service shops* an interesting alternative for the province, as it involves participation of private actors. This has the advantage of not only diluting rivalry between municipalities but also bringing in know-how and specific skills which are often lacking in small communities.

- Provide financial incentives from the central government to small-sized local authorities to help them overcome their reluctance to co-operate.

Strengthening the role of civil society in the co-production of services

The following recommendations are made:

- Local authorities can help make information on volunteering opportunities readily available to the local population. Even though the umbrella organisation for voluntary organisations in the province, *Consulta*, partly fulfils this

133|

role, more public support is needed. This may require public information campaigns targeted at audiences other than the typical well-educated volunteer. Authorities can also improve access to the voluntary sector by providing voluntary organisations with office space in local and provincial agencies. For example, one-stop shops seem an appropriate solution to establishing a physical and virtual presence for voluntary organisations.

- Local businesses can also support volunteering by providing flexible working hours to make volunteering easier for their employees. Businesses could even second staff for a fixed period of time to voluntary organisations. The Sienese business community could also play a larger role in sponsoring social projects, although small-sized local companies will never be able to match the funding provided by Monte dei Paschi. Unfortunately, voluntary organisations in the Province of Siena do not tend to consider alternative sources of funding besides Monte dei Paschi or local authorities.

- Finally, by reporting more on the activities and problems of the voluntary sector, the regional and local press have a lot of power to help that sector. Establishing a regular flow of information exchange between *Consulta* and the four major newspapers in the province and the private television station *Canale Toscana* could raise public visibility of volunteers.

Voluntary organisations themselves should assess whether they carry out their tasks in the most efficient and effective way.

- *Horizontal co-ordination between the myriad voluntary organisations operating in the Province of Siena needs to be improved.* Many organisations work in the same field, but there seems to be little knowledge of who does what.

- *There is a lack of project partnerships between voluntary organisations.* For example, *Club Alpino* acknowledges that there are problems in maintaining hiking trails and protecting them from the threats of commercial logging and tourism. Yet, even though the Siena chapter of the National Environmental Association (*Legambiente*) has expertise and experience with environmental policing there is no co-operation between the two organisations to solve the problems.

- *There should be a stronger concern for efficiency and effectiveness within voluntary organisations.* So far, the steering boards of voluntary organisations have focused only on activities and how to finance them, not on achieving results. A stronger focus on results would encourage co-ordination and even co-operation between voluntary organisations in the province.

This requires reducing institutional, financial and behavioural barriers that limit civil society participation.

Reinforcing managerial reforms

While it is too early to assess the results of the managerial reforms begun in 1999, the limited capacity of small municipalities to implement them is worrisome. Following are several recommendations to help generate that capacity and carry through with the reforms.

- Participate in regional and national learning laboratories to learn from the successes and failures of other local authorities in Italy that are more advanced in terms of budget and human resource management. Because human resources are more important than sophisticated management instruments, keep staff motivated and upgrade their qualification levels as demands on them increase.

- Institutionalise the management of change. The steering group and/or working groups should include representatives from different levels of local authority, as well as representatives of trade unions and staff councils, on the steering group and/or working groups in order to ensure wide-spread buy-in.

- Keep staff informed about the scope and nature of planned changes, and their impacts on staffing and the workplace.

- Invest in training in order to ensure the effective implementation of executive management plans, management control systems and performance evaluations.

- Decentralise operations in order to integrate financial and staffing responsibilities at "cost centres" and "responsibility centres".

- Do not measure everything – it is not necessary and can lead to a new "measurement bureaucracy".

- Train public managers and elected officials to talk to their citizens rather than on behalf of their citizens. For example, the City of Siena has no objective data that can tell whether its citizens are satisfied with the Siena Card or not, but it deduces from the high number of users that they do like it. Therefore, it is high time for all local authorities to undertake surveys and other forms of market research to get objective data on the needs, preferences and perceptions of citizens.

Table 26. **Summary of technology options**

Access technology	Infrastructure	Range (from local exchange or base station to customer premises)	Indicative digital transmission rates	Comments
ADSL, HDSL, VDSL	Copper wire	5 km	Upstream: 256 kbit/s Downstream: 6 Mbit/s	Requires copper wire local loop Cost effective for urban areas only
DAMA	Geostationary satellite	No limit	9.6 kbit/s, 16 kbit/s, 19.2 kbit/s	Radio spectrum required
HCRCS	Fixed radio	50 km Up to 9 repeaters 50 km apart	14.4 kbit/s, 19.2 kbit/s	Radio spectrum required 28.8 kbit/s planned[3]
HFC	Optical fibre and co-axial cable	Local[1]	Up to 10 Mbit/s	Cost effective for urban areas only
ISDN	Copper wire	Up to 5 km from exchange	64 kbit/s, 128 kbit/s, 2 Mbit/s	
LEO	Orbiting satellite	No limit	9.6 kbit/s	Radio spectrum required
Microwave radio	Fixed radio	Multiples of 40 km-no limit	Up to 155 Mbit/s	Radio spectrum and line of sight required
MEO	Orbiting satellite	No limit	[2]	Radio spectrum required
Powerline	Electric power lines	Limited to existing electricity network	Up to 1 Mbit/s	Commercial viability yet to be proven
PSTA via modem	Copper wire	Up to 5-10 km from exchange	From 2.4 kbit/s to 56 kbit/s depending on condition of the local loop	
VSAT	Geostationary satellite	No limit	Upstream: up to 512 kbit/s Downstream: up to 30 Mbit/s	PSTN and ISDN can be used for upstream links radio spectrum required
Wireless local loop (WWL) (narrowband)	Fixed radio	70-90 km	Wireless IP 19.2 kbit/s	Radio spectrum required
Proprietary CDMA			Asynch. 28.8 kbit/s 64 kbit/s	
Wireless local loop (broadband) LMDS	Fixed radio	Limited	Up to 6 Mbit/s	Radio spectrum required

1. Range determined by number of people using the service rather than the characteristics of the cable.
2. No indicative transmission rates available as no service yet in operation.
3. HCRCS is now capable of 14.4 kbit/s and 19.2 kbit/s. Over time it is expected to be capable of 28.8 kbit/s.
Source: The Allen Consulting Group and Telstra.

Notes

1. See OECD (2001d), *Information and Communication Technologies and their Implications for the Development of Rural Areas.*
2. With the term *"digital divide,"* we refer here to the existing gap in opportunities to access advanced information and communication technologies between geographic areas and/or individuals at different socio-economic levels.

Chapter 5

Developing Sustainable Tourism in Siena

Introduction

High numbers of visitors and a reputation as a tourism destination are signs of the success of this sector in Siena. However, a closer analysis of tourism patterns in the province reveals weaknesses that hamper the development of sustainable tourism. These weaknesses stem mainly from the model of "cultural" tourism, prevalent in the province, which shares some features with mass tourism. This model promotes visiting a limited series of sites quite rapidly. The objective is to confirm tourists' stereotypical expectations rather than allow them to stay longer and discover the areas' lesser-known resources.

The consequences of such an approach seem evident in Siena. Tourism flows are far from evenly distributed in time and space in the province. The World Heritage sites of Pienza, Siena and San Gimignano have serious problems of congestion, exceeding their carrying capacity in the high season and resulting in environmental deterioration, social rejection, consumer dissatisfaction and significant problems for service provision.

Also to blame is the lack of a common and integrated strategy for tourism development in the province. The actors – private and public – do not operate in a co-ordinated manner. Indeed, the present success owes more to tradition (Siena and San Gimignano were included in the Grand Tour, so visitors have seen them for two centuries as part of the European must-see list) and to marketing by the foreign press and foreign tour operators than to internal efforts.

The province can no longer afford to let tourism take place in an ungoverned manner. It needs to manage both the positive and negative aspects of tourism. Siena must construct a model of sustainable tourism development that diffuses tourist concentrations, spreading both the benefits and the costs more widely. Such a model would also help conserve natural and cultural resources for the future. Fortunately, the province has the exceptional wealth of highly diversified, yet currently underused, tourist attractions needed to construct the model. These attractions focus on a variety of amenities, including heritage, landscape, farming, gastronomy and spas. However, maximising these resources in pursuit of sustainable tourism will require overcoming several obstacles.

Tourism in Siena: resources and opportunities

Uniqueness of Sienese tourism resources

Siena is an internationally known tourist destination. It evokes images of sun-drenched landscapes, historical towns, the Palio and intact medieval villages. Siena has indeed managed to preserve an integral rural landscape and a valuable cultural heritage throughout the centuries. Nonetheless, most current and prospective visitors to the province are seemingly unaware of the province's unique asset: the exceptional density and quality of cultural, architectural and environmental assets throughout the province.

Fine examples of Medieval art and architecture, Renaissance art, Etruscan remains as well as a wide variety of hilly landscapes and woods, can be found all over the province and are very popular with foreign tourists. Domestic tourists, on the other hand, tend toward the province's abundant thermal resources, most of which are located in Chianciano, although there are smaller spas in other localities (Table 27).

Current trends in tourism development

The capacity of tourism attraction of Siena, its potential for future development and the threats it faces, cannot be properly understood independently of the global trends affecting tourism (Box 12). New types of tourism based on special interests in nature and culture are growing rapidly as a proportion of total tourism and are closely linked to rural amenities (landscapes, mountains, rivers, ancient monuments). Because such amenities are more evenly distributed than the resorts that cater to mass tourism, regions ignored by mass tourism and excluded from resort strategies now have a special opportunity.

Virtually all these trends are applicable to Siena. Nonetheless, taking advantage of those trends remains a major challenge. Improvements in transport and telecommunications have the competition for tourists fierce. Many rural (and non-rural) destinations offer their tourism products to the global market. Siena thus competes not only with its neighbouring provinces in Tuscany, but with regions around the world.

Is tourism development sustainable in Siena?

With more than five million tourists visiting the province each year, tourism in Siena is widely seen as a success. But there is a growing awareness that the number

Table 27.   **Tourist presence in the Province of Siena**

	Italians	Foreigners	Total (estimate)	2nd homes
Art/business				
Hotels	488 497	421 196	909 693	
Other	195 087	240 612	435 699	
Total	683 584	661 808	1 345 392	465 000
Business/art				
Hotels	102 588	33 863	136 421	
Other	4 997	10 683	15 680	
Total	107 555	44 456	152 101	66 000
Mountains				
Hotels	64 855	2 334	67 189	
Other	2 989	18	3 007	
Total	67 844	2 352	70 196	195 000
Spas				
Hotels	1 209 111	210 887	1 419 998	
Other	107 663	63 306	170 969	
Total	1 316 7444	274 193	1 590 967	318 000
Country hills				
Hotels	97 205	121 619	218 824	
Other	60 149	254 425	314 574	
Total	157 354	376 044	533 398	694 000
Other				
Hotels	7 553	853	8 406	
Other	4 097	5 778	9 875	
Total	11 650	6 631	18 281	47 000
Total				
Hotels	1 969 779	790 752	2 760 531	
Other	374 982	574 822	949 804	
Total	2 344 761	1 365 574	3 710 335	1 785 000

Source: ISTAT, ANCI (Associazione Nazionale Comuni Italiani) and SMP estimates.

of visitors is no longer a valid indicator of successful tourism. Instead, the sustainability of tourism (and other economic activities) has become a critical objective in OECD countries. This new approach views tourism development as a valuable tool for local development as long as it has a positive impact on the local economy and community, and as long as it ensures that natural and cultural resources are preserved. In the words of the 1987 report, *Our Common Future*, prepared by the United Nations' World Commission on Environment and Development, sustainable tourism should *"meet the needs of the present without compromising the ability of future generations to meet their own needs"*.[1]

Box 12. Qualitative trends in tourism

- More tourists desire to participate in recreation, sports and adventure and learn about history, culture, nature and wildlife of areas they visit. Tourists are more physically and intellectually active now than previously.
- More tourists wish to pursue their special interests and hobbies. There are many types of special interest tourism based on nature and wildlife, archaeological and historic sites, arts and crafts, cultural patterns, economic activities and professional interests.
- "Roots" tourism of tourists visiting their ancestral home areas is becoming important in many places. Nature, cultural and adventure tourism are rapidly growing forms of tourism development.
- More tourists are seeking new destinations and new tourism products. This provides many opportunities to develop new tourism areas and improve and expand existing destinations.
- More tourists are concerned about maintaining and improving their health and there is much development of health resorts and spas. Conventional hotels and resorts are including exercise facilities. There is renewed interest in traditional medical treatments and these can form the basis for health resorts and special interest tourism.
- Many tourists are taking more frequent but shorter vacations throughout the year. This provides the opportunity to develop more tourist destinations, and for destinations to offer facilities and activities for tourists to use during different seasons throughout the year.
- More older and active retired persons, many of whom are affluent, are travelling. However, younger and middle aged people are still travelling in large numbers. More disabled persons are travelling as tourists and facilities and services are being designed to handle handicapped tourists.
- Tourists are becoming more experienced and sophisticated in their travel habits and expect good quality attractions, facilities and services, and good value for money in their travel expenditures.
- Business travel and conference/meeting tourism will continue expanding and can bring benefits to many places. Many persons travelling on business or to attend conferences and meetings also function as holiday tourists during part of their stay in an area, and they often bring their spouses with them.
- More tourists are becoming environmentally and socially sensitive and seek well-designed, less polluted tourist destinations, bypassing badly planned destinations that have environmental and social problems.
- More tourist destinations are adopting the planned and managed approach to developing tourism and wish to develop good quality tourism that avoids environmental and social problems and optimises economic benefits.
- Older tourist destinations are being upgraded and revitalised to meet present-day tourists' expectations, with this renovation being carried out in a carefully planned manner.

Box 12. **Qualitative trends in tourism** (*cont.*)

- The tourism sector is making increasing use of modern technology, in areas such as reservation services and marketing. Internet, for example, is becoming an important information and marketing tool.

Source: Guide for Local Authorities on Developing Sustainable Tourism, WTO, 1998.

This implies that:

- Economic goals must be set beyond the short-term, ensuring a high level of tourist satisfaction so that tourist destinations maintain their marketability and popularity over time.

- Social goals must be set by the community as a whole if the benefits of tourism are to be widely shared throughout the community.

- Environmental goals must be taken into account so that resources – natural as well as historical and cultural – are preserved for the future, while still bringing immediate benefits to the community.

Unfortunately, the current state of tourism in Siena puts sustainability at risk.

A *cultural mass tourism*

A significant portion of tourism in Siena is based on classical art and culture and shares many of the characteristics of mass tourism. These "fast consumption" visitors view a limited number of sites on the must-see list and show little interest in further exploring the province. A significant proportion of visitors in Siena stays only a short time and many stay only one day. The average stay in the province is 3.4 days. In the Municipality of Siena, the main tourism centre, the average stay is just 2.5 days.

The concentration of visitors at the most popular places leads to congestion in some areas (such as Siena and San Gimignano) while other areas that possess invaluable amenities (such as the Merse and Crete areas) go unnoticed. Congestion has negative social, economic and conservation implications. Excessive tourism creates resentment and rejection among locals. It can also lead to a "crowding-out" effect. That is, as tourist services replace the traditional functions of historical centres, property prices, rents and taxes typically rise so high as to force locals

143|

Figure 13. **Arrivals per municipality in the Province of Siena**
1999

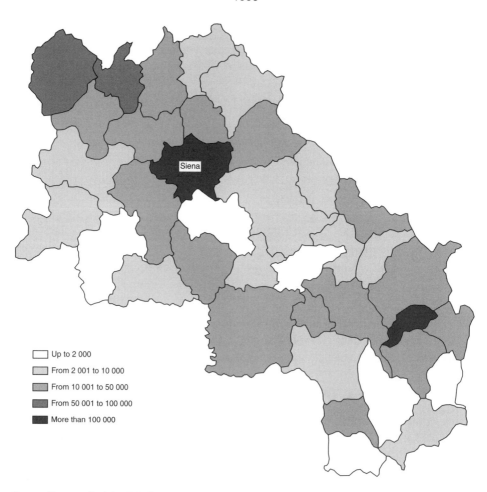

Up to 2 000

From 2 001 to 10 000

From 10 001 to 50 000

From 50 001 to 100 000

More than 100 000

Source: Rapporto Statistico della Provincia di Siena, anno 2000.

and non-tourist businesses to move in search of more affordable accommodation. Finally, it can ultimately drive visitors away as they begin to shun overexploited tourism sites in search of authentic experiences.

The historical centre of San Gimignano has experienced just such an increase in retail shops. The excessive shopping facilities and congestion detract visitors from sightseeing and can lead to tourist dissatisfaction, environmental deterioration

Figure 14.   **Average stay per municipality in the Province of Siena**
1999

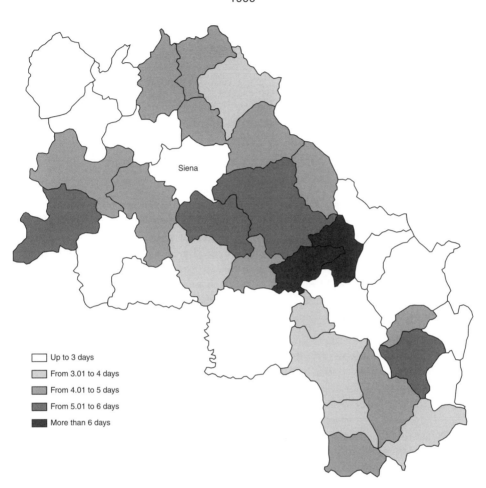

Source: Rapporto Statistico della Provincia di Siena, anno 2000.

and a tarnished image of such a major historical site. Furthermore, the shops market low-cost products, manufactured in other parts of Tuscany and Italy or supplied by the international souvenir industry, which are not at all linked to local traditions. Because San Gimignano is a UNESCO World Heritage Site, preservation, planning and real estate development are regulated. Commercial activities, however, are not. In Italy, the Bersani Law reduces the power of local authorities to regulate trade in commercial areas. Nonetheless, the Municipality of Montalcino has recently approved a regulation that requires that a "commercial impact assessment" be conducted prior to obtaining authorisation for new commercial establishments in its historical centre. This compulsory procedure aims to ensure the compatibility of certain trade or service activities with the protection and valorisation policies of its historical centre. Certain commercial activities (tourist guides and souvenirs, large grocery retail shops, construction materials, petrol stations and others) are prohibited in the historical centre.

Who benefits from tourism?

The benefits of tourism notwithstanding, the costs it imposes on a region can be quite large. If tourism is to be sustainable, investments are required to provide adequate local infrastructure and to diversify and enhance the tourism product. Some of the costs can be met by user fees (e.g., for parking and admission to museums). Other costs must be covered by the government. Unfortunately, the availability of government funding in the province seems limited. New mechanisms need to be found. The City of Siena uses the Siena Card as a way of raising funds. This city debit card allows users to pay for services, parking fees and public transport fares. It uses a differential pricing system for domestic and foreign tourists, charging higher admission fees to foreign tourists and lower fees or no fees to domestic visitors. The card helps raise some revenue, but not enough.

Consideration has been given to establishing a special tourist tax for development funding purposes in Siena City. Tuscan local governments do no have the power to raise funds through this kind of tax, although it is possible that such power will be given local authorities in the ongoing devolution process. The private sector, however, opposes the tax, in the belief that the level of taxation is already high and any additional tax would be bad for business. Representatives of the private sector argue that any additional tax would be passed on to the tourist, raising the price, discouraging tourism and leading to an overall loss in tax revenue. According to the counter-argument, a special tourist tax designated environmental or historic preservation, and explained to tourists, might be acceptable to them. The Balearic Regional Government in Spain intends to apply an "ecotourist tax" to be used specifically for environmental conservation and improving the tourism product.[2]

Huge investments are required for preserving cultural heritage. Unfortunately, museum entry fees are one of the few direct sources of income generated by cultural tourism for the benefit of cultural heritage conservation. Additionally, some may argue that cultural tourism, properly managed so that the integrity of heritage is not threatened, is obviously positive for cultural heritage, since it motivates local authorities, voluntary associations and the private sector to get involved in its pro-

146

tection and maintenance. Nonetheless, cultural tourism patterns in the province, where most tourists are interested in a limited series of cultural amenities, means that funding stands a better chance of being directed to the most visible cultural resources, to the detriment of the less visible ones. This creates therefore a vicious circle since the chance for the latter to become popular tourist attractions will be slim.

Unexploited synergies

The Province of Siena has many things to offer tourists. In addition to the popular sites, it has gastronomy and craft products and traditions that could prove attractive to tourists, yet are currently unexploited. High quality food products, such as wine (Chianti, Brunello di Montalcino, Vino Nobile de Montepulciano) and olive oil, have international reputations and markets (Chapter 6). These products contribute to the image and promotion of Siena, and some specialised tourism activities based on wine (*e.g.*, "wine trails") are starting to be developed. There is also a wealth of other less-known, yet high quality products with significant potential. Products such as Pecorino de Pienza and Sburrata cheeses, Finocchiona salami, etc., are specific to Siena's culinary tradition, but are not always found in restaurant menus, which tend to be standardised. There are natural synergies and some initiatives are being implemented. Many municipalities in the mountains of Amiata organise festivals and tours combining gastronomy, visits to local museums and churches and chestnut and mushroom picking. Nonetheless, more integrated efforts could be made at the provincial level. Craft production is even less linked to tourism development. Although the province has a strong tradition of production – objects made of travertine marble, ceramics and crystal – most of the crafts that can be found at tourist sites are souvenir items produced in other Italian regions or abroad.

Planning and managing tourism

The negative impacts of congestion, the costs of infrastructure, and unexploited synergies all point to the critical weakness facing tourism development in Siena: the lack of an integrated and long-term strategy. Sustainable tourism, like all sustainable development, requires effective co-ordination of policies and actors, in order to achieve a balance between economic, social and conservation objectives. Unfortunately, in Siena, only short-term tourism development policies, strategies and plans are being implemented. Consequently, development takes place *ad hoc*.

This is due, in part, to a complex tourism governance structure and a large number of private operators, most of whom are small and dispersed according to the typical pattern of rural tourism. The associations and consortia that do exist are very fragmented. As far as the public sector is concerned, regional, provincial

147|

and municipal authorities all participate to some extent in the management and planning of tourism activities, although not always in a co-ordinated fashion. For example, tourism promotion for the province is split between three different and unlinked agencies.

The tourism sector's current success should not be seen as a rebuttal to the argument for planning. That current success relies mainly on traditional tourism circuits – for the UNESCO sites of the province – and on the chance discovery of areas such as the Chianti. Continued success cannot be assumed or taken for granted. Tourism consumers have shown how easy it is to find substitute destinations and change their holiday patterns, as was the case for southern European tourism at the time of the conflict in Yugoslavia. Furthermore, current practices are leading to the undesired overcrowding of parts of the province and to other sustainability problems. Finally, the market is becoming more and more competitive. Tourist destinations around the world are aiming to attract tourists instead of waiting for them.

Therefore, tools are needed to define a global and coherent view for future tourism in the province. That view will need to be established in close co-operation with all stakeholders and will need to integrate with the province's overall development strategy. A strategic planning process is being initiated in the province (see Chapter 3). The Draft Strategic Plan for the province considers tourism a critical issue for sustainable development in Siena. It is timely to carry out a strategic planning exercise on tourism.

Drafting and implementing a tourism strategy

How can this integrated and long-term strategic plan be drafted and implemented? Sustainable tourism strategies usually entail a six-stage development and implementation process (OECD 2000a).

1. Collection and analysis of statistical and policy evidence concerning tourism, the wider socio-economic scene, the state of the natural environment and the cultural heritage.

2. Detailed community consultations with the existing tourism industry and related industries such as farming, forestry and transport. Advocates of nature conservation and of the promotion of cultural interests should also be involved. Official bodies of all kinds should be asked to add their views and experiences. In part, these procedures help to structure a holistic approach, and to develop tourism as a broad tool for both conservation and development. In part, the public discussions, which strategy development engenders, act as an educational stimulus to prompt better understanding of tourism's potential role. The strategy-making process

seeks out potential entrepreneurs – movers and shakers – who will help inject new life into the economy. Most importantly, in this phase and in Phase 4 described below, is the role of consultation in:

- developing a sense of ownership of the strategy on the part of the people and enterprises in an area; and
- acting as a kick-start to the development process itself, by encouraging new ideas and entrepreneurship.

3. Development of a draft strategy that includes a discussion of broader development and conservation values and goals and an assessment of best policies for the area (covering accommodation, product development, markets and marketing, organisation, support services and training/ advice). The draft strategy usually draws upon successful techniques used elsewhere in the world. In determining conservation aims, it considers concepts such as limits of acceptable change, carrying capacity and zoning. It also uses zoning to mark out areas where development efforts will have the best chance of success in a market economy. There is also a detailed implementation plan. Wherever possible, alternative ways to proceed are presented.

4. A second round of consultation amongst the stakeholders consulted in Phase 2 above. This second round allows for:

- the dissemination of the ideas and proposals in the strategy to again promote the sense of ownership by stakeholders, to aid the eventual implementation of the strategy, and to act once more as an educational forum and development tool; and
- tuning of the strategy to reflect local views and wishes.

5. Implementation of the strategy, typically over three to five years. If the project mode is used to deliver all or any part of the strategy, effective exit strategies should be devised for those projects.

6. Evaluation and review on an annual basis, ensuring the ongoing relevance of the strategy to both market and local conditions, and to build in penalties for non-performance.

Dynamics of monitoring and evaluation

It will be essential to establish, as part of the province's sustainable tourism plan, carrying capacity standards for specific places. Carrying capacity refers to the level of tourism development and visitor use that can occur without resulting in serious environmental, socio-cultural or economic problems, or being perceived by tourists as diminishing their enjoyment of a given area or site. Considerations for establishing carrying capacity standards are described in Annex I of this report.

Even when carefully planned, developed and managed, tourism can generate unexpected sustainability problems. It is essential that the environmental, socio-cultural, and economic sustainability of tourism and its resource base be continually monitored. This monitoring process will detect any problems before they become serious, and allow for remedial action if necessary. Annex II lists the core indicators of sustainable tourism adopted by the World Tourism Organisation. Based on these core indicators, more specific indicators can be established for Siena to use in monitoring sustainability. Monitoring tourism sustainability is generally the responsibility of the tourist offices in co-ordination with other government agencies and the private tourism sector. In order to carry out effective tourism monitoring, as well as successful management and marketing activities, it is essential to develop a sophisticated tourism management information system. Such a system should be organised at a provincial level in connection with municipalities that carry out tourism activities, as well as with Tuscany's regional and national tourist offices. Besides monitoring, a tourism management information system provides a database that is essential for other analytical purposes such as marketing and product development.

Types of tourism particularly relevant for the Province of Siena: farm, spa and cultural tourism

Agriturismo

Agriturismo (farm tourism) offers significant advantages for the province from a sustainability point of view. It broadens the types of tourist attractions and activities offered by the province. It appeals to tourists eager to learn more about local cultural patterns and economic activities. And it provides a stimulus for forestry and environmentally friendly activities. And because the benefits of agriturismo are more evenly shared throughout the province, it plays a revitalising role in the most deprived areas of the province, generating additional income for farmers and local communities with no other substantial economic activities. Finally, agriturismo increases the average length of tourist stay (5 days in 2000).

The Province of Siena is the second most important area in Italy for agriturismo. Bolzano, Siena, Perugia, Florence and Grosetto are, in decreasing order, those with the highest concentration of agriturismo units, together accounting for 41% of the national total (ISTAT, 1998). In early 1998, there were 440 farm holiday centre operators listed in the regional registry, up 26.8% from the previous two-year period. Today, agriturismo offers 5 200 beds, or 32% of the region's tourist beds. Arrivals increased by 37% in the 1999-2000 period.

The vitality of agriturismo can be explained by several factors. On the offer side, the need to diversify agricultural activities and the direct and indirect incentives

Table 28. **Evolution of *agriturismo* in Tuscany**
1993-1997

Province	Companies in 1993	Companies in 1997	Percentage change in the number of companies 1993 to 1997
Siena	186	392	111
Prato	4	7	75
Pistoia	16	31	94
Pisa	45	114	153
Massa	2	25	1 150
Lucca	17	42	147
Livorno	25	81	224
Grosseto	40	197	393
Florence	86	213	148
Arezzo	55	124	124

Source: IRPET.

deriving from the previous Rural Development Plans and LEADER programs, have undoubtedly played a significant role. The opportunities offered by Tuscany's regional A*griturismo* Law (L.R. 17 October, No. 76) have also strongly supported farm accommodation, giving *agriturismo* status to farms where tourism activities do not account for more than half of the invoicing. This entitles them to a preferential tax treatment – a 4% rate compared with an average rate of 27% for other types of accommodation.

Finally, *agriturismo* is popular with farmers because it provides an additional source of income, both through room and board sales and through direct-to-consumer sales of agro-food products (cheese, wine, olive oil, fruit products, vegetables, meat and poultry) at higher prices than on the wholesale market.

On the demand side, the growing popularity of countryside tourism has been a boon to Siena's *agriturismo* operators. A great part of Siena's landscape is agricultural, highly aesthetic, with a variety of hills, plains and woods, and many ancient farmhouses.

Given the sector's dynamism, the challenge for development of *agriturismo* in Siena lies in weaknesses related to quality standards and to co-ordination with other tourism activities. Rural accommodation faces the dual challenge of meeting quality, hygiene and safety expectations of urban consumers while maintaining an authentic rusticity. Although standards are generally satisfactory in the province, some countryside facilities and services have not met acceptable standards and will need to be upgraded. Facility descriptions are sometimes inaccurate or the comfort and quality are not up to foreign tourists' expectations. This situation is understandable to some extent, as the agroturismo operators are not trained tourism professionals. Nevertheless, quality issues must be resolved. Furthermore, since cost is generally not the main concern for agroturismo consumers, there is great potential for creating a higher value product.

In order to provide an adequate range of tourism services in the province, co-ordination and networking must be integrated into local and regional promotion networks. Internet information and reservation facilities must also be improved.[3]

Another significant issue likely to tarnish farm tourism's image in Siena is the uneven compliance with regulations. On some farms, tourism activity accounts for more than half of revenue; on some, farm activities are almost non-existent. Some operations, despite regulations to the contrary, do not accept reservations for less than two nights. A number of farms are not even licensed to provide catering and accommodation services. All this suggests that better law enforcement by the municipal government is necessary.

Spa tourism

Siena's spa system, one of the largest in Italy in terms of guest capacity, is adapting unevenly to major changes affecting it. On the supply side, cuts in public health system expenditures reduced the subsidies for thermal treatments and caused a drop in the number of spa visitors and in their spending.

On the demand side, other changes have reduced consumption of spa services. First, the elderly – traditionally the biggest spa users – not only enjoy better health than in the past, but also have access to a wider selection of therapy options. Second, and more significantly, the growing concern for health and well-being among people of all ages can prove a boon to the spa sector. Visitors interested in relaxation, fitness and beauty represent a new market for spas, if they are willing and able to adapt. High-quality health resorts – offering a combination of health treatments as well as recreational and entertainment facilities and activities – are increasing in number throughout Europe and the United States.

To take advantage of these changes, the Sienese spa system needs to undergo major changes itself, although a distinction should be made between the high-capacity resort of Chianciano and the smaller spa centres – some of which are of Mediaeval origin – scattered across the province. Different paths are being followed by some small spas, which are adapting successfully to the new situation, developing into integrated health resorts and proposing a quality product focusing on fitness and well-being. However, in high volume spas such as Chianciano, hotels compete with low prices and struggle to maintain their level of occupancy.

To help facilitate this restructuring, the Siena provincial government intends to promote a development plan in concert with all sector operators and local administrations. This is in accordance with the Regional Plan of 2001-2005, which allocates resources to co-finance projects in order to obtain a quality environmental thermal mark. This plan aims at fostering a "well-being" district, encouraging the sector to move towards a more innovative spa model and integrating the spa sector into the broader tourism offer in Siena. National Laws (59/97 and 127/97) have transferred share assets to the Region of Tuscany, and a privatisation process for the management of public-owned spas is progressing.

Cultural tourism and the valorisation of cultural resources

The diversified and unique artistic and cultural heritage in Siena is one of the province's main assets. But, to what extent are these valuable resources used in a productive manner? Cultural resources are increasingly deemed a valuable tool in local development, not just in pure economic terms but also in reinforcing local identity.

Traditionally, cultural assets were treated as passive elements. Given their artistic and historical value they deserved to be protected and preserved for future generations. They also needed to be shared with the public through museum exhibitions. All this required public financing, which was justified due to their nature as public goods and to their non-marketable value. This mindset has evolved, and cultural assets today are perceived as a economic assets, able to generate income and jobs and contribute to their own financing.

Italy, with a wealth of cultural heritage, is taking seriously this new approach to cultural resources. For a long time, cultural heritage policy had merely been a conservation policy, the central government being the main body involved. Beginning, however, in 1993 with the Ronchey Act (which aimed at revitalising sites and museum services for tourists), cultural policy has changed. More recently, and following the British example, funding for the conservation of cultural heritage has started coming from the national Lottery, rather than from the public budget. Additionally, at the time of this report, there were government plans to increase tax relief levels in order to further involve the private sector and to further liberalise the management of museums.

Reference needs to be made to the specific context of Tuscany regarding the management and valorisation of its cultural heritage. While responsibility for the protection of cultural heritage remains with the central government, the ongoing process of decentralisation in Italy has given the regions increased competencies in cultural heritage, notably regarding valorisation and management. Decisions on cultural assets are now implemented through concerted programming between *sopraintendenze* (regional offices of the ministry), the regions and local entities. Regional and local authorities in Tuscany have been particularly active in promoting valorisation strategies of their rich cultural resources, including historical towns and architecture, archaeological sites and arts and crafts.[4] They have focused on a number of integrated small projects in a territorially balanced manner, rather than investing in more visible, isolated mega-projects. Municipalities, interested in increasing their cultural capacities and optimising the positive effects of tourism, have been active participants.   153|

Tuscany has also attracted external resources for the valorisation of this heritage. For example, a significant amount of European funding has been used in recent years to refurbish and reopen small historical theatres, often of Renaissance origin, in many small towns. Regional theatre circuits have also been created, increasing visitation at the theatres. Regional data showing the increase in theatre attendance in Tuscany confirm the success of this initiative.

There is still a huge unrealised potential in the valorisation of Siena's cultural resources. Although there are several interesting initiatives in place (Box 13), the province does not seem to have an integrated plan for the valorisation and

---

Box 13. Cultural valorisation initiatives in Siena

Arte all'Arte

Arte all'Arte (www.arteallarte.org) gathers works of art by famous contemporary artists – especially produced for this event – in five towns of the Province of Siena and the town of Volterra in Pisa. The initiative provides an art route, an art catalogue (with international circulation) and a visitors' guide that describes the towns and surrounding countryside and recommends restaurants, wineries, local products and hotels. The initiative shows alternative artistic uses of local materials. Local craftsmen also participate. For example, in 1999, in Colle Val d'Elsa, the "crystal capital" of Tuscany, Tobias Rehrberger installed 200 lamps made out of coloured crystal and blown by local craftsmen.

Sistema dei Musei Senesi

A good example of valorisation of heritage is the recent creation of a museum network (Sistema dei Musei Senesi) http://musei.provincia.siena.it/. Items previously kept in several municipal and parish museums are to be exhibited in a series of 25 museums scattered over the territory. The idea is to increase tourists' experiential value of the province while relieving the carrying capacity problem of the most popular destinations. It does this by redirecting the 200 000 visitors of the main museums in the city to less popular areas. Each museum provides links to other museums in the network – an organised serendipity that helps visitors discover other museums and resources. For example, a tourist's interest in terracotta, mining, or the Toscan countryside introduced in one of the main museums can be investigated in depth at these topical museums off the beaten track. The system is a first step in guiding interested tourists to a Siena itinerary or path. Didactic activities are also being developed to attract specialised tourism. The initiative illustrates the key role that museums can have in understanding and interpreting the history and identity of a territory.

Source: OECD.

promotion of its cultural heritage. Its cultural heritage continues to mainly benefit a type of unmanaged cultural tourism, which is really a variant of mass tourism. True, and sustainable, cultural tourism requires a strategy, otherwise the pattern of mass consumption would lead to a devastation of the resources.[5]

The province also has great unrealised potential in linking its cultural heritage to other productive activities such as scientific research or new forms of art.[6] As an example, Florence has linked multimedia production to its artistic and architectural heritage, resulting in the creation of many small multimedia companies. Siena has a strong cultural vocation, with its long-standing tradition of artistic creation and the activities of its university, which could be the basis for development of a "cultural cluster" of related productive activities. Because there are few operators such as event organisers, art galleries and multimedia producers, private sector incentives would be needed. In addition, strong linkages between public and private stakeholders, universities, museums, and voluntary associations would have to be formed.

Recommendations

Fighting congestion: managing tourism flows

Managing tourism flows is a key issue for tourism sustainability in Siena. Some sites in the province suffer from overcrowding; others languish for lack of visitors. Actions to better manage tourist flows can be divided into two categories: those that restrict tourism and those that stimulate it (CISET, 1998) (Table 29). Regardless of the approach taken, efforts should be part of a co-ordinated strategy involving different policy areas, as well as public and private stakeholders in the province.

Table 29. **Management of tourism flows: strategies from the demand and supply side and possible tactics**

Strategies, tactics	Supply	Demand
Control	Restricting the offer/the area of visit, in time and space, so as to reduce tourism pressure (*e.g.* limited access to museums, traffic plan, coach restrictions in the city centre, etc.)	Limiting the use of local resources by increasing the cost of visit or introducing restrictive policies (*e.g.* compulsory booking, entrance fees, etc.)
Stimulus	Increasing the offer/the area to visit, in time and space, so as to favour the spread of visitor flows (*e.g.* promotion of alternative attractions/city routes, off-season events, etc.)	Rationalising the use of local resources by stimulating visitors' interest for alternative itineraries and/or attractions, through effective promotional policies

Source: CISET, 1998 (adapted from van der Borg and Gotti, 1995).

Restricting tourism supply

A possible strategy in order to decrease numbers of visitors and obtain a better management of their impact on the visited sites requires restricting tourism supply. Thus, time, space or access restrictions can be implemented, such as restricting parking in city centres and near tourist sites. Nonetheless, in Siena City, traffic and parking could be more controlled. In the old historical centre of Siena City, for example, parking is allowed near the Duomo and therefore tends to spoil the visit. City traffic planners should reduce the amount of traffic and parking in the historical centre and concentrate it on the outskirts of the centre. Shuttle bus services should be used to bring people into the centre.

Restricting tourism demand

A control of tourism may also be realised by acting upon tourism demand. This may be done by increasing the cost of tourist visits, or through other restrictive methods, such as the compulsory electronic booking system for museums (such a system has already been introduced in Siena City for school tours). Tourism flows in the congested cities can also be managed through "urban trails". These trails guide visitors, through trail maps and signs, on logical walks through the urban area that encourage distribution of the visitors in the urban area.

Enlarging the tourism offer and stimulating demand

The creation of new tourism products offers the greatest possibilities for creating a more sustainable model of tourism.

- *Create customised vacations that combine countryside, cultural visits, gastronomy and shopping.* By linking the region's assets to the growing demand for authentic experiences, the province can increase the length of stay, spread tourists out, and capture more tourist revenue. To support customised, experiential tourism, the province must link the varied resources and develop good interpretative facilities that help tourists appreciate what they are visiting. Doing this will require co-ordination between tourism operators, craftsmen, farmers, museums, municipalities, etc. Special interest tourism requires combined initiatives from the public and private sectors, although the government might need to take the lead role in initiating ideas, improving or developing the tourism product and facilitating development in general.

- *Promote ecotourism.* The province contains several nature reserves and sites of environmental interest. Ecotourism, which is currently being developed by the provincial government, will provide an additional resource for visitors interested in nature, can help spread tourism and can help justify and pay for conservation of the natural environment.

In order to attract visitors to the enlarged tourism offer, a co-ordinated marketing strategy is required, implying the need to make information on all the province's tourism possibilities transparent and accessible. This will require the joint efforts of the different tourism promotion agencies, the municipalities and private operators. Another interesting possibility lies in creating networks or systems that lead visitors from one attraction to the next. Initiatives such as Arte all'Arte or the Sistema dei Musei Senesi operate in this fashion.

Better valorising cultural tourism resources

Taking advantage of, and conserving, the province's cultural resources can contribute to sustainable tourism in Siena.

- The province should commit itself to a planned valorisation and conservation of its cultural resources. The plan should define guidelines for a more sustainable model of cultural tourism; should specify a greater role for the public sector; and should involve cultural institutions, local authorities, universities, voluntary associations and private operators.[7]

- Monte dei Paschi funds should be used to reinforce the plan. That is, funds should be limited to those efforts that are linked to the overall strategy defined in such a plan.

- Innovative products that have fewer negative impacts on the cultural sites should be created. These could include special interest tours, combined classroom and field investigation study programs, seminars and workshops and participatory excavations or restorations.

Developing a unique marketing image and branding

Marketing alone cannot lead to a sustainable tourism sector in the province; it must go hand-in-hand with the other recommendations listed in this chapter. However, marketing to create a unique image and brand for the province is important.

- Marketing efforts must be carefully co-ordinated among the public agencies involved, in connection with the government tourist offices and the private tourism sector. The province Website is a reflection of how fragmented the supply of tourist attractions and the current efforts of the various actors are. At present, it only offers links to each of the three tourism promotional offices, which, in turn, give information only on the specific part of the province they cover, with no links to the other offices.

- Create a tourism marketing co-ordination committee to encourage greater co-ordination on promotion, and to design a marketing strategy as well as a common promotional thematic approach (logo, slogans, etc.). Another approach would be to set up a joint promotion board, with funding from the provincial and municipal government and the private sector. The board would be responsible for co-ordination of all major promotional efforts for the province.

Creating synergies with locally produced crafts and foods

Stronger linkages between tourism and other local economic sectors such as agro-food production and the craft sector can only enhance the economic benefits of tourism.

- Improve and expand local production of craft items for sale to tourists, thus reinforcing the craft sector and increasing local benefits of tourism.
- To do this will require special craft research and training programmes and financial incentives.
- Provide venues for craft workshops and sales in town centres. Some municipalities in the province are already doing this.
- Establish "craft trails", where craftsmen can be seen at work. Again, some municipalities have already done this.
- Many typical Sienese agrofood products can be enhanced through tourism and also be used in the promotion of the different areas of Siena, as they are strongly linked to the history and traditions of the province.

Improving the quality of tourist offerings

The remarkable resources of the province allow Siena tourism to be marketed as an overall high-quality product. Nonetheless, the province's tourism offer shows an uneven level of quality, particularly in accommodation and catering services.

- Relieve congestion at the most popular sites. Doing so will reduce the negative consequences of mass tourism and improve quality at those locations.
- Enforce compliance with the standards that have been defined at the regional level. This will, of course, require effective government monitoring of quality standards.[8]
- Provide training to Siena's tourism operators to ensure that a high level of professionalism is achieved and that visitors' quality requirements are met.
- Provide incentives to develop better quality, but not necessarily larger, hotels. Provide incentives to refurbish existing hotels as well. Examples of providing high quality accommodations in historical centres can be found in the Spanish *paradors* and the Portuguese *pousadas* models.[9]

Enhancing agroturismo

Several things can be done to improve facility and service standards in the agroturismo sector to take advantage of increasing demand.

- Establish appropriate and internationally acceptable facility and service standards, disseminate them via manual, video and/or Internet to all relevant company managers. Enlist the provincial tourism office or a local tourism college.
- Organise short training courses on standards for company managers or employees. These training programs could be organised by the provincial tourism office in co-ordination with the local tourism office of the concerned area.
- Conduct annual inspections of companies to check compliance with facility and service standards.
- Encourage companies to provide guests with an evaluation form to rate satisfaction with facility and service. Company managers should then use evaluations as a guide to undertake improvements.
- Establish a complaints department in the tourist office for guests to use when they have serious complaints about facilities and services. The complaint department would handle all tourism complaints, not just those related to *agroturismo*.

Revitalising the spa sector

Revitalisation of the spa tourism sector in Siena would help move the sector toward sustainability.

- Emphasise clients' needs and demands in terms of quality and atmosphere.
- The Chianciano spas should broaden their offerings to include such things as a high quality cultural centre. Performances could be set up featuring internationally known entertainers, and meeting/conference facilities could be developed. Expansion and development of new hotels could include meeting facilities.
- Smaller spas should offer a combination of their own services and other types of tourism activities, taking advantage of the wealth of resources available in each sub-area of Siena. Health or fitness stays in spas could be combined with trekking tours or cultural visits. Cooking and wine-tasting courses could be organised, taking advantage of the significant gastronomic and oenological tradition in Siena.

Notes

1. Quantity has typically been the goal of mass tourism strategies. Mass tourism has often been developed without taking into account the specific culture and resources of the areas concerned, leading in many cases to extensive urbanisation and to the depletion of important resources. Furthermore, the regions in which mass tourism strategies have been followed have not always retained the benefits of tourism. In many cases, these strategies have been defined at a central government level. Powerful tour operators have played a key role in attracting high volumes of tourists with low purchasing power. Local entities have been excluded from the decision-making process. As a result of the current debate on sustainable tourism and the relative decline in mass tourism consumption, national and regional tourism plans are being refocused, and tourism has become a major component within local development strategies, particularly in rural areas. Spain, perhaps the leading example of central government-led mass tourism strategies in the 1960s, has declared the upgrading of the quality of its tourism offer as its main objective (FUTURES Programme 1992). Calvià, a mass tourism resort in the island of Mallorca, has developed its own Agenda 21. The French region of Languedoc-Roussillon, where the coastal mass-tourism strategy has failed to create stable jobs and income for sustained growth, or to protect its coastline, now promotes natural and cultural amenities in its internal rural areas.

2. This *ecotasa*, approved in April 2001 and still waiting for its Constitutional validation, would charge EUR 1 (ESP 166 386) per day for each tourist older than 12 staying in tourist accommodation.

3. "Holidays on a Farm" is an interesting farm tourism organisation in Austria (*www.farmholidays.com*). It groups farmers involved in tourism in each province, within provincial associations and federal associations, allowing a better dialogue with other tourist organisations. It uses a quality classification system based on 150 criteria such as room size, comfort, ecological factors, house location, state of the buildings, etc. It also promotes specialised products such as nature and health farms, wine farms, as well as baby and children farms. Online reservations are available for many farms.

4. Although the 1939 Law of Cultural Heritage Protection operated at a national level, the extent of conservation has varied across Italian regions. In Tuscany, there was usually a consensus to protect local heritage, as it was considered a collective good and in the community's interest to do so. In the south of Italy, where politics were more often dictated by particularism and clientelism, historical heritage has deteriorated and been neglected for many years.

5. In the mid-1990s the World Tourism Organisation estimated that cultural tourism, including tours of cultural/historic attractions, had increased by 15% annually would continue to do so throughout the next decade.

6. At the time of writing, there were plans in the municipality of Siena to create a European Centre for Art Restoration.

7. The municipality of Ferrara has developed a strategic approach to cultural tourism that adds to the valuable artistic and architectural heritage of the city. Two specialised agencies, *Ferrara Arte* and *Ferrara Musica* manage the visual and music events. A partnership between the municipality and Ferrara University has led to the creation of the first Museum of Architecture in Italy, and to the production of multimedia linked to the architectural heritage of Ferrara.

8. Integrated quality management is new to tourism development. It focuses on consumer satisfaction while taking into account the three dimensions of sustainable development. It also seeks to achieve a positive impact on the activities of tourism professionals and the local communities involved in the process. Recommendations and case studies on quality management for rural and urban destinations can be found in *Towards quality urban tourism: Integrated quality management* (IQM) *of urban tourist destinations* and *Towards quality rural tourism: Integrated quality management* (IQM) *of rural tourist destinations*, European Commission, 2000.

9. These historic hotels have been developed in old monasteries, convents, palaces and other historic buildings. The architectural style, character and furnishings of the buildings have been kept. Their restaurants typically offer a selection of the area's traditional dishes.

Chapter 6

Differentiated Agricultural Products

Introduction

Despite the considerable economic success of many agricultural producers in the province, the majority of cultivated land area is dependent on Common Agricultural Policy (CAP) subsidies to remain economically viable. The combination of market-driven and subsidised agriculture highlights the policy dilemma regarding the relative value of commodity and non-commodity outputs of the sector. Although the wines of Montalcino, Montelpuciano and Chianti are renowned throughout the world, vineyards in Siena account for only 9% of the utilised agricultural area. In contrast, the latest available estimates have the cereals, fodder, oilseed and protein crops subsidised under the CAP accounting for 71% of the utilised agricultural area that generates roughly an equal split between market and subsidy revenue for many of its farmers.[1] The integral rural landscape that is a considerable asset to the province would be dramatically different in the absence of agricultural subsidies. The policy challenge, to which actors in Siena are cognisant, is to increase the competitiveness of producers dependent on subsidies and foster entrepreneurial efforts to uncover new sources of value. Additionally, it is recognised that some form of transfer might still be required to ensure the provision of these non-commodity outputs and so instruments that would allow for such compensation are also being considered. The purposes of this chapter are to identify best practice examples ensuring the market viability of agricultural production through the development and certification of differentiated agricultural products as well as strategies for responding to changes in the CAP that are likely to ensure provision of the substantial non-commodity outputs currently associated with agricultural production.

Provision of possible non-commodity outputs of agriculture

The special role that agriculture has played in the territorial development of the province is well understood. Along with producing commodities, agriculture is the most critical activity in *"Landscape Conservation"*. Farmers maintain about 50% of the total regional area in Tuscany. Local people are convinced that the quality of

163|

life is tightly linked to the quality of the environment and to the landscape. This has been highlighted by the recent debates engendered by the consultative process surrounding the *Piano Territoriale Coordinamento*. Although there was strict agreement among members of Sienese society regarding strong links between the quality of life, the environment and the rural landscape, farmers expressed concerns regarding their potential legal responsibility in satisfying the requirements of "landscape preservation" as a potentially unfunded mandate. The very source of the problem was the presumed acceptance of these strong links by the authors of the PTCP and a lack of consultation with farmers' associations to fully examine the implications that this planning tool would have on behaviour and imposed costs. Since there are no instruments for intervention on the landscape, the actions of farmers are determinative. Plans in the PTCP regarding the maintenance of terraces that conflicted with production plans to introduce new techniques were the main source of contention. Some of the larger wineries had chosen to introduce mechanisation in some of their vineyards that was not feasible with the small walls and windbreaks of traditional practice. These changes in production practice were inconsistent with the marketing of these products that was still reliant on the image of traditional Tuscany vineyards. Resolution of this conflict was dependent on demonstrating that the value of the product was linked to an image of traditional landscapes and that the strategy of imposing the burden on others for its maintenance created an unsustainable free-rider problem. There is now an understanding that the image must be maintained by the production process if the image makes an important contribution to the value of the product. The example highlights the complexity of the problem in which competitiveness, production practices, and the amenity values associated with production are inter-linked.[2]

While it is impossible to approximate the cropping patterns and extent of cultivated area in the counterfactual of no CAP subsidies, it is generally agreed that the current subsidy scheme has contributed to an integral, idyllic rural landscape. However, claims as to the authenticity of the current landscape are questionable as the extensive mono-cropping observed in some parts of the province was not characteristic of Tuscany at any time prior to the CAP. The sharecropping system that was ubiquitous in the southern Tuscany countryside prior to the Second World War was reliant on a diversified cropping pattern. This resulted from each farm's reliance on draught animals for ploughing, the requirement to meet the subsistence consumption needs of farm families and the absence of economies of specialisation providing no incentive for landlords to stipulate monocropping of individual holdings (Pratt, 1994). Both the technological and organisational economies related to cropping patterns have changed in the postwar period that have contributed to the market rationality of monocropping. Among these, the development and diffusion of labour-saving mechanisation, substituting chemical fertiliser for the rotation of crops and composting to ensure soil fertility, and the existence of subsidies obviating the need to diversify as a strategy to guard against price risk have been critical. The above evidence does not contradict the claims that the CAP has contributed to a pleasing rural landscape, but it does open up questions as to the value of preserving the current cropping patterns over all others. The images of the *bel paesaggio* from the 16th century or the interspersed vines and trees on sowable fields of the *alberata* landscape that has been in decline since the 1920s suggests that different landscapes are both conceivable and could be highly valued. The central challenge is to envision farming systems that will both contribute to the aesthetic value of the landscape while maximising the economic competitiveness of agriculture. Indeed, it appears that the value that both residents and tourists place on an integral landscape is not merely a desire for "scenery" but relates directly to the contribution of the landscape to an agrarian way of life. That is, the value of the landscape relates not only to it being picturesque but it also being authentic. Commentators on the rural landscape have noted that *"[t]he value of land and the rural life with which it is associated comes down to... the intuitive feeling that local life is connected to the web of living things"* (Gottfried, 1996).

The argument is also made that agriculture in the province makes a significant contribution in the form of environmental services. This is clearly a contentious issue that would require analysis far beyond the scope of this review. However, there is some experience in the province suggesting that land abandonment of former cultivated areas had resulted in serious erosion problems that adversely affected downstream producers. From this perspective, the current subsidy scheme can also be thought to contribute to reducing erosion risk under the alternative of the loss of subsidy resulting in land abandonment. This issue's complexity, however, results from the range of alternatives that might be available and the responses of producers to differing incentives. While cultivation would be preferred to land abandonment in the short run, alternative land uses such as forests or grasslands demonstrate much lower rates of soil erosion in international studies relative to agriculture (Pimentel, 1993). As the debate over the PTCP demonstrated, the linkages to positive non-commodity outputs of agricultural production will also be determined by choices of production method as the move to greater mechanisation in some vineyards produced erosion problems. Experience in the province thus suggests that the link between agricultural output and the provision of environmental services is weak in the absence of restrictions on production methods.

The multifunctions of agriculture are evident in the province, but this alone is not a sufficient justification for maintaining production subsidies as it fails to envision the possibility of better targeted policy instruments or the role of entrepreneurial capacity of farmers. As the above examples demonstrate, there is often a weak link between the level of commodity production and the provision of non-

165|

commodity outputs currently associated with agriculture. In addition, production subsidies will inadvertently contribute to negative non-commodity outputs such as pesticide or nutrient leaching. The single instrument to promote positive externalities from the multifunctional perspective is too blunt to address the potential negative consequences of the policy. An alternative is to remunerate farmers for specific actions that are positive externalities of agricultural production. Such payments may be justified by the need to remunerate the provider of a public good; in particular when that good has a high non-use value which cannot be expressed in market terms. Examples of "amenity management contracts" include the Swiss "contributions for ecological services" that encourage socially desirable production methods such as organic agriculture, measures to increase animal welfare such as paddock grazing and free-range poultry farming and the conservation of biodiversity (Article 31b of the Agriculture Act, 1992). These contributions involve remunerating, on a contractual basis, the supply of ecological services beyond those prescribed by current legislation. Another example of this type of policy instrument is the *Contrat Territorial d'Exploitation* (Territorial Management Contract) in France that enables farmers to enter into five-year contracts with local authorities to ensure the provision of non-market benefits. Although available to all farmers, priority is given to proposals requiring collective action of small and medium-sized farms. Initial case study analysis of this initiative, however, cautions that monetary incentives should reinforce socially desirable practices, not substitute for the shared norms that define acceptable professional and community practice (Beuret, 1999).

Indeed, the possibility that monetary compensation of non-market services may be antagonistic to promoting positive externalities needs to be considered in light of the norms and intrinsic motivation of farmers in the province (see Frey and Oberholzer-Gee, 1997 and Vatn, 2001). The economically rational response to extrinsic incentives attached to desirable non-market outputs would be for an increased supply of those outputs. But if the motivation for their supply has been derived previously from intrinsic motivation related, say, to one's conception of the appropriate role of farmers, then extrinsic incentives may have perverse effects. This may be especially important in Siena where farmers have maintained a strong sense of autonomy and entrepreneurship. The debate over the PTCP and landscape preservation demonstrated that farmers have a strong sense of their role as stewards of the landscape, and while guarded about imposition of additional costs, may not embrace financial inducements to elicit behaviour that already exists. Vatn notes the importance of promoting the production of non-commodity outputs in an atmosphere of co-operation rather than one of control, given the complex and often relational nature of these goods:

> "Creating a common culture is not only shaping identity. It is also a way of simplifying communication. It reduces the level of transactions costs through a reduced need for control and

makes it possible to utilise the creativity of the individual farmer and her community to pro-duce high quality goods" (Vatn, 2001, p. 9).

While consideration of possible intrinsic motivations does not obviate a possible role for public subsidy, it further reinforces the priority given to market and quasi-market means for finding sustainable solutions.

The capability for farmers in Siena to adapt to a new policy environment more dependent on the creative capability of farmers is clearly augmented by the considerable value associated with an integral Tuscan landscape, the large influx of tourists that provides more opportunities for direct marketing and the considerable experience with product labelling throughout the province to add value by linking products to the territory. The farm sector in the province thus starts from the privileged position that farmers are already well aware of the alternative sources of value that exist beyond conventional commodity sales – a realisation that has yet to be demonstrated in many rural areas. The following discussion elaborates on strategies that have been successfully implemented in the province, strategies that are currently being pursued but have yet to demonstrate definitive success and strategies that are currently being developed. Indeed, there is a significant gap between the perception of feasible strategies to increase the viability of farming activities through increases in added value and current practice in the province. That gap represents a significant development opportunity, and success in securing EU funds and Territorial Pacts is evidence of this.

Successfully implemented strategies

Farm tourism

The regional law promoting farm tourism has provided one means for internalising part of the benefit from the non-commodity outputs of agriculture. By promoting the development of the sector through the special tax advantages of farms, the legislation has helped to create a market in which individual consumers can explicitly express their demand for landscape or cultural heritage amenities associated with a farm through the purchase of tourism services. The enabling national legislation was provided by Law No. 730, the "Regulation of *Agriturismo*" of 5 December 1985. The key points of the law recognise the ability of farming to produce valuable outputs other than commodities while making clear that tax advantages are attached to an ability to support the primary agricultural activities. Specifically, *agriturismo* signifies reception and hospitality by agricultural enterprises in connection with and complementary to their main cultivation, sylviculture and animal breeding practices, which must remain their prime activities. In 1994 the Region of Tuscany promulgated the first regional law regulating farm holiday activities (L.R. 17 October, No. 76) and in 1997 made some amendments to

167|

the 1994 law (L.R. 2 July, No. 48). While the topic of *agriturismo* is discussed in greater detail in Chapter 5, its importance for agriculture in the province is its ability to provide a market solution to the valorisation of the non-commodity outputs of farming.

It is from this perspective that the favourable tax treatment that the farm tourism sector enjoys with respect to conventional tourism activities must be understood. *Agriturismo* status is given to farms where tourism activities cannot account for more than half of the invoicing. The tax rate applied to this activities is 4% compared to an average rate of 27% (ranging between 20% to 42%) applied to other forms of accommodation. It is widely observed that these incentives have helped to revive the life and splendour of old farm housing that is a prized amenity of the built rural environment. Although the differential tax treatment of farm tourism relative to all other tourism activities may be thought to distort individual incentives, these must be assessed in relation to the second-best circumstance of positive externalities from the activity. Indeed, to the extent that failure to penalise a polluter comprises an implicit subsidy, failure to compensate providers of a positive externality comprises an implicit tax (Latacz-Lohmann and Hodge, 2001). The tax-favoured status of farm tourism would appear to be a reasonable resolution if the social valuation of these amenities is not fully internalised. The danger that the favourable tax treatment of farm tourism may lead to significant distortions is lessened considerably by the requirement that income coming from the tourism sector should not exceed 50% of the revenue from the farm. This has the combined desirable effect of limiting the size of single farm accommodations as well as preserving substantive farming activity. In this way, the scale of the tourism services provided on the farm are constrained to a level consistent with the amenity values desired by farm tourists.

Labelled typical products in the Province of Siena

Typical products, because of their link with the territory and its traditions, have been a factor of rural development in the area. Siena is a region with a strong traditional agricultural culture and producers in this province have earned recognition for both wine with DOC and DOCG labels and other agriculture and foodstuff products with denomination of origin or geographical indication (Table 30).[3] Case studies of Chianti Classico and Brunello di Montalcino highlight the circumstances surrounding the success of two wines that have achieved international acclaim. Development of differentiated products carrying special geographical denominations can also play an important role in less prestigious sectors, such as the olive oil or meat sector. The case of a regional IGP label (Tuscany Olive Oil) followed by the development of other labels with stricter geographical limits inside the Province of Siena is also examined.

168

Table 30. **Typical products in the Province of Siena**

Wines	
Chianti Classico	DOCG
Brunello di Montalcino	DOCG
Nobile di Montepulciano	DOCG
Vernaccia di San Giminiano	DOCG
Olive oil	
Chianti Classico Oil	PDO
Terre di Siena Oil	PDO
Tuscany olive oil	IGP
Cheese	
Formaggio	PDO
Pecorino	PDO
Toscano	PDO
Meat	
Prosciutto	PDO
Toscano	IPDO
Vitellone	IGP
Bianco dell'Appennino	IGP
Centrale	IGP
Others	
Castagna dell'amiata	IGP

Source: Mission to Siena.

The Chianti Classico case

• Historical overview

The name Chianti as related to wine was first found in a document dated 1404. In 1924, 33 small, medium and large vineyard owners and wine producers based in Radda in Chianti decided to group themselves in a *"Consorzio per la difesa del vino Chianti e della sua marca di origine"* (Consortium for the Defence of Chianti Wine and its Territory of Origin) to monitor (*tutelare*) Chianti Classico wine production, sold under the *Gallo Nero* brand, a symbol of the old military league of the Chianti Region. In 1930, an Italian law allowed producers to develop consortia with the aim of monitoring typical products. In 1932, seven sub-districts comprising the Chianti wine district were defined; that included five municipalities in the Province of Siena and four municipalities in the Province of Florence. At that time, Chianti Classico as one

169

of the seven sub-districts was recognised as the oldest geographical area of origin and it retains its original borders to this day. This area corresponds with the Chianti geographical zone, an area of 70 000 ha located between Florence and Siena. It is a hilly area, with altitudes between 200 and 600 metres. Of a total 10 000 ha of vineyards, about 70% are devoted to the production of Chianti Classico DOCG.

Chianti Classico obtained the DOC recognition in 1967, at which time a code of rules was established. The production of Chianti wine required adherence to a number of strict rules, including the type of grapes used,[4] limits on output per plant and per hectare, exceeding a specified alcohol content, the enforcement of a five-year period before new vineyards could produce wine, and a minimum of nine months before the wine could be sold. In 1984, the DOCG recognition was obtained and a stricter code of rules was imposed for the Chianti Classico wine. In 1987, the consortium split into the *"Consorzio Vino Chianti Classico"*, which monitors and supervises the Chianti Classico product, and the *"Consorzio del Gallo Nero"* (later called *Consorzio del Marchio Storico – Gallo Nero*), which promotes the product through the Gallo Nero brand.

Chianti Classico sold 25 million bottles in 2000 for a total turnover of ITL 300 billion. It is a global business, as 67% of the turnover come from exports. The main foreign markets are Germany (28%), United States (27%) and United Kingdom (17%). In the last two years, the price of Chianti Classico loose wine has been stable at ITL 550 000 a quintal. The price per bottle of a Chianti Classico is approximately three times the average price of a Chianti bottle.

Table 31. **Chianti Classico**

Territory extension (Chianti area)	70 000 ha
Total vineyards extension for DOCG wine	7 200 ha
Vineyards owned by consortium's members	5 412 ha
Producer members of consortium	85% (600)
Total production (2000)	291 406 hl
Number of traded bottles	25 million
Total turnover	ITL 300 billion
Percentage of turnover from exports	67%
Percentage of turnover from Italian market	33%

Source: OECD elaboration on Consorzio del Marchio Storico Chianti Classico figures, 1999.

• Indirect economic effects

The economic effects of Chianti Classico in the region must take into account a number of other interrelated activities. These include bottling and selling the product locally, and the growing importance of agro-tourism, tourism and restoration. The spill-over effect is not just material, in terms of economic activities linked to the wine production, but also immaterial, in terms of the product's reputation which has impacts on the region's reputation. A positive image of Siena and the Chianti Region is helping to build the wine's reputation, but at the same time the Chianti Classico's wine reputation is consolidating the very positive image of these geographical areas (both Chianti Region and Siena), thereby strengthening their attracting force. Total indirect economic effects of Chianti Classico production, linked to agro-food, craft, restoration and tourism (both agro-tourism and tourism) activities are estimated at almost three times the product's total turnover.[5]

Table 32. **Chianti Classico economic system**

Total employees in Chianti Classico firms*	2 430
Total employees in Siena's area (55%)	1 340
Total turnover of agriculture firms linked to the Chianti Classico system	ITL 830 billion
Total turnover of firms linked to Chianti Classico firms in Siena	ITL 450 billion
Total year investments in agriculture firms linked to the production of Chianti Classico	ITL 165 billion
Total year investments in Chianti Classico – Siena's area	ITL 90 billion
Total Chianti Classico selling points	320
Total Chianti Classico selling points in Siena	145

* Consortium estimates based on the ratio between hours of work and hectolitre of wine in 2000.
  This includes other sources of profit such as olive oil, cereals and agro-tourism (estimated by Chianti Classico Consortium).
  Consortium 2000 estimate (AGRIPROGEST).
Source: OECD elaboration on Consorzio del Marchio Storico Chianti Classico figures.

The Brunello di Montalcino case

• Historical overview

Brunello wine was introduced for the first time at the end of 19th century as the result of research efforts by a group of local producers, including Biondi-Santi acting as one of the leading forces. Around 1870, Ferruccio Biondi-Santi began to plant in his vineyards a clone of the Sangiovese variety known as Brunello. In a period when Tuscans generally preferred young red wines, Biondi-Santi decided to subject the wine to an ageing process involving a period of maturation of four years in oak casks, completed by a period of bottle ageing. The culture of a mono-variety wine was born and already in the beginning of the 1890s Brunello was known and appreciated abroad. But its development was interrupted by two world wars. In the 1950s, Brunello's production was limited to a relatively small number of bottles. In the same period, from a social point of view, at the end of Mezzadria Agreement, the Montalcino area followed the same pace in the demographic revolution as did other central Italian areas with a population decrease going from 10 000 inhabitants during the 1950s to 5 000 at the end of the 1960s. It was at this time, however, that in addition to some

Table 33. **Brunello di Montalcino**

Territory extension (Montalcino area)	24 000 ha
Total vineyards extension	3 000 ha
Total vineyards extension for DOCG wine	1 400 ha
Olive oil extension	3 000 ha
Cereals	4 600 ha
Woods	12 000 ha
Producers	210
Producers/bottlers with their own brand	67% (141)
Total production (1999)	68 751 hl
Member of the consortium	98% of total production
Total turnover	ITL 250 billion
Bottles produced (average 1999-2000)	4 200 000
Percentage of turnover from exports	67%
Percentage of turnover from Italian market	33%

Source: OECD elaboration on Brunello di Montalcino Consortium figures.

long standing local producers, new investors in the wine sector coming from Rome, Milan and foreign countries arrived in this area. In a buoyant Italian economy, people were attracted by the very competitive price of the land. Some local producers as well were able to buy the land thanks to a policy of facilitated credits.[6] It was also during this period that the government began to impose quality regulations on the wine and passed Law No. 930 of 1963, which introduced denominations of origin for wines.

The Ministry of Agriculture defined the geographic area of Brunello wine in 1932. In 1966, Brunello was one of the first Italian wines to obtain the DOC denomination. In 1967, producers grouped together in *"Consorzio del vino Brunello di Montalcino"*. A strict code of rules was defined governing not just grapes and techniques of production, but also the ageing of wine. In 1980, Brunello di Montalcino was the first Italian wine to be recognised as a DOCG wine. In the beginning of the 1980s, Banfi, an important American producer invested significantly in Brunello wine, giving an important example of a business-oriented, innovative producer. Banfi introduced major innovations both in the techniques of production[7] and in the marketing strategies used. In the last ten years, the code of rules has changed twice. The main changes introduced were the following: the selected grape harvest (selecting grapes between those for the *annata* production and those for the *riserva* production); the obligation to bottle the wine in the specific area; and the obligation to age the wine in durmast tanks for two years (instead of three years).

Today, Brunello di Montalcino wine is produced by 204 producers, 98% of which are members of the consortium. Fourteen hundred hectares are registered in *Brunello di Montalcino's Albo* (register). About 64% of the total production are exported, with the United States, Switzerland and Germany the major importers. Approximately 20% of the production are sold locally: 10% direct from the winery and 10% in specialised wine shops in the Montalcino area.

Table 34. **Outlets of Brunello di Montalcino wine**

	%
Direct selling	10
Specialised local wine shops and restaurants	10
Sold in other Italian regions	15
Sold outside Italy	65

Source: Mission to Siena.

• Indirect economic effects

The economic effects of the Brunello di Montalcino production in the Montalcino area are linked to a number of interrelated activities, from the local selling and the bottling of the wine, to the growing importance of agro-tourism, tourism in general and restoration. The spill-over effect on tourism is clearly evident in the case of Montalcino. Geographically isolated, and far from the usual tourist interests, Montalcino has become a destination for tourists mainly because of its production of a typical product, Brunello wine. At the same time, other products profit from the reputation of both Brunello wine and the Montalcino area; these include olive oil produced in Montalcino, honey and local fruit jams. Local people claim that Brunello wine made Montalcino a tourist destination in contrast to San Gimignano where an attractive tourist destination "made" the reputation of *Vernaccia di San Gimignano* wine. One CENSIS study estimated that one million tourists visited Montalcino in 2000.

Table 35. **Evolution in Brunello di Montalcino production**

	Producers	Producers/bottlers	Vineyards (ha)	Total production (hl)	Wine production/ha
1969	41	13	53.6	2 302	42.92
1979	83	41	624.2	28 418	45.52
1989	118	87	910.9	41 178	45.21
1999	192	135	1 344.1	68 751	51.14

Source: Consortium of Brunello di Montalcino.

Main elements of the success of Brunello di Montalcino and Chianti Classico

In addition to the favourable climate and geographical situation (a positive mix of soil, climate and altitude makes both Montalcino and Chianti Classico excellent areas for the production of wine), it is possible to determine other factors for the respective success of these products. Common elements of success include *strong associative behaviour*, a focus on *quality*, and *the ability to balance innovation with tradition*. In Chianti, producers joined together in the first consortium at the beginning of the 20th century. This was possible thanks to the capability of recognising in Chianti Classico wine a local and common richness and the necessity for producers to group together to monitor the product's quality and to develop a common market strategy. The consortium played a strong associative role, assuring the necessary collaboration between different actors of the food chain and offering important services to its members. The history of association in Montalcino is somewhat shorter with producers joining together to obtain the DOC recognition in the 1960s. In the last years, the consortium has been very active in the promotion of this wine, playing a role that not many small producers could play. Another strong element is the relationship between the product and territory. The image of this wine has changed together with the image of the territory. This area endured a demographic crisis in the 1960s, engendering feelings of isolation and marginalisation of those who decided to stay. Tourists today appreciate the isolation as well as the geographical location (overlooking a valley) of Montalcino, so that what was once considered as a negative characteristic, is today considered a very positive one (even an amenity to be protected).

Another common element of success was a clear strategy based on the *quality* of the product. Since the beginning, both Brunello di Montalcino and Chianti Classico were produced in a small limited area. Monitoring the quality and the ageing of the wine were key elements of producers' strategy in both areas. Behind the control system established for DOC and DOCG wines, firms had quality control systems to monitor the product from the cultivation of grapes to the bottling of the wine. In Chianti, the consortium also set in motion intensive research for improving the quality of the grapevines and cultivation practices through the Chianti Classico 2000 Project. It is estimated that up to two-thirds of the district's vineyards will have to be replanted to replace old vines planted in the 1950s and 1960s. In addition to requiring a considerable investment from grape growers, the replanting also presents the possibility for substantial improvement in the clones of the Sangiovese, Canaiolo and Malvasia Nera varietals. Research collaboration begun in 1988 between the consortium, researchers from universities in Tuscany and the Ministry of Agriculture has identified the most promising clones and cultivation techniques on the basis of experiments at 14 test vineyards throughout the district. The collaboration has allowed for a scientific evaluation of alternatives that would have been beyond the means of any individual member of the consortium, providing highly valuable information for a capital investment decision having a long-term effect on the quality of Chianti Classico wine. The ability of the consortium to experiment with new viticultural and winemaking techniques with

174

minimal risk to individual producers confers a considerable competitive advantage to its members in a sector characterised by quality competition rather than price competition.

Indeed, it would appear that a *mix of innovation and tradition* is essential to maintaining competitiveness in the premium wine sector. Even the oldest estate of Brunello, Biondi-Santi, had a very innovative approach. The capacity of this product to adapt to changes is demonstrated by the evolution of its code of rules. In fact, there is a strong debate within the consortium between those wanting to maintain a traditional product and those who want to innovate. To date, a good balance has been maintained. This tension in Chianti has been manifest in the two different market orientation strategies. Some firms opted for a differentiation strategy, investing in a large array of products and in their quality. These companies have invested in the development and promotion of their brands.[8] Other firms opted for a niche strategy, selling to specific local markets and to single clients (importers); they use the consortium's brand Gallo Nero. No firm has adopted cost saving strategies. Where companies have opted for a differentiation strategy, they have invested important sums on research and innovation; those opting for niche strategies (smaller sized companies) use tradition as a key element in their success. They use their small size and their flexibility to adapt to market changes. In so far as research is concerned, they tend to use the consortium's services. The first group of companies has brought an element of innovation and modernity, and the second group of firms has been more important in preserving traditions. The consortium has helped this mix of innovation/tradition to work successfully, playing an important role in developing a cohesive working relationship between companies with different needs and offering a range of services recognising these differences.

Olive oil

• The olive oil sector in Tuscany

Tuscany olive oil is a niche product. In 1999/2000, Tuscany produced 200 000 quintals of olive oil, representing 2.7% of the total Italian production (7.2 million quintals), with Florence followed by Grosseto and Siena, as the main producers. The olive oil sector in Tuscany suffers from both the fragmented nature of the food chain's structure and high production costs, the latter partially linked to sophisticated strategies in view of obtaining a high quality product. Traditionally, those from Tuscany have cherished the special taste of oil produced in the region. The close link between urban and rural areas has made local consumption important and it is one of the principal reasons why olive oil production continues to exist in the region. People used to go to the countryside to buy their olive oil directly from the producers. This situation changed somewhat when, after the crisis which befell this sector in 1985 (caused by a severe frost or *gelata*), people began to buy industrialised olive oil in supermarkets. At present, only 65% of the total production are commercialised, with the rest consumed directly by olive growers and collectors (self-consumption) or sold locally (direct selling) to local people visiting firms or to tourists.

The main food chain actors are[9] the olive growers, olive millers, blenders and bottlers. Many farmers cultivate olive oil trees in Tuscany, together with other cultivation. The last Census (1991) counted 70 000 farms with an average size of 1.26 ha that produced, in combination with other products, olive oil. About 9.6% of regional SAU (*Utilised Agricultural Area*) were dedicated to this production. During the 1990s, this sector went through a consolidation process that included new plants, and the renovation and rationalisation of old plants. In general, the local population is showing a renewed interest in olive oil production for several reasons. It is possible to cultivate this product in conjunction with another product; it is relatively easy to cultivate and the population appreciates its favourable influence on the landscape. Olive oil has, in fact, a strong impact on the character of the Tuscany landscape. Normally, olive growers bring their olives to oil millers who act as service deliverers: the product is then commercialised through various short channels (self-consumption, consumption by an inner circle of friends and family, and through direct selling). Some co-operative oil millers are able to sell their product through more important commercial channels (shops, supermarkets). Blenders and bottlers are highly polarised; there are a few important leading firms which blend and bottle the oil coming from different regions, or which produce olive oil with olives originating from a variety of regions.

Table 36.   **Olive oil food chain in Tuscany and in Siena**

	Year	Tuscany	Siena
Production area (ha)	1998	93 361	14 706
	1999	97 041	18 711
	2000	98 920	20 289
Production of pressed oil (ql)	1998	165 326	15 059
	1999	194 321	19 780
	2000	123 970	n.a.
Number of active oil mills	1997/1998	417	54
	1998/1999	425	53

Source: Irpet, Third Report on Agriculture Economics in Tuscany, May 2001.

EU policy for olive oil is based on a system of quotas. The general EU quota is shared between national quotas. Subsidies per unit of production were reduced in the last 1998 policy revision. The special aid system for small producers was abolished. At the same time, EU approved the EU Regulation 2815/1998 establishing that the origin indicated on extra-virgin olive oil is the geographical place in which the processing (milling) takes place and not where the olives are grown.[10] This means, for example, that under EU legislation an olive oil produced with imported olives, but milled in Italy, can be sold under the "Made in Italy" label.

Given the many difficulties faced by olive oil producers in Tuscany, along with the ongoing process of reform of EU policy and the abolition of the special aid system for small producers, it was decided to adopt a differentiation strategy through the use of denomination of origin labelling. Producers felt that it was necessary to improve information to consumers who were unaware that Tuscany olive oil could in fact be milled of olives coming from other regions. Large producers were promoting these oils as traditional products, trying to attract consumers by using the reputation established by the Tuscany region.

- The Tuscany olive oil IGP

On the urging of the Tuscany region, the Ministry of Agricultural Policy initiated the procedure in 1994 to obtain the PDO recognition at EU level for Tuscany olive oil. In 1997, the national DOC was granted to Tuscany olive oil, although it was later suspended. In the same year, the EU refused to recognise Tuscany olive oil as a protected denomination of origin because of the weakness in the link between the product and the geographical environment and because of the non-uniformity of different extra-virgin olive oil produced in the region.[11] In February 1998, the EU decided to grant the geographical indication (IGP) to Tuscany olive oil and the name was registered in March 1998. Producers can obtain the IGP certification and they can also ask for an additional geographical mention corresponding to specific areas (*e.g.*, Tuscany olive oil, Colline Senesi).

Producers in Tuscany have demonstrated a consistent interest in IGP certification. Some provinces were more attracted than others were. The main producers are Grosseto, Florence and Livorno, with the Province of Siena playing a less important role. Today, the IGP "Toscano" represents 33% of national certified olive oil production (which is just 1% of the total national production). The main outlets for IGP Tuscany olive oil are supermarkets[12] and a large quota of total production which is exported (60%). The main importers are the United States, Japan and Germany.

177|

Table 37. **IGP Tuscany olive oil**
1998/1999 – 1999/2000

	Unit	1998/1999	1999/2000
Members of consortium	Number	6 300	8 500
Members with certification	Number	n.a.	3 000
Area registered	Hectares	35 440	45 000
Potential production (including self consumption)	Quintals	40 000	44 400
Released certifications	Number	72	170
Additional geographical mentions	Number	3	2
Certified production	Quintals	5 574	15 363
Certified production from Siena	Per cent	8%	4%

Source: Irpet, Third Report on Agriculture Economics in Tuscany, May 2001.

Table 38. **Operators asking for IGP certification**
1999/2000

	Certifications		Quantities	
	Number	%	Quintals	%
Agriculture farms	33	19.8	337	2.2
Co-operative millers	72	43.1	9 029	58.8
Agriculture farms with mill	6	3.6	234	1.5
Private millers	11	6.6	578	3.8
Bottling firms	45	26.9	5 118	33.7
Total	167	100.0	15 363	100.0

Source: Irpet, Third Report on Agriculture Economics in Tuscany, May 2001.

• IGP impacts

Although the results of this very recent denomination[13] are not as definitive as with the wine case studies above, several suggestive observations are possible. The main effect of the IGP differentiation strategy was the positioning of the Tuscany olive oil on long distance distribution channels and foreign markets. A part of olive oil produced in Tuscany is still sold locally to both local people and tourists. Direct selling from the producer to the consumer allows the producer not to lose an important source of revenue. This oil is generally sold, however, without the IGP label. The use of IGP denomination has opened new interesting markets for olive oil produced in Tuscany in that it can now be sold in large national and international supermarkets. The IGP denomination has lessened consumer confusion as to what Tuscany extra virgin olive oil is so that supermarkets are much more confident introducing Tuscany IGP extra virgin olive oil in their product line. This has also required a consistent reorganisation of the supply chain facilitated by the important role of co-operative oil millers.

Since 1997,[14] it is possible to observe an increase in price of Tuscany olive oil on the Florence market (commercialisation at wholesale level or *commercializzazione all'ingrosso*) following the denomination recognition and, also, an increasing price gap between non-IGP and IGP oil in favour of the IGP oil.[15] This positive effect on the price has profited mainly production taking place in geographical areas with a minor affirmed reputation (*e.g.*, Maremma area). This is directly linked to another important effect. The use of IGP certification has provoked a reallocation of the benefit coming from the Tuscany reputation between different provinces. In this first period those areas of Tuscany region that did not profit from a partic- ular notoriety and that did not use the geographical reputation as a promotion leverage, profited from the common regional name in a consistent way. Some of these areas, due to the nature of the soil, are particularly apt for the introduction of new production techniques. This is not the case of other sub-regions that, because they are located in valleys, are less adapted to the introduction of new techniques although this characteristic is strongly appreciated by tourists.

The participation to IGP Tuscany certification was quite limited in provinces that, having already an important tourist reputation, preferred to develop their own labels. This was the case of Siena's olive oil producers that contributed with a limited percentage to the total IGP Tuscany olive oil production in 1998/1999 (8%). This production was even lower in 1999/2000 (4%). Even the use of the special geo- graphical mention Colline Senesi was limited. Nevertheless, this province has seen the affirmation of two EU recognised denominations of origin for extra-virgin olive oil: Terre di Siena DOP and Chianti Classico DOP.[16] These denominations have been recognised as DOP and they have strict product and processing stan- dards established by the code of rules.

Table 39. **Olive oil with special designations in Province of Siena**

Designation	Classification	EU registration date
Tuscany Olive Oil	IGP Special mention Colline Senesi	March 1998
Terre di Siena Oil	DOP	November 2000
Chianti Classico Oil	DOP	November 2000

Source: Mission to Siena.

Box 14. **Terre di Siena DOP and Chianti Classico DOP**

Terre di Siena (DOP). Following Law 169/1992 on protected designations of origin for olive oil, Colline Senesi olive oil obtained the Italian DOC recognition. In November 2000, Terre di Siena olive oil was recognised as a DOP by the European Union. The code of rules was established and a third independent inspection body was chosen: Societa "Agro Qualita" srl. In 2000, total certified Terra di Siena extra virgin olive oil production was 64 ql, produced by eight firms. The consumer price was about 40% higher than conventional industrialised olive oil. About 30% are sold directly to consumers; approximately 20% in supermarkets and approximately 50% in small shops specialised in typical products.

Chianti Classico (DOP). The *Consorzio Olio Extra Vergine d' Oliva della Zona del Chianti Classico* was created in 1975. In 1992, the consortium asked for recognition of the EU DOP, which was obtained in 2000, with the recognition of *Olio Chianti Classico* DOP. As of 31 December 2000, 141 producers were members of the consortium, with 176 484 olive trees registered. In 2000, certified extra virgin olive oil production was 750 ql. In 2000-2001, the consortium received 468 applications requesting certification. As a result of the consortium's services (monitoring of the production and quality through a territorial computer system) and its promotional activities, it is foreseen that in five years the consortium should control 90% of tradeable olive oil production taking place in this area.

Source: OECD mission to Siena.

Implemented strategies showing promise

Organic agriculture as a product differentiation strategy

Organic agriculture in Siena

In 2000, only 5% of total agriculture land (SAU) in Tuscany was organic agriculture. The number of firms registered in the regional register of organic operators, however, has grown rapidly over the last years, with many farmers converting their agricultural activities from conventional to organic. This is a dynamic sector in Tuscany, particularly amongst young and innovative farmers. In 1999, Siena accounted for 17% of the total agricultural land cultivating organic agriculture in Tuscany, ranking third in this domain after Florence and Grosseto. The main organic agricultural products in Siena are cereals, pasture/livestock and olives. This reflects in part a heightened

Table 40. **Organic agriculture in Province of Siena**

Organic agriculture actors (total 1999)	209
Of which:	
Organic farms	86
Organic/conventional farms	6
In transition farms	81
Processors	35
Distributors	1
Organic agriculture cultivated area (ha/1999)	6 406.0
Cereals total organic area	2 628.0
Of which:	
Effective organic area	2 160.5
In transition area	467.4
Market garden total organic area	17.6
Of which:	
Effective organic area	16.8
In transition area	0.8
Fruits total organic area	160.3
Of which:	
Effective organic area	65.3
In transition area	94.9
Vineyards total organic area	274.7
Of which:	
Effective organic area	241.6
In transition area	33.1
Olive groves total organic area	593.8
Of which:	
Effective organic area	453.9
In transition area	139.8
Industrial cultivation total organic area	
Of which:	
Effective organic area	375.7
In transition area	20.3
Pasture/livestock total organic area	1 925.2
Of which:	
Effective organic area	1 444.4
In transition area	480.8
Others total organic area	410.2
Of which:	
Effective organic area	385.0
In transition area	25.2

Source: ARSIA, Agricoltura Biologica in Toscana, Report No. 1, April 2000.

interest of Italian consumers in the credence attributes of products.[17] As a result, distributors are giving additional shelf space to certified and organic products. Organic agriculture adds value to the product by controlling production processes

---

Box 15. **Organic agriculture and *lotta integrata* agriculture**

Organic agriculture. All agronomic techniques and breeding techniques based on natural interaction between live organisms, climate and human actions, excluding the use of synthesis chemical products. In Italy, as in all EU countries, organic agriculture is regulated by EU Regulation 2092/1991, completed by EU Regulation 1804/1999 on organic *zootecnologia*.

Lotta integrata. The integrated agricultural production integrates natural resources and natural mechanisms of production with the use of synthetic chemical products. The use of synthetic chemical products is controlled and limited as much as possible to minimise negative impacts on the environment and on human health. This processing method is regulated by EU Regulation 2078/1992 and provides incentives recognising environmentally friendly methods of production. In Tuscany, products produced through the *lotta integrata* method are sold under the A*griqualita* trademark. Products must respect the code of rules established by the region. An independent third body authorised by the region performs inspection to ensure conformance with these standards.

Box 16. **Procedure of inspection for products under organic agriculture**

Private inspection bodies are authorised by the Ministry of Agricultural Policies to control and certify products produced by organic agriculture. The Ministry of Agriculture registers all inspection bodies. Some obtain accreditation by SINCERT, an accreditation body. In Tuscany ARSIA (A*genzia Regionale per lo Sviluppo e l'Innovazione del settore Agricolo-forestale*) supervises all recognised inspection bodies in their control activity and is responsible for the regional register of organic agriculture operators.

---

and frequent requirements for a relatively short commercialisation life. Once a producer decides to go into organic agriculture, his farm must go through an inspection process. If the producer was involved in conventional agriculture, there is an obligatory transition process.[18]

- Choosing between organic or typical product strategies: organic extra virgin olive oil

An interesting example of differentiation into organic agriculture is provided by a group of small and medium-sized firms in the area of Val d'Orcia that produces olive oil under an organic label. In 1991, the *Olivicoltori Italiani Associati* started a project with the aim to sensitise small and medium-sized local firms to a differentiation strategy. The project had two main objectives: to help small and medium-sized producers to become competitive on the market and to obtain an ecological valorisation of the Val d'Orcia area. The project was implemented due to the actions of a group of dynamic firms that felt the necessity to innovate in a way compatible with their territory and their limited size. The Val d'Orcia environment, because of its physical and climatic characteristics, was particularly adaptable to organic agriculture. Initially, ten firms were interested in joining this project, but only seven were selected. In 1999, another 26 firms were in the process of converting from conventional to organic agriculture in order to obtain organic certification. The role of the association is important for informing the various opportunities offered by the organic method, as well as assuring market outlets and an extra margin linked to the premium price. Organic products are presently sold in supermarkets and specialised small shops (for both organic products and typical products). The margin for these products is 20% higher than for Tuscany IGP olive oil and 40% higher than for conventional industrialised olive oil. Total commercialised production in 2000 was 200 000 kg. Its success is linked to a wider strategy of offering high quality products, projecting a good territorial image, and promoting tourism and farm tourism in the area. This project is intended to be a pilot project and new initiatives are underway in other provinces of Tuscany. It is important to note that even though the product could obtain both Tuscany IGP and organic labels, producers felt that the combination might dilute its differentiation as an organic product. As a result, only one label was sought.

- Reasons for success

  – The association played an important role in convening a small number of firms to initiate this project and these firms, in turn, have played the role of leaders (*trainanti*). The association was also important in terms of facilitating communication between firms and in developing a common strategy through its constant attentiveness to the needs and desires of producers. Finally, the association was able to provide both technical assistance (*e.g.*, the problem of maintaining soil fertility) and promotional services.

  – The strategic choice of starting with a group of innovative and dynamic leading firms was successful, and this has generated an imitation process.

  – The association has combined two strategies: that of valorisation of a product, such as olive oil, and that of ecological valorisation, for example the Val d'Orcia. The central idea guiding this development is that a good quality product is linked to a wider quality strategy.

183|

- Firms, even if assisted by the association for which their services have been paid, are competitive, and this without receiving subsidies.

- Weaknesses

- With an ever-larger market and with supermarkets giving increasing space to organic products, the quantity produced is too low. This is linked to a wider organisational problem of the olive oil supply chain in Tuscany.
- There is a problem of information. People very often do not know what an organic product is and are not prepared to read a label so as to better inform themselves.
- The credibility of this strategy is based on a good control system. Consumers are very attentive to any problems that may come up in the control system and a problem in one organic food chain can have an impact on other organic products.

The "Green" Territorial Pact: combining private initiative with social purpose

Territorial pacts are a recent participative planning tool in Italy with the objective to strengthen economic development by combining a shared vision of social purpose with the entrepreneurial initiative of private and public actors for realising this vision (see Chapter 3 for a further discussion). Several of these pacts have focused exclusively on primary production limited to activities related to agriculture and fisheries. The Green Siena Territorial Pact is an initiative of the Province of Siena. The objective of this territorial pact is to increase the employment and investments in agriculture and farm tourism with the intention to integrate high-quality agriculture based on typical products, environmental protection and high-quality tourism. In particular, it is hoped that the territorial pact will promote a developmental path of agriculture that manages to establish a balance between the use and protection of natural resources. Therefore, the objectives of Green Siena are fully in line with the agricultural policies of the European Union. Originally, the Province of Siena had intended to establish an intersectoral pact, including industry, services, agro-industry and tourism in order to improve the economic and social cohesion in the province. However, priority was given to Green Siena after modifications to national legislation in 1998 opened the possibility of including primary activities in territorial pacts. In addition to the Provincial Administration of Siena, Green Siena is supported by 20 municipalities in the Province of Siena, one municipality in the Province of Florence, the Chamber of Commerce of Siena, representatives of the bank and credit sector, representatives of the trade union worker organisations and of the professional entrepreneurial unions (API Toscana, Confesercenti, CNA, Coltivatori Diretti, Confcooperative, Unione Agricoltori, Confcommercio, Confederazione Italiana Agricoltori, Lega delle

Cooperative, Confindustria, Confartigianato). Seventeen of the 21 municipalities signing Green Siena fall within Objective 2 of the EU. In total, the pact includes a population of 179 426 inhabitants that are distributed on a surface of 2 389 km with a population density of 75 inhabitants per km^2. The territory covered by the pact is characterised by a dichotomy: on the one hand, there are four municipalities (Poggibonsi, Siena, Monterriggioni and Colle Val d'Elsa) which cannot benefit from European Objective 2 funds and which concentrate 60% of the population in their area, including the largest part of the manufacturing industry and services. On the other hand, the 17 other municipalities are characterised by a small population density and a local economy based on agriculture and agri-tourism. They are eligible for European funding as defined by Objective 2. Approximately 130 operators proposing investment initiatives of ITL 90 billion joined the agreement. In addition to these private parties, public infrastructure activities total approximately ITL 28 billion.

The "Green VATO" was signed in 2001 as a response to the earlier exclusion of agriculture and fishing from the VATO 2000 Pact initiated in 1997. The central objectives of the pact are to promote innovation and modernisation in the agricultural and fishing sectors through entrepreneurial initiatives. "VATO Verde" was prepared by various bilateral and multilateral protocols between public and private actors, establishing special conditions conducive to the promotion of agriculture and fishing in the area. "VATO Verde" identifies activities in 17 different areas, including training based on curricula jointly developed by public, private and civil actors. Of the initial 306 private and 23 public projects submitted to "VATO Verde", 257 private projects and 10 public infrastructure projects were accepted on the basis of furthering the social objectives of the pact and identifying responsible parties for implementation of the project. In terms of investment, this amounted to ITL 179 billion with ITL 169 billion for private projects and about ITL 10 billion for public works. The private projects are expected to create 373 direct jobs.

Emerging strategies

Quality strategies for commodity production

While agricultural producers in the province see linking the product to the territory as a plus, it is also understood that this is much more difficult for products not traditionally sold to final demand. The common theme is to root all production in a strong commitment to quality to meet supply chain or final consumer requirements. In the case of the cereal sector the differentiation strategy has to be linked to a vertical integration strategy. This means not just to produce cereals, but to try to develop firms or co-operatives for the production of processed food such as "quality pasta", "quality biscuits", or "quality bread." The farmers' associations serving cereals producers are cognisant, however, of the need to increase

185|

market orientation so that the product meets international standards even if there is no intention to export. This means consistent delivery of product meeting customers' unique requirements. For example, fresh pasta requires highly coloured durum wheat in order to offer consumers a product with particularly inviting visual appearance. Biscuits, on the other hand, require good baking performance and thus specific content of glutins. Until now this has meant that many food-processing firms have turned to international supplies, since Italy does not provide wheat with the necessary quality specifications. Meeting these demands will require shifting cultivation to more valued varieties and away from varieties that are well suited to the local growing conditions but do not possess the qualities required by the local food industry. The specific quality strategy involves adoption of Hazard Analysis Critical Control Point (HACCP) principles in combination with quality assurance registration to the International Organisation of Standardisation Series 9000 (ISO 9000) standards (Box 17).

Linking production to a rigorous standard that addresses both food safety and customer satisfaction is seen as the best way to increase the market orientation of farmers and improve the viability of the cereals sector. Strategies for vertical integration would then allow this production to be linked with the territory in the form of quality products for final demand. As a new added-value strategy in Siena, a conventional labelling strategy oriented around "typical production" is obviated. However, there are other means of guaranteeing the credence attributes of a good and these alternatives are being considered for future initiatives. Providing assurance to consumers regarding these credence attributes can be provided by third party certification schemes such as ISO 14000. Although primarily identified with environmental management systems, certification provides a validation of claims made regarding various attributes of the product related, for instance, to origin, production method or environmentally friendly practices. In fact, the flexibility of the standards does not guarantee a specific level of "greenness" of the certified products, so conforming with ISO 14000 is a poor signal of environmental or organic attributes. Rather, the standards do guarantee that claims made regarding attributes of the product have been verified by an independent third party. Though of questionable value in mass retailing, certification could be very valuable in business-to-business sales or in specialised retail where purchasers will invest more time in understanding the nature of product claims. The generic standards that lend great flexibility to ISO 14000 also make the costs of certification prohibitive for individual farms owing to the considerable effort required for formulating the EMS. In contrast, either labelling as organic or typical products merely requires adherence to a fixed set of regulations governing production. While both ISO 14000 and typical or organic product labelling require third party inspection to ensure adherence, the audit of the EMS under ISO 14000 will be more costly due to the uniqueness of the system for each firm. Organisational

Box 17. **Integrating HACCP and ISO 9000 in an increased product quality strategy**

"Increase quality" is a common prescription for maintaining the competitiveness of agricultural producers in high-wage countries throughout the European Union. Since *quality* is a multidimensional term, to be useful the prescription must also precisely define its intended meaning, identify which dimensions are most likely to increase demand or result in a price premium and identify cost-effective strategies that are likely to achieve the desired increases in quality. The quality strategy that has been developed by the commodity growers – mainly wheat – reflects this interest of implementing changes in production and distribution that will be valued by their specific customers that may be different from quality strategies pursued by the wine, olive oil or other typical product sectors.

Five dimensions of product quality can be defined and this delineation is helpful in making sense of various quality strategies and the tools that may be most effective in pursuing them (Hooker and Caswell, 2000, p. 59):

1. Food safety attributes: foodborne pathogens, heavy metals, pesticide residues, food additives, naturally occurring toxins, veterinary residues.

2. Nutrition attributes: fat content, calories, fiber, sodium, vitamins, minerals.

3. Value attributes: purity, compositional integrity, size, appearance, taste, convenience of preparation.

4. Package attributes: package materials, labelling, other information provided.

5. Process attributes: animal welfare, biotechnology, environmental impact, pesticide use, worker safety.

For wheat producers selling to food processing firms, the main interests are with respect to providing a standardised product that consistently meets the food safety, nutritional attributes and value attributes. Implementation of the HACPP principles are central to satisfying the food safety criteria especially related to storage activities but having the effect of reducing risks throughout the production cycle. This approach requires producers to document and analyse the different stages of the production process, identifying key points at which hazards arise and putting into place site-specific strategies to manage them. However, HACCP by itself does not provide a credential guaranteeing that the other relevant quality attributes of interest to customers are being met consistently. Integrating HACPP with an international quality assurance system as embodied in ISO 9000 is seen as the most effective way to orient the product to a standard based in customer satisfaction to supplement food safety.

From a business strategy perspective, the essential question is whether costs of implementing these two systems are merely additive or whether organisations might be able to derive synergies from their joint implementation. From a cost-saving perspective there do not appear to be any advantages to joint implementation of the two systems, as they do not share any common elements. The focus

187

Box 17.   **Integrating HACCP and ISO 9000 in an increased product quality strategy** (*cont.*)

of HACCP is a disciplined application of science to identification and control of food safety hazards while ISO 9000 is a document-based system ensuring that all processes affecting quality are implemented consistently. Rather, the synergies from joint implementation would appear to derive from the explicit requirements of ISO 9000 addressing various management issues that are recognised as important to the implementation of HACCP but providing no measurable characteristics for assessing implementation. For example, the guidelines for HACCP state that the full commitment and involvement of management and the workforce are essential but provide no basis for evaluating this recommendation. In contrast, ISO 9000 requires that the quality policy is defined by management that is understood, implemented and maintained at all levels of the establishment, that responsibility and authority for personnel are assigned, and that the system is reviewed at defined intervals to assess effectiveness. Recommendations in the HACCP guideline regarding training and the documentation of work instructions are also substantive elements of the ISO 9000 standards. Thus, conforming to the ISO 9000 standards should contribute directly to HACCP effectiveness.

---

innovations that have allowed co-operative associations to obtain umbrella registrations for their members in quality assurance – with members being audited on a random basis and the co-operative on a regular schedule – could be extended to environmental management systems.

Common requirements

The role of producer associations

Importantly, it does not appear that the subsidy scheme has dampened Sienese farmers' desire to organise and collaborate to derive the maximum return from their farm businesses. Siena provides an instructive example for other rural regions as this ability will become more critical to the viability of rural areas if subsidies are greatly reduced. This capability for organising is best displayed in the farmers' associations and agricultural co-operatives that have been successful in supplying real services to their members, securing reduced prices due to collective buying of farm inputs, and maximising the return from spot markets by providing storage facilities and market analysis. These real services include technical assistance, consultancy, tax and accounting services that become critically important to the survival of smaller producers. Bargaining power they provide with respect to wheat producers is especially important. Indeed, to the extent that economies of scale in marketing and distribution are likely to become increasingly important in food retailing, producer associations of small to medium-sized farms may be the only viable means to maintain a market presence. Efforts in national, regional and local agricultural policy to facilitate this central role of producer associations will be important.

The possible diversification of individual holdings will make greater demands on associations' ability to co-ordinate, market and provide real services to an increasingly heterogeneous membership. Current activities of the associations have concentrated on the supply of technical tools for a limited range of outputs and in collecting the product to enhance value on market. The co-operatives involved in packaging and selling members' wine with the co-op's brand name provides a clear example of this strategy of providing a channel for promotion and distribution – completing a service that farmers need. One likely impact of CAP reform will be to extend the qualification of typical products such as wine and olive oil to qualify cereals and animal husbandry based on a quality certification or organic or whole farm reconversion. However, the associations also have a potentially important role to play in fostering the entrepreneurial activities of farmers. Increasingly, it will be the ability to follow emerging market trends that will allow farmers to realise viable opportunities. Alternative crops identified include flax, linen, hemp, wild wheat, saffron and fruit and vegetables. This last option would appear to warrant much closer study given the very limited cultivation of 630 hectares (0.3% Utilised Agricultural Area) of vegetables currently in the province that seems low considering substantial short channel demand for such produce in a region with a strong gastronomic allure. It is important to emphasise the niche market aspect of potential strategies that would be dependent on providing highly specialised produce to restaurants and the growing number of cooking schools appealing to international tourists. But in entering potential niche markets, the services that the associations provide to farmers and their ability to protect added value and market share would become even more critical to the viability of individual efforts.

Enhanced consumer information

Clearly, the presence of a quality label and the origin of the products will have little impact on affecting choices of consumers if few know what the labels represent. It is in the area of enhanced consumer information that higher levels of government will be most efficacious in implementing policy. There are strong public goods aspects of enhanced consumer information suggesting that national or supranational authorities would be the appropriate level for co-ordinating educational campaigns that empower choice, distinct from efforts of product promotion.

189

There should be a greater effort from EU, national and local institutions to improve consumer knowledge of PDO/IGP and organic labels. A recent Nomisma research[19] study indicates that only 29% of those actually doing the food shopping in Italy know what a PDO product is and only 18% know what an IGP product is. In the case of designation of origin products, consumers often do not know that these products are not just linked to a specific geographical area, but that they are also produced according to a detailed code of rules (*disciplinario*). This point is particularly interesting in a period when food safety is a preoccupation of many consumers. Both designations of origin and organic products can be tools to reassure consumers by making the code of rules establishing the processing and the characteristics of the product accessible to the general public. While an individual producer's Webpage could provide pertinent information in this respect (discussed below), it is important that general knowledge of product attributes is more widely dispersed so that consumers are at least aware of potentially relevant information. The recently convened National Conference on Alimentary Education by the Italian Ministry of Agricultural and Forestry Policy and the Ministry of Public Instruction was a timely and appropriate initiative that should be encouraged. The ability of a proposed International Centre on Labelling of Typical Products to address these common problems of information – in addition to problems of regulation and competition policy – should be evaluated with respect to its potential contribution to rural development. In addition, such a centre would also be able to provide a clearinghouse for best practice related to production, marketing, and enhancing the organoleptic attributes of typical products.

In addition, applications of new information technologies by producers also introduce the possibility of increasing consumer knowledge regarding production processes, quality standards and other attributes that may be independent of any direct marketing strategy. Certification of a minimum and/or specific standard of quality would appear to be one of the best ways to overcome the major drawback of e-commerce where buyers are denied the opportunity to visually inspect or evaluate a sample of the product. E-commerce presents an advantage in that, contrary to selling a product off the shelf, a large amount of information of potential interest to consumers can be made available on the Webpage. Providing visual images of the origin, a description of production techniques, the requirements of organic certification, etc., is not feasible at the retail level. On a Webpage, a potential consumer can obtain the information that satisfies his or her specific needs. It is just this sort of information that a label at retail tries to encompass, but often with little success. As suggested above, consumers still have little knowledge of what a PDO/IGP or organic product is. But the code of rules establishing the processing and the characteristics of the product for either designations of origin or organic products can be fully described providing an important source of reassurance accessible to knowledgeable consumers.

The major benefit of e-commerce for producers is that they can capture a share of the revenue formally taken by the distribution chains. This is a way for many small and medium-size producers to achieve long-distance channels of commercialisation that they would never otherwise be able to reach.[20] It is true, however, that for these small and medium-size producers there could be a problem of sustainability of the choice to sell on the Web. This is the reason why, for this kind of marketing, the role of a consortium or co-operative as co-ordinator is a potentially important one. Such associations could play a role of interface, co-ordinating different producers' goods on the same central source. This role is also important for the organisation linked to the setting up of a Webpage, especially if the aim is to sell the product (and not just promote the product on-line). In this case, the logistics can be costly and would be more affordable for a group of producers.

As concerns the products analysed in this study, in the case of Brunello di Montalcino the consortium's director is unsure whether they will start to sell on the Web as supply of the product is limited and they prefer to give priority to signed agreements. It was also noted that this product has a number of long-term loyal clients; going on the Web should not undermine these relationships. The situation is different for Chianti Classico wine. The *Consorzio del Marchio Storico Chianti Classico* has created a shop on line, selling different types of Chianti wines, olive oil and other products such as honey and vinegar. Ten firms are already selling through the Webpage both in Italy and in other EU countries.

Differentiated product strategies and rural development

Differentiation strategies through labelling of products, both PDO/IGP labels and organic labels, has allowed farmers to add value to their products and to compete at local, national and international levels in an entrepreneurial and self sufficient way. Products under designations of origin labels, because of their special link to a territory, are particularly interesting from a rural development perspective. In the case of geographical indication, proof must be given that the specificity of the product is due to the location. In the case of designations of origin, the product must also have a close tie to the locality and thus ensuring that production, processing and packaging take place within the specified geographical area and that its qualities and characteristics are due exclusively or essentially to its geographical environment, including natural and human factors. Through the application of a niche market strategy, the recognition of a denomination can allow a group of producers to build up a common reputation. However, it must be appreciated that the PDO (Protected Denomination of Origin) or IGP (Protected Geographical Indication) labels are first and foremost a recognition of success. It is necessary to have a good product (possibly based on a tradition) and only then is it possible to have a label recognising past investment. As a source of valuable

191|

information for consumers, this strategy may then allow for the valorisation of these quality attributes in the market. It is the quality of the product itself (which will establish its reputation) that must be the initial factor which producers seek to establish and maintain.

In rural areas, the socio-economic impact of the use of a denomination can be stronger than the extra-margin obtained by the producer. The fact that, in the case of denominations of origin, the whole processing of the product takes place in the limited area of origin means that a number of economic activities are also localised (for example, bottling in the case of wine and oil). There can also be spill-over effects with other activities such as "small shops selling typical and traditional food products", restaurants serving traditional/regional meals, and agro-tourism selling typical products. The spill-over effects are not just material, in terms of economic activities linked to production, but also immaterial in terms of reciprocal effects of the product's reputation on the reputation of the territory and *vice versa*.

From a social perspective, the development of typical products, in association with other factors, can help to successfully develop a strong cultural identity as well as offer a community dimension that helps strengthen local development approaches. In the Chianti Classico case, it is clear that this common cultural identity was built up around the idea of the territory as a common good, capable of offering services such as a high quality landscape, traditional products and interesting business opportunities. This was possible also due to the capability of local people to co-habit with other people coming from other areas and sharing the same perception of the territory.

Of course, these potential benefits will only be realised if the control and protection of a label is credible; if the requirements for certification are substantively related to specificity, tradition and place of origin, and if consumers are aware of the special attributes that are conferred by a label. A quality product can be achieved if inspection systems work properly and if the first actor of the inspection system is the farmer followed by the other operators at different levels of the food chain. Systems of control applied for both PDO/IGP products and organic products must undergo strict monitoring (see Annex III). Existing mechanisms of control are based on the interaction between many actors (national and local institutions; the consortium of producers; inspection and police bodies) and on a multi-step procedure; the result is a complex system in which there still exists a certain degree of failure. Many operators interviewed expressed the need to improve existing quality control systems, especially for organic agriculture products. They denounced the fact that too often the producer knows when the control by the inspection body takes place and the fact the control body is paid by the producer on the base of certified quantities. Another problem seems to be the level of competency of the inspection body (in the case of organic products and of non-wine PDO/IGP products, this is an external body). In the case of DOC and DOCG wines, inspection is a responsibility of the consortium. To be successful, it is important that such inspections are not only conducted by the consortium and the *Camera del Commercio* inspection activities, but that firms also have their own quality control systems to monitor the product from the initial cultivation of the grape to the bottling of the wine. For well known wines, such as those analysed in this report, the problem lies in the difficulty to monitor the product once it is commercialised at the shop and supermarket levels. This is particularly problematic when the product is exported.

Standards for typical products can generate considerable tension with respect to the relative importance of tradition and innovation in the definition of quality. This is most evident in the wine sector where the organoleptic attributes of a wine will be critical to the price premium provided on the market. While the recent experience of the consortia in Siena has demonstrated considerable flexibility in adjusting stipulated production methods to produce wines that better match consumer demands, the standards did give rise to a revolt. Some of the most renowned wines from the area, often commanding very high prices, were paradoxically bottled as common *vino da tavola* (table wine). First appearing in the 1970s, these "Super-Tuscan" wines were a response to growing frustration with wine of origin laws governing production of Chianti that were not perceived as promoting quality wine making and that banned the use of varietals not traditionally grown in the area such as Cabernet Sauvignon. The evolution of consortium regulations and Italian wine law over the past 30 years has effectively reconciled the sources of the former clash as the quality orientation has increased significantly and a newly added classification introduces greater flexibility for wineries wanting to experiment with different varietal make-up. IGT (*Indicazione Geografica Tipica* or Typical Geographic Indication) establishes tighter controls than table wine with regard to origin, varietal make-up and vintage but are less restrictive than DOC or DOCG wines with respect to precise varietal make-up and production. Although the Super-Tuscans have been brought back to the fold of geographical labelled wines (either through IGT or for some the creation of new DOCs), it was the considerable established reputation of these wineries that was critical in their ability to sell premium wine as *vino da tavola*. In this case, the "exit" of frustrated producers contributed to the positive evolution of the wine laws and regulations. The much more common situation will be of individual producers lacking name recognition and in these cases reconciling innovation and tradition will be dependent on effective "voice" of affected producers.

Common Agricultural Policy reform

Even though representatives of the farming sector express confidence with respect to the entrepreneurial capacity of Sienese farmers in satisfying market

193|

driven demands of consumers, it is also recognised that the market by itself may not be able to support the level of non-commodity outputs that consumers have come to expect under the Common Agricultural Policy (CAP). In line with recent reforms under Agenda 2000 and more sweeping reforms envisioned for 2006, the farming sector in the province is also adopting the view that public support of agriculture should promote those things valued by society. While it is generally accepted that this will mean a complete phase-out of subsidies linked to production and possibly also to direct payments linked to cross-compliance contracts, the most likely alternative policy path is still unknown. This uncertainty against the backdrop of the maintenance of the status quo makes policy innovation at the local level particularly risky if future levels of support are conditioned on current activities. Given the problems of transition from subsidised to market driven agriculture, there is a strong social interest in promoting just such policy experimentation. This interest has been partially supported by the ability of member countries to modulate a share of direct payments. However, explicit recognition of a transition period leading up to 2006 would encourage more systemic experimentation without imposing potential future costs on innovators.

The uncertainty over the future of agricultural policy allows little more than delimiting the broadest range of possible scenarios. Given impending enlargement of the EU and commitments to satisfy trade liberalisation agreements, local actors deem the one extreme of maintaining the status quo highly improbable. At the same time there is the belief that the other extreme of eliminating all support for agriculture equally improbable given public pronouncements of a "European model of agriculture". At this stage a contingent evaluation as to the workability of hypothetical reform proposals is the most productive means for exploring options.

Bond schemes, i.e., issuing a negotiable instrument to the farmer at a point in time that represents the cash flow of future subsidies if they were continued, are rejected outright by relevant actors in the province as being inimical to preserving an agrarian landscape in the countryside. The advantages of such a scheme are its simplicity and finality allowing the net present value of future flows of income that would have been provided as subsidy to be either re-invested in the modernisation of farms or transferred to other sectors. Such a policy would eliminate the need for farmers to engage in unproductive activities of growing specific crops or maintaining herds to guarantee continued subsidy. However, this finality is also the greatest disadvantage perceived locally, effectively eliminating any future policy leverage on the decisions of (current) farmers. Land abandonment on a massive scale is the feared outcome. This concern is a bit ingenuous; bringing into question the viability of farming even with the substantial infusion of capital that would be made available. Discussion of bond schemes animated the idea that the role that farmers play in the province is that of stewards that provide landscape services. These services to now have been compensated by subsidies to agriculture. But the absence of subsidies – or their lump sum pay-off – would remove the incentives for their provision.

The transparency of the bond scheme makes it clear that CAP reform is not merely a problem for agriculture but one that also impacts many non-agricultural activities in the province. Supranational transfers currently mitigate this interdependence that will need to be articulated and possibly negotiated as the reform of policy progresses. In this respect, the Province of Siena is in an enviable position to experiment with forums for investigating this interdependence given the recent adoption of the *Piano Territoriale Coordinamento* (PTC). Although the principle of using resources to support farmers making a valuable contribution to the preservation of an agrarian landscape is consistent with the PTC, the appropriate instruments for generating revenue and compensating farmers need to be developed. With respect to the generation of revenue there is a general aversion in the province to a tourism tax used either for compensating farmers for landscape services or covering the considerable overhead costs of tourism. An alternative to forced taxation would be to facilitate voluntary contributions that are earmarked for "preservation of the Tuscan landscape", say through a line item that could be checked off on hotel bills. A valuation study in the province could estimate the willingness-to-pay of tourists to determine the revenue that might be made available in this way.

Mechanisms for allocating compensation to farmers create significant moral hazard problems in an environment primarily concerned with increasing the market responsiveness of farmers. But while the moral hazard problems of opportunistic individuals should be appreciated in devising policy, ways of promoting the creative contributions of farmers should not be abandoned to respond to the lowest common denominator. The idea of a safety net for farmers may be a productive way for structuring programs designed to promote the non-commodity outputs of agriculture that is gaining currency in many OECD Member countries. Whether or not farming is a unique economic activity is at the centre of international debates regarding the legitimate societal role of agricultural policy. However, in attempting to promote the entrepreneurial capability of farmers, policy should recognise the particular resource and temporal constraints that do not constrain ventures in other sectors. In contrast to ventures in the new economy, a minimum level of continuous maintenance will be required to ensure that the fixed factor of land is productive. The traditional way of conceiving of this maintenance is through the family farm, which implies that individual risks will be greater given substantial levels of past investment. However, the societal returns to this maintenance may significantly exceed the private returns of maintaining this capacity if the maintenance produces valuable landscape services. The important distinction with current agricultural policy is that the interest in maintenance is not tied to a predefined composition of agricultural production. Rather, the societal interest

195|

works in parallel with the objective of maintaining some capability for farmers to respond entrepreneurially to market demands. The ideal program would make no payments when entrepreneurial efforts were successful in fully covering the costs of production and supplement incomes when costs not fully covered up to a maximum of compensating for a minimal level of maintenance.

The increasingly bimodal distribution of farm sizes (Table 18 in Chapter 2) suggests that proposed reform to the CAP directed to very small farms could play a role in preserving part of the rural landscape. *"Lump-sum payments"* based on *"proof of environmentally friendly maintenance of production capacity"* to small holders has been put forward by Franz Fischler, the European Commissioner responsible for agriculture. While the threshold for small holders has not been defined, an upper limit of EUR 2 500 for this measure would apply to more than two-thirds of all EU agricultural holdings. As a very rough approximation, 47% of all farms in Siena have five hectares or less. But even if all of these farms fell within the threshold criteria such an initiative would only apply to 4% of the utilised agricultural area. At the other end of the spectrum, some of the largest producers are operating in sectors not affected by the CAP. For those large farms specialised in cereals, oilseed or protein crop production, the proposed limits on the amount of subsidy to any one farm would substantially reduce incentives for planting these crops. But it is generally assumed that these farms should be better able to adapt to a shift to market-oriented agriculture. Small and medium-sized farms that fall outside the threshold of small holdings but may also have a hard time adapting to market-oriented agriculture present the most difficult case. A safety net scheme for this intermediate group would affect a significantly larger share of the utilised agricultural area (anywhere between 12% to 30% of cultivated land depending on how this category is defined) that may justify an outcome oriented formula for determining the level of support in any given year in contrast to the unconditional lump-sum proposal for smallholders.

The *Contrat Territorial d'Exploitation* in France and Countryside Stewardship Scheme in the United Kingdom provide productive examples of how the non-commodity outputs from agriculture can be secured on a contractual basis. In France, the Agricultural Law of Orientation promulgated in 1999 takes into account the multipurpose dimension of agriculture and sets up a contractual step for ascribing assistance, through land management contracts (*Contrat Territorial d'Exploitation*). Individuals or groups of farmers enter into 5-year contracts with local authorities administering CAP funds. Half of the funds for the program (EUR 0.3 billion) come from national sources, of which 65% will come from reallocation of existing funds and 35% from new funds. The remainder is generated by the modulation of EU direct payments, a process that allows EU Member states to levy up to 20% from direct payments and to reallocate the resulting amount to finance rural development and environmental measures. In the United Kingdom, the Countryside, Stewardship Scheme is the

196

Government's main scheme for the wider countryside, which aims, through the payment of grants, to improve the natural beauty and diversity of the countryside, enhance, restore and recreate targeted landscapes, their wildlife habitats and historical features, and to improve opportunities for public access. It operates outside environmentally sensitive areas. Farmers and land managers enter 10-year agreements to manage land in an environmentally beneficial way in return for annual payments. Grants are also available towards capital works such as hedge laying and planting, repairing dry stone walls, etc.

The impacts of both these programmes to date have been modest. By the end of 2000, 4 201 contracts for territorial management were approved and 2 604 were signed in France. Although this number is below the ambitious target set in July 1999 when the framework law was adopted of 50 000 by the end of 2000, the fact that contracts have been signed in every single *département* would indicate that the mechanisms to implement this new policy are in place. The government's current target is that 100 000 contracts be signed by the end of 2001. In the United Kingdom roughly 1 000 contracts have been signed each year since the programme's inception in 1991, affecting a total of more than 140 000 hectares.

Current experience with territorial pacts in the agricultural sector has been very promising, but the instrument is designed for investment projects that are not well suited to a service contract. (Territorial pacts are discussed in greater detail in Chapter 3). Both the VATO Verde and Siena Verde pacts have focused on environmentally friendly initiatives in the agriculture sector. The "Green Siena" Agreement has pursued the following strategic targets: development of high-quality cultivation; development of biological crops; protection and improvement of natural environment; diversification of agricultural company activities, especially through tourist activities (farm tourism), processing of agricultural products and handicraft, and through the production and retail sale of products. The pacts have been able to promote structural adjustment in the agriculture sector related to modernisation and conversion to organic production consonant with the aims of EU policy. While the organisational architecture of the pacts is instructive for the representation of diverse interests in defining social purpose, the provision of capital in order to fulfil social objectives in the form of, say, the creation of jobs, lacks the type of mutual obligation inherent in a service contract demonstrated in the CTE or UK Stewardship Scheme.

Successful implementation of the territorial pacts combined with the rich history of consultation and associative relations in the province make it is possible to conceive of Tuscan variants of the service contract framework. Indeed, the democratic process embodied in the consultation table involving a plurality of actors addresses several of the principal weaknesses identified in the other service contract schemes. Most importantly, the actors representing citizens' interests would be from the various sectoral and functional groups at the consultation table rather than representatives of the national ministry. Most importantly, this would contribute important local capabilities for the specification and evaluation of eventual contracts. By exploiting the local and collective decision-making capacity of the consultation table, both the principle of subsidiarity and the potential to discover unanticipated possibilities are introduced that are notably absent in the farmer-ministry negotiation. To the extent that an infusion of supranational funds masks the true interdependencies between farmers and Sienese society, a service contract signed with the representatives of national authorities maintains a similar detachment even considering domicile of the national representative in the province. Rather, the central challenges posed by social valuation of the non-commodity outputs of agriculture are defining the objectives of the contract, determining how satisfactory execution of the contract is evaluated and determining which parties are authorised to sign in the name of citizens. All of these challenges may be more tractable at the consultation table in comparison to national or supranational desks. Finally, in the situation where intrinsic motivation plays an important role in directing the practices of farmers, associational forms for defining duties and responsibilities as conventions of appropriate behaviour will be preferable to their explicit specification as legal obligations.

The great diversity of rural areas involved in agricultural production throughout the EU suggests that block grants to agricultural districts, arrived at through consultation, may be the most appropriate allocation of funds to meet sustainable development objectives consistent with concerns of subsidiarity and target efficiency. Unfortunately, in most cases the majority of the alleged consumers of the non-commodity outputs of agriculture are distant, or at least not resident in any districts that might be created. There is thus an important role for the state as mediator between consumers and providers of these non-commodity outputs. In the case of Siena much of this complex relation collapses as the interests of many of the ultimate consumers in the form of Italian and international tourists are mediated by the local tourism industry. This perspective, alongside considerable local experience in processes of consultation and the recent creation of the PTC for disciplining land use policy, reinforces the value of Siena as a test case for examining associative and contractual forms for assuring the provision of the non-commodity outputs from agriculture. This does not assume that the instruments developed would provide a blueprint for reproduction throughout the EU. Indeed, the rationale for the block grant scheme derives from the inability to force very different rural contexts into a one-size-fits-all policy. Rather, the context in Siena provides a clarified collection of interests, disciplined in their discussion of land-use policy by a prior process of consultation, that is likely to generate considerable insight into processes required for a workable reform of agricultural policies.

The distinction between subnational and national or supranational policy-making bodies is very useful for delineating the positive and normative dimensions of the multifunctionality debate. The analytical framework developed by the OECD for examining the policy implications of multifunctionality is premised on the positive dimension that examines multifunctionality as a particular *characteristic* of an economic activity such as agriculture (OECD 2001*h*). Determining whether there are multiple interconnected outputs or effects of an activity, the social desirability of these interconnected outputs and whether they are valued in markets or are characterised by market failure are the principle objectives of this analysis. The framework leads to a series of empirical questions:

- Is there a strong degree of jointness between commodity and non-commodity outputs that cannot be altered, for example, by changes in farming practices and technologies or by pursuing lower cost non-agricultural provision of non-commodity outputs?

- If so, is there some market failure associated with the non-commodity outputs?

- If so, have non-governmental options (such as market creation or voluntary provision) been explored as the most efficient strategy?

If and only if all the questions are answered affirmatively, is there a positive basis for considering public policy intervention. Not only are the data requirements for answering these questions onerous but the threshold criteria for intervention are also quite stringent. However, the questions force a serious consideration of the alternative provision of non-commodity outputs that are not reliant on subsidies to agricultural production. It thus provides the most unequivocal determination of whether national or supranational agricultural policies should tolerate some level of trade-distorting effects in the interest of providing non-commodity outputs of agriculture that are socially valued.

The second way of interpreting multifunctionality is in terms of multiple roles or objectives assigned to agriculture. In this normative view, agriculture as an activity is entrusted with fulfilling certain functions in society. Consequently, multifunctionality is not merely a characteristic of the production process; it takes on a value in itself. Maintaining a multifunctional activity or making an activity "more" multifunctional, can be a policy objective. It is at the subnational level that any pursuit of multifunctional objectives can be better rationalised with both the specific characteristics of agriculture and differences in interaction between these multifunctions and the unique economic and social characteristics of each region. Clearly, those areas that have progressed farthest in the industrialisation of agriculture are likely to assign very different multifunctional objectives relative to, say, a mountain community. Having a better understanding of the characteristics of the local farming sector and its interaction in the wider community, the normative approach would benefit from detailed knowledge of specific local characteristics. The central criticism of the multifunctionality argument has been the highly conditional nature of the claims made regarding positive multifunctions; *e.g.*, agricultural

199|

production may provide environmental or landscape benefits but higher benefits at lower social cost may be provided by alternative land uses. These conditional claims can be more definitive at the local level where there is some similarity in topography and a shared history of "acceptable practice" or where rival farming practices can be meaningfully compared with respect to the joint determination of production efficiency of commodity and non-commodity outputs.

In the final analysis, appropriate policies for agriculture must consider both the ethical dimension of the implicit social contract along with considerations of economic efficiency. Arguably, it is the implicit social contract that has animated discussion surrounding agricultural policy reform. In many OECD countries "sustainability" has displaced food security as the primary objective of agricultural policy, expanding concerns to the continuous environmental and social viability of farming. This paradigm shift has also recognised that economic viability – completing the sustainability triad – is not a simple function of agricultural production as the ability to produce undifferentiated goods exceeds consumer demand. Thus, at the market level agriculture must find ways of adding value to products by responding to consumer demands. Public support to foster the entrepreneurial capability of the sector would come from a definition of unique characteristics of farming activities that justify some insulation from simple market tests determining which activities survive and which become extinct. At the societal level, this will require expanding the ability to appropriate values attached to farming activities that are not expressed in markets. Recent national legislation (rationalisation of measures in the Agricultural, Agri-food, Agri-industrial and Forestry Sectors Law) identifies some of these issues as they relate to multifunctional aspects and sustainable development priorities of the agriculture sector. The requirement at the local level is for forums between farmers and all other interested parties in the community to experiment with transparent initiatives that can then be assessed with respect to this emerging social contract.

From agricultural policy to rural policy

Although this chapter has addressed strategies to increase the viability of the agriculture sector it is clear that the health of the farm and non-farm economies in rural areas are inexorably linked. The OECD high-level meeting on rural development in 1995 emphasised that agriculture continues to play a defining role in rural landscapes and that it is essential to recognise agriculture as one component of a comprehensive rural development strategy. In terms of policy synergy it was noted that an integrated rural development policy could actually help to facilitate agriculture adjustment by stimulating a broader range of non-farm activities. This approach offers a means whereby agricultural labour released through structural adjustment may remain in rural areas and for improving economic viability for rural residents, remaining on small farms, engaged in part-time farming. The Cork

Declaration that resulted from a European conference on rural development in 1996 elaborated on such an integrated approach encompassing agricultural adjustment, economic diversification, management of natural resources, enhancement of environmental functions and the promotion of culture, tourism and recreation. The new Rural Development Regulation (RDR), adopted at the Berlin Summit in 1999, endeavours to implement this integrated approach by defining rural development as the "second pillar" of the Common Agricultural Policy. At least in rhetoric, the CAP now comes closer to the recommended policy in OECD Member countries that rural development should be addressed through an integrated approach to rural development policy rather than through agricultural policy alone.

However, identifying rural development as the "second pillar" of the Common Agricultural Policy devalues this interdependence and early empirical work suggests that non-farm initiatives under the second pillar account for less than 1% of CAP funds (Bryden, 2000). Indeed, the move to stress rural development rhetoric in the CAP appears to be driven more by meeting trade liberalisation agreements and the budgetary implications of Eastern enlargement than by a realisation that non-farm rural development is an essential facilitating element of agricultural development. A more substantive commitment to the non-farm accompanying measures in the RDR is needed to acknowledge the importance of the non-farm sector by bringing its funding level closer to the approximate 10% share of CAP funds devoted to "rural development". The principle of subsidiarity is supported by constructing the RDR as a menu of accompanying measures that the appropriate national or regional authorities can select in line with specific needs. Thus, the reluctance to separate a portion of CAP resources from the farm sector lies with national and regional authorities where it can more easily be addressed rather than at EU level. Among the accompanying measures that may be especially relevant for facilitating rural development in Siena are menu items for 1) basic services for the rural economy and population; 2) village renewal and development and conservation of rural heritage; and 3) tourism and craft investment. While funding levels of non-farm activities approaching the 10% "rural development" share would come closer to the integrated approach espoused in the Cork Declaration and OECD policy recommendations, it still privileges sectoral policy over territorial policy in roughly inverse proportions to the economic importance of farm and non-farm sectors in the majority of predominantly rural areas.

Unfortunately, the legal framework of the European Union strongly supports this sectoral bias over a more holistic territorial approach. The support of agriculture and farming are Treaty objectives that provide a tactical explanation for why rural development is introduced as an "accompanying measure" to agricultural market policy. This framework also reinforces the lobbying efforts of economic interests that would lose out in a genuine reform of policy. However, there is

201|

ample evidence at the local level that farmers are keenly interested in proactively responding to the internal and external forces that are driving the need for reform. This suggests that farmers may be an allied interest in pursuing a territorial approach to "a living countryside" rather than a blocking coalition bent on maintaining sectoral subsidies. Given that alignment of these interests will become increasingly difficult at larger territorial scales, Siena may provide a unique opportunity for a pragmatic test of the advisability of the OECD recommendations on rural and agricultural policy as also embodied in the Cork Declaration.

Redirecting a larger share of CAP funds to non-farm activities would not be without conditions in order to avoid prohibitions on state aids regarding competition policy. This is an important consideration in relatively successful provinces such as Siena where rural development is not necessarily an extension of social and economic cohesion policy. Thus, redirection of aid away from agriculture may still run foul of the competition provisions that would have no claim to the possible exception for *"aid to promote the economic development of areas where the standard of living is abnormally low or where there is serious unemployment"* [Article 87 (3) EC]. Two other possible exceptions are more in line with the current economic realities and objectives for development in the province. Aid to facilitate economic activities or to promote the conservation of culture that does not adversely affect trading conditions appears consonant with the Rural Development Regulation on non-farm activities including public service provision, the conservation of heritage and tourism and craft investment. A more credible commitment to the second pillar would provide needed resources for a more holistic rural development strategy that might include initiatives to make schools in sparsely populated areas the delivery node of life-long learning curricula or restoring and improving the interpretative content of the more disperse cultural and heritage resources found throughout the province.

Recommendations

Increase the market viability of a larger number of farming operations to assure the provision of non-commodity outputs of agriculture. Specific strategies to realise this include:

- *Tax incentives for the development of farm tourism should be continued as an effective means for internalising returns from the non-commodity outputs of agriculture and diversifying sources of income for the farm economy.* The current legal requirement that not more than half of farm revenue comes from tourism related activities is a useful restriction. If enforced, it ensures that this form of tourism development is on a scale consistent with the amenity values of agricultural production. It also minimises distortions to the allocation of tourism resources throughout the province. Enforcement may become more difficult as perceptions of "easy money" in the tourism sector increase but becomes more essential to ensure that those currently abiding by the restriction continue to do so in the future. Quasi-voluntary compliance is the name given to the observation that individuals are willing to comply with restrictions if they are reasonably sure that others are also complying. This assurance is undermined if violators routinely go unpunished. Compliance may decline due more to an aversion of being a "sucker" than to a rational calculation of the relative costs and benefits of complying or not complying. Thus, enforcement of this restriction would be a service both to the genuine farmers who want passionately to pursue their agricultural interests and to the rest of the tourism sector that is unfairly disadvantaged by the abuse of this incentive.

• *Typical product strategies that add value to agricultural goods by establishing a connection to the territory should be enlarged where practicable and encouraged across the full range of production activities.* The observations that the cultivated area of Controlled Denomination of Origin (DOC and DOCG) makes up a small share of agricultural land in the province and the price premium enjoyed by many wines produced there immediately suggests an enlargement strategy. However, there are a number of individual and collective constraints that limit the practicality of this strategy. The individual constraint that a consortium weighs in considering enlargement of the cultivated area of a denomination is the dilution of the value to members of the intellectual property embodied in the label.[21] This has a strong moderating influence on the speed of enlargement that is in line with the quality orientation of this production. As a sector that has strong seasonal demand for experienced labour with a significant spike during harvest time, there are also labour market limits to significant expansion. The constraint that is perhaps most amenable to a swift slacking is allocation of national quota of the area that can be planted to wine grapes by the EU. Any enlargement to areas that are not currently growing grapes would require that these rights be purchased from other areas in Italy. Taken together, these constraints suggest that any enlargement of the current DOC areas would proceed quite slowly, if at all, and certainly at much too slow a pace to compensate for areas that may be brought out of production in response to eventual CAP reform. More amenable to policy is the support of quality strategies in non-DOC areas producing wine grapes to bolster their economic viability. Strategies may benefit from the phenomenon surrounding the Super-Tuscan wines that have opted for the less stringent *Indicazione Geografica Tipica Toscana* (IGT) classification in the interest of greater production freedom to innovate. Although the exceptionally wide range of quality (and price) contributes to consumer confusion over what an IGT classification actually represents, the wine press is cur-

203

rently keen to identify "discount" or "up-and-coming" Super-Tuscans that have yet to achieve stratospheric status and price. This increases the probability that quality wines with an IGT Toscana classification will be appropriately valued in the market.

- *Efforts to diversify the range of labelled typical products should be actively promoted.* Such a strategy presents opportunities for increasing competitiveness over a wider area of cultivated land that would fully utilise the human capital of farmers currently operating in the province. Although the range of labelled products currently extends to olive oil, and includes some meats and cheeses, there are currently a number of other traditional products that could also benefit from the legal protection and consumer information embodied in a label. Any such initiative would be facilitated by better co-ordination in the sale of authentic Sienese products so that the added value consumers derive from a product attached to the territory is represented in price premiums. Given the uncertainty surrounding the size of the price premium of a label and the significant up-front costs in securing a typical product classification, just such a demand orientation will be required to make appropriate decisions based on the costs and benefits of possible labelling.

- *Product differentiation through quality or organic certification should also be actively pursued, which may be applicable to both commodity production and production for final demand.* The potential for this strategy to tap into EU and national funds for the modernisation and upgrading of farm businesses has already been demonstrated in Siena and these efforts should continue to have a high priority. Both the structural funds from the EU and CAP subsidy premia for farms in the process of whole farm organic conversion have made a significant contribution to environmentally friendly farming practices in the province. Price premiums in the market for organic products have also been driven by heightened consumer awareness of food safety issues – though not necessarily resolved by the conversion to organic production – and the limited capability of producers to alter production practices in the short to medium term. With respect to quality control certification, increased market orientation will require a farming sector that is more attuned to satisfying customer demands and standards such as ISO 9000 will be required to persuade food processing firms that primary producers can perform as promised. The experience with the "Green" territorial pacts demonstrates the effectiveness of combining private initiative with social purpose and such tools may be instrumental in expediting the various agreements that are required to initiate modernisation in agriculture.

- *The province should build support for the creation of an International Centre on Labelling of Typical Products with the mission of enhancing consumer information regarding typical products, addressing competition and trade issues surrounding typical products, and developing strategies for maximising the contribution of typical products to the rural development objectives of Member countries.* The information mission of the centre would be a pure public good that has lacked substantial provision at the national or subnational level given an understandable preoccupation with "promotion". Especially in light of the concerns regarding a high-quality food supply, information on the justifiable claims of typical products would provide a valuable service to European consumers. Concerns with respect to competition policy and external concerns regarding trade could also benefit from an objective assessment of the issues that transcends national borders. Finally, an observatory of the mutual interdependence of typical products and rural development would provide insight into how agricultural production can be reintegrated into the cultural, natural and economic systems of rural communities.

Public support from the subnational, national or supranational level to underwrite provision of non-commodity outputs from agriculture should be consistent with the principles of subsidiarity and target efficiency. Specific strategies to be pursued include:

- *Impress upon Italian and EU officials the importance of a transition period so that innovative actions at the local level in the period prior to eventual reform do not automatically disqualify farmers from future participation in the modified* CAP. The objectives and solutions for an economically competitive agriculture sector are inherently complex in stark contrast to the much simpler problem of increasing agricultural yields to ensure food security. Finding policy solutions in a complex environment must recognise the importance of enabling experimentation at the local level to mobilise the rich information sources and creativity of a diverse set of actors, along with a heightened ability for all localities in the system to learn from successful and unsuccessful initiatives. Unfortunately, incentives for experimentation in the current CAP framework are nil, and in fact there is a strong degree of programmatic lock-in where farmers are dissuaded from pursuing potentially economically viable alternatives that receive no public support. "Wait-and-see" is the rational economic response in the current environment that squanders immense human resources, many of which are well disposed to "explore and endeavour". The implicit penalty on innovative behaviour should be removed by defining a transition period that would allow farmers to revert back to pre-transition activities if they find these to be more remunerative after reform.

- *Investigate options for mobilising the entrepreneurial capability of farmers.* An environment that has been premised on eliminating market risk for farmers presents a difficult starting point for initiatives to promote entrepreneurship.

205

Options will thus have to begin by considering those factors that differentiate entrepreneurial risks in agriculture from other sectors and whether there is a public interest in insulating farmers from some of these risks. Redirecting CAP subsidies for production to a farm safety net scheme that ensures a minimum level of subsidy to maintain the productive capability of small to medium-sized farms deserves further attention. The creative resources engendered by associative relations in producer co-operatives and farm associations should also be fostered, especially with regard to the real services these organisations provide that will become more critical in a market driven agriculture. Advances in e-commerce present the possibility that short-channel distribution in the form of direct marketing could leverage recurring long-channel sales. This possibility has greater promise in Siena than in most other rural environments.

- *Investigate local instruments for underwriting the provision of non-commodity outputs currently provided by agricultural production.* Substantial supranational transfers through the CAP have dulled the true interdependence of other sectors with agriculture. This interdependence needs to be explicitly examined. The fact that many of the beneficiaries of the non-commodity outputs of agriculture are physically present and experience these outputs directly suggests that the beneficiary pays principle may be an appropriate and highly efficient way of ensuring a desirable level of provision. A tourism tax or means for soliciting voluntary contributions should be investigated. However, as the relationship between the level of non-commodity outputs and agricultural production is weak, these discussions should also investigate those non-commodity outputs that are valued and how they can be produced at lowest cost. In this respect, provincial experience with consultation and negotiation across public and private sectors would be a valuable resource in the constitution and specification of service contracts for the provision of non-commodity outputs.

- *Find support for participatory farming systems research with the objective of increasing the social returns from agricultural production that also increases the competitiveness of farming.* The PTCP confirms that positive multifunctions are an objective – not merely a characteristic – of agricultural production for Sienese society. There is thus a strong public interest in the farming sector adopting production techniques of agricultural goods and commodities making the largest contribution to these non-commodity outputs. There are currently no incentives for farmers to experiment with alternative farming systems that might produce these desired effects nor do individual farmer-entrepreneurs have the capabilities or scope to assess the relative viability of rival alternatives. The absence of market tests regarding the superiority of alternative farming systems producing non-commodity outputs suggests that the social returns to this type of research would be very high. An interest in authenticity suggests that the history of agriculture in the province may provide a wealth of ideas that were dependent on the sustainable co-evolution of social, economic and ecological systems. Investigating their contemporary viability would thus provide a rich source of insight and potentially feasible innovations.

Notes

1. In 1997, vines and olive trees produced 34.3% of gross saleable product of agriculture and forestry in the province whereas cereals and other sowable crops produced 27.3%.

2. It is important to recognise that there is a very weak relation, if any, between a designation of origin's code of rules and its environmental impact. While small walls and windbreaks of traditional practice could be an obligation included in the code of rules of these wines, it was not explicit. This demonstrates that denomination of origin certification does not prohibit innovation *a priori*. Labels of geographical indication have similar implications for environmental impact. However, tradition is an important product attribute under certificate of specific character (see Annex III). Italy recognised *Traditional Products* through Decree No. 350, 8 September 1999. To be recognised as traditional, a product needs processing methods and stocking methods that have been applied for at least 25 years. This kind of product is recognised at national level, but is not covered by EU Regulation 2080 and 2081.

3. Controlled Designation of Origin (DOC) and Controlled and Guaranteed Designation of Origin (DOCG), see Annex III.

4. Mainly *uva a bacca rossa sangiovese* (75-90%), *canaiolo* (5-10%) and *uva a bacca bianca trebbiano e malvasia* (2% and 5%).

5. See Consorzio del Marchio Storico Chianti Classico, "le Cifre del Chianti Classico", unpublished report, 2000, S. Casciano V.P., Florence, Italy.

6. Some of them switched in this period from Chianina meat production to Montalcino wine production.

7. For example, the winery was the first to introduce steel fermentation tanks to the area.

8. They used the firm's brand together with the Gallo Nero consortium's brand.

9. See Belletti, G. (2001) "Le prospettive offerte da DOP e IGP per la valorizzazione degli oli extra-vergini d'oliva" in *Olivo e olio: suolo, polline*, DOP, ARSIA, Regione Toscana.

10. At the time of writing there were indications that this regulation would be revised. On 17 May 2001 the EU Parliament stated its intention to review Regulation No. 2815 (concerning commercialisation rules on olive oil) prior to its expiration in November 2001. On 19 June the Council of Agriculture Ministries that labels should clearly report the origin of the product and the geographical place in which the processing (milling) takes place if they are different.

11. This decision produced a strong reaction as other regional PDO were recognised as *Umbro* olive oil or *Ligure* olive oil.

12. Supermarkets sell IGP Tuscany olive oil under their private supermarket labels in addition to *fattoria* and *confezionatori* labels.

13. IGP Tuscany olive oil has just undergone two olive oil seasons (1998/1999-1999/2000).

14. It was during this period that the national denomination of origin was recognised.

15. See Belletti (2001), "Le prospettive offerte da DOP e IGP per la valorizzazione degli oli extra-vergini d'oliva", in *Olivo e olio: suolo, polline, DOP*, ARSIA, Regione Toscana.

16. The geographical area of "Chianti Classico" extra virgin olive oil DOP is the same of the Chianti Classico wine, defined in 1932.

17. See Nomisma (2000), *Prodotti Tipici e Sviluppo Locale, Il ruolo della produzione di qualità nel futuro dell'agricoltura italiana*, VIII Rapporto Nomisma sull'Agricoltura in Italia.

18. This is normally a three year period in which the producer has to follow the organic agriculture rules, he is submitted to the inspection procedure but goes on selling the product at the same price and without certification (even if the product can be labelled as coming from a farm in transition to organic agriculture).

19. See Nomisma (2000), *Prodotti Tipici e Sviluppo Locale, Il ruolo della produzione di qualità nel futuro dell'agricoltura italiana*, VIII Rapporto Nomisma sull'Agricoltura in Italia.

20. See OECD (1997), "Private sector mechanisms for dealing with price variability: opportunities and issues". In Appendix 1 on Virtual Commodity Markets in relation to online marketplace it is written: "*This type of marketing could be of substantial importance to the small producers in more remote areas who face difficulties due to limited market size.*"

21. The first limitation to the enlargement of already existing DOCG wines is the existence of a code of rules clearly establishing the limited area of production. This is the basic philosophy underlining the existence of these products. The respect of these constraints is seen as the source of their quality. For existing PDO/IGP the only reasonable possibility would be to use those areas that, even if included in the limits established by the code of rules, are still underused.

Annex I

Establishing Carrying Capacities*

Establishing tourism carrying capacities is based on the concept of maintaining a level of development and use that will not result in serious environmental deterioration, socio-cultural or economic problems, or be perceived by tourists as depreciating their enjoyment and appreciation of the area or tourism site. Carrying capacity analysis is a basic technique being widely applied in tourism and recreation planning (and also wildlife management) to help achieve sustainable development by systematically determining the upper limits of development and visitor use, and optimum use of tourism resources. Any type of development results in some environmental changes. Carrying capacity analysis typically is based on not exceeding the levels of acceptable change. Numerous tourism areas in the world show evidence of having exceeded their carrying capacities. This has resulted in environmental, social and sometimes economic problems, with a decrease in tourist satisfaction and consequent loss of deterioration of tourist markets.

In practice, determining carrying capacities is often not easy or precise, depending on the factors involved. It is based on assumptions that are made and perceptions of the levels of acceptable change. Carrying capacities may also change through time and can be increased by taking certain actions. However, it remains a very useful technique in guiding planning for sustainable tourism. Carrying capacities can be established for both undeveloped tourism areas and those that already have some development, and perhaps even reaching or exceeding their saturation levels. It is often the more developed destinations that have become concerned about their capacity levels. Carrying capacities can best be calculated for specific development sites and small tourism areas. At the national, regional and larger tourism area levels, they must be considered more generally. Often at an area-wide level, capacities are based on a total of the capacities of individual sites such as major tourist attractions or resorts.

The measurement criteria presented here are for establishing carrying capacities primarily of tourist destinations. The capacities of transportation facilities and services used by tourists travelling to their destinations are also important to analyse. Each area and its type of tourism are unique and development objectives will vary from one place to another, especially with respect to local concepts of what are acceptable levels of change to the physical and socio-cultural environment. Also the types of tourist markets affect measurement levels. However, some common criteria exist for virtually all places. Some criteria can be evaluated quantitatively while others must be evaluated qualitatively. In determining capacities, the major factors to be considered are described in the following sections.

---

* See World Tourism Organization (1998*a*), *Guide for Local Authorities on Developing Sustainable Tourism*.

The indigenous physical and socio-economic environment

This refers to the capacity of development and visitor use that can be achieved without resulting in damage to the physical (natural and man-made) environment and generating socio-cultural and economic problems to the local community, while still benefiting the community and maintaining a proper balance between development and conservation. Exceeding saturation levels will lead to permanent damage to the physical environment or socio-economic problems, or both. The criteria for determining optimum capacities include:

Physical

- Acceptable levels of visual impact and congestion.
- Point at which ecological systems are maintained before damage occurs.
- Level of tourism that helps conserve wildlife and natural vegetation of both the land and marine environments without degradation.
- Level of tourism that helps conserve archaeological, historic and cultural monuments without degradation.
- Acceptable levels of air, water and noise pollution.

Economic

- Extent of tourism that provides optimum overall economic benefits without economic distortions or inflation.
- Amount of economic benefits accruing to local communities.
- Level of tourism employment suited to the human resources of the local communities.

Socio-cultural

- Extent of tourism development that can be absorbed socially without detriment to the life styles and activities of the local communities.
- Level of tourism that helps conserve and revitalise, where desirable, arts, crafts, belief systems, ceremonies, customs and traditions.
- Level of tourism that will not be resented by local residents or pre-empt their use of attractions and amenity features.

Infrastructure

- Adequate availability of transportation facilities and services.
- Adequate availability of utility facilities and services of water supply, electric power, waste management of sewage and solid waste collection, treatment and disposal, and telecommunications.
- Adequate availability of other communities' facilities and services such as those related to public health and safety, and of housing and community services for employees in tourism.

The tourism image and product

This refers to the levels of development and number of tourists that are compatible with the image of the tourist destination and tourism product, and the types of experiences that visitors are seeking. If the area exceeds saturation levels, the environment and attractions, which visitors have come to experience, will be destroyed or degraded. Tourist satisfaction will decrease, and the destination will decline in quality and popularity with a loss or deterioration of the tourist markets. The criteria for determining optimum capacities include:

Physical

- Overall cleanliness and lack of pollution of the destination.
- Lack of undue congestion of the destination including its attractions.
- Attractiveness of the landscape or townscape including the quality and character of architectural design.
- Conservation and maintenance of ecological systems, flora and fauna of the natural attraction features.
- Conservation and maintenance of archaeological, historic and cultural monuments.

Economic

- Cost of the holiday and "value for money".

Socio-cultural

- Intrinsic interest of the indigenous community and its cultural patterns.
- Quality of the local arts, crafts, cultural performances and cuisine.
- Friendliness of residents.

Infrastructure

- Acceptable standards of transportation facilities and services.
- Acceptable standards of utility services.
- Acceptable standards of other facilities and services.

For each of the criteria, measurement standards must be decided for each particular area. For example, a measurement standard for the amount of sandy beach area and frontage for each tourist staying at a beach resort can be established based on various assumptions of what is acceptable environmentally and necessary to maintain tourist satisfaction.

Seasonality is a major consideration in the concept of carrying capacity. The saturation level of tourist use of a destination is often reached during the peak periods of use, and not during the low season or on an average annual basis. Therefore, carrying capacity must be calculated for the peak period of use. Approaches can be applied to reduce use during the peak period and even out seasonality during the year. This achieves a more optimum use of attractions, facilities, services and infrastructure. For some types of natural attraction features, visitor use may need to be carefully managed, sometimes controlled with respect to establishing maximum numbers of visitors, or prohibited during an ecologically critical period, such as animal breeding seasons. At any type of attraction site, effective organisation of visitor use and flows through the site can reduce congestion at certain points.

213|

Annex II

Core Indicators of Sustainable Tourism[1]

Indicator	Specific measures
Indicator	**Specific measures**
1. Site protection	Category of site protection according to IUCN[2] index
2. Stress	Tourist numbers visiting sites (annually and peak periods)
3. Use intensity	Intensity of use during peak period (persons per hectare)
4. Social impact	Ratio of tourists to local residents (annually and peak periods)
5. Development control	Existence of environmental review procedure or formal land use and building controls over development of site and use densities
6. Waste management, etc.	Percentage of sewage from site receiving treatment and other indicators such as on water supply
7. Planning process	Existence of organised regional, municipal and local plans for the tourist destination
8. Critical systems	Number of rare, endangered and threatened wildlife species
9. Tourist satisfaction	Level of satisfaction by visitors (questionnaire-based)
10. Local satisfaction	Level of satisfaction by local residents (based-based)
11. Tourism contribution to local economy	Proportion of total economic activity generated by tourism

Composite indices

A. Carrying capacity	Composite early warning measures of key factors affecting the ability of the site to support different levels of tourism
B. Site stress	Composite measures of levels of impact on the site (its natural and cultural attributes due to tourism and other sector cumulative stresses)
C. Attractiveness	Qualitative measure of those site attributes that make it attractive to tourism and can change over time

Notes

1. See World Tourism Organization (1996), *What Tourism Managers Need to Know: A Practical Guide to the Development and Use of Sustainable Tourism*. This publication also contains more detailed indicators for different types of tourism environments.
2. International Union for Conservation of Nature (World Conservation Union).

Annex III

Labelling of Typical Products

The concept of typical products is recognised by Italian consumers.[1] Some consumers associate typicality with organoleptic attributes, others with geographical origin and its link to a specific territory, and yet others with traditional methods of production. Italy for many years has had extensive legislation on products with protected designations of origin covering wine and other agro-food products.[2] The preceding analysis concentrated on those denominations that have been the object of both national and EU legislation and that benefit from a structured system as well as juridical protection. In fact, once the product has been recognised as a protected designation of origin or protected indication of origin, it is automatically recognised and protected in all EU countries against misuse of any kind. Although other typical products are not included in the following definitions, it should be noted that these could have a significant impact in terms of rural development.[3]

In 1992, the European Union, of which Italy is a member, recognised three denominations for all non-wine products: Designations of Origin, Geographical Indications (EU Regulation 2081/1992) and Certificates of Specific Character (Box 18). In so far as wine is concerned, Italy is in line with EU legislation and it recognises three categories: Typical Geographical Indication, Controlled Designation of Origin and Controlled and Guaranteed Designation of Origin[4] (Box 19).

For agro-food products sold under a special designation, some degree of co-ordination is required between the actors involved. The need, at the end of the processing stage, to arrive at a product with specific characteristics, necessitates monitoring at all stages of the production chain. Even if there are some differences between wine and the other products, it is possible to rank some characteristics.[5]

- The enterprises producing the good must be organised in a representative association (a single firm cannot reserve the designation for its own purpose).

- In order to qualify, the product must comply with a product specification (*disciplinario*).

- The product must go through a quality control process and a certification process.

- These products are registered at both the national and EU levels.

In so far as product specifications are concerned, in the case of certificates of specific character, the product specification must include the name of the product, a description of the method of production, the nature of the raw materials used and aspects allowing for an appraisal of its traditional characteristics. In so far as designations of origin are concerned, product specification must include the name of the product, the definition of the geographical area, a description of the production method, details describing the link to a geo-

---

Box 18. **EU designations for agricultural products other than wine: definitions**

Designation of origin: The name of a region, a specific place or, in exceptional cases, a country, used to describe an agricultural product or a foodstuff originating in that region, specific place or country and the quality or characteristics of which are **essentially or exclusively due to a particular geographical environment with its inherent natural and human factors**, and the production, processing and preparation of which take place in the defined geographical area.[1]

Geographical indication: The name of a region, a specific place or, in exceptional cases, a country, used to describe an agricultural product or a foodstuff originating in that region, specific place or country, and which possesses a specific quality, reputation or other characteristics attributable to that geographical origin and the production and/or processing and/or preparation of which take place in the defined geographical area.

Certificate of specific character: *"Specific character"* means the feature or set of features which distinguishes an agricultural product or a foodstuff clearly from other similar products or foodstuffs belonging to the same category. In order to appear in the register of certificates of specific character, an agricultural product or foodstuff must either be produced using traditional raw materials or be characterised by a traditional composition or mode of production and/or processing reflecting a traditional type of production and/or processing (Articles 2 and 4).

---

1. Also considered as designations of origin are certain traditional geographical or non-geographical names designating an agricultural product or a foodstuff originating in a region or a specific place and which fulfil the conditions referred to above (Article 2, paragraphs 2*a* and 3).

Source: OECD (2001*a*), "Appellations of origin and geographical indications in OECD countries: economic and legal implications".

---

graphical environment or origin and information of the monitoring (inspection) structures of the whole production line.

Both non-wine products (agricultural products and foodstuffs) under EU Regulation 2081 and wines under DOC or DOCG denominations must be submitted to a quality control. For the first group of products, Article 10 of Regulation 2081/92 states that inspection structures have the function of ensuring that agricultural products and foodstuffs bearing a protected name meet the requirements laid down in the specifications. An inspection structure may comprise one or more designated inspection authorities and/or private bodies approved by the Member state. Those bodies must offer adequate guarantees of objectivity and impartiality. For DOC or DOCG wines, there are two kinds of controls. The

217|

Box 19. Italian "designations of origin" for wine

Controlled Designation of Origin (DOC) and Controlled and Guaranteed Designation of Origin (DOCG). In Italian law, "designation of origin" means any geographical name of a viticultural area producing a product of quality and renown belonging to a number of producers. The geographical name that comes after the letters DOC or DOCG may be followed by the name of the vine variety or other terms. DOCG status is awarded to DOC wines at least five years of age, of high quality and of national and international repute.

Typical geographical indications are represented by a geographical name used for table wines and corresponding to a usually very extensive viticultural area that may be specified by vine variety, type of wine or colour. IGTs are not allowed to use the names of areas used by DOCs and DOCGs. In ascending order, Italian wines are classed as IGT, DOC or DOCG.

Source: OECD (2001a), "Appellations of origin and geographical indications in OECD countries: economic and legal implications".

---

first aims at testing determined chemical, physical and organoleptic characteristics of the product; the Camere di Commercio generally conducts this. The second control system concerns the processing of the product and aims to ensure that producers respect the established codes of rules. The consortium conducts this latter control.

Box 20. Procedure of inspection for products under EU Regulation 2081(non wine products) – Italy

The Ministry of Agricultural Policy is the national authority in charge of co-ordinating inspection activities.

Producer consortia play a general role of monitoring and supervising each controlled designation product.

An independent inspection body, formally appointed by the Ministry of Agricultural Policy carries out the control, with the aim of verifying if the producer respected the established code of rules.

The Ispettorato Centrale Repressioni Frodi and the relevant local authorities oversee the inspection work conducted by the three independent bodies.

Box 21. **Procedure of inspection for DOC and DOCG wine products – Italy**

The Ministry of Agricultural Policy is the national authority in charge of co-ordinating inspection activities.

Producer consortia play a general role of monitoring and supervising each controlled designation product. At the same time they carry out control concerning the processing of the product and aim at controlling if the producer respected the established codes of rules.

Camere di Commercio taste determined chemical, physical and organoleptic characteristics of the product.

The Ispettorato Centrale Repressioni Frodi and police bodies can always decide to check the product, both the processing and the final characteristics.

Notes

1. See Nomisma (2000), *Prodotti Tipici e Sviluppo Locale, Il ruolo della produzione di qualità nel futuro dell'agricoltura italiana*, VIII Rapporto Nomisma sull'Agricoltura in Italia.
2. See OECD (2001a), "Appellations of Origin and Geographical Indications: economic and legal implications", country chapter on Italy.
3. The Italian Ministry of Agriculture has been working on a classification of national agro-food traditional products.
4. These definitions are based on Law No. 164 of 10 February 1992 on new rules governing designations of origin for wines which transposes European Regulation (EEC) 823/87 in Italian Law and replaces the earlier Law No. 930 of 1963.
5. This analysis is based on EU Regulation 2080 and 2081.

Bibliography

EUROPEAN ASSOCIATION FOR INFORMATION ON LOCAL DEVELOPMENT (AEIDL) (1997),
Marketing quality rural tourism, European Commission, Brussels.

ALLEN, P.M. (1994),
Cities and Regions as Self-Organizing Systems, Gordon and Breach Science Publishers, Amsterdam.

AMMINISTRAZIONE PROVINCIALE DI SIENA (2000a),
Osservatorio Economico Provinciale, http://osservatorioeconomico.provincia.siena.it, Siena.

AMMINISTRAZIONE PROVINCIALE DI SIENA (2000b),
Piano Territoriale di Coordinamento della Provincia di Siena, www.provincia.siena.it/ptc, Siena.

AMMINISTRAZIONE PROVINCIALE DI SIENA (2000c),
Rapporto statistico provinciale senese, http://osservatorioeconomico.provincia.siena.it/resources/rapp_stat2000.htm, Siena.

AMMINISTRAZIONE PROVINCIALE DI SIENA (2001),
Piano Territoriale di Coordinamento della Provincia di Siena, Siena – PTC, Amministrazione Provinciale di Siena, Siena.

ARSIA (2001),
Agricoltura Biologica in Toscana, Report No. 4, July, Florence.

BASSANINI, F. (2000),
"L'Italie: Notre révolution silencieuse", in Fauroux, Roger and Spitz, Bernard, Notre État: Le livre vérité de la fonction publique, Robert Laffont, Paris, pp. 148-173.

BELLETTI, G. (2000),
"Origin labelled products, reputation and heterogeneity of firms" in The Socio-economics of Origin Labelled Products in Agri-food Supply Chains: Spatial, Institutional and Co-ordination Aspects, Economie et Sociologie Rurales, INRA.

BELLETTI, G. (2001),
"Le prospettive offerte da DOP e IGP per la valorizzazione degli oli extra-vergini d'oliva", in Olivo e olio: suolo, polline, DOP, ARSIA, Regione Toscana.

BEURET, J.-E. (1999),
"Une 'ethique de la terre' manifestee par des conventions: des C.T.E. comme substituts ou complements?", Mimeo, Ecole Nationale Supérieure Agronomique de Rennes, Laboratoire Systèmes de Production et Développement Rural.

BRYDEN, J.M. (2000),
"Is there a new rural policy?", paper presented at the international conference: European Rural Policy at the Crossroad, 29 June – 1 July, Aberdeen, Scotland.

CISET (1998),
In Manente, M. (2000),"Visitor and mobility management in an urban development strategy" in *Tourism*, Vol. 48, No. 3/2000/213, Institute for Tourism, Zagreb.

CNEL (2000),
Secondo Rapporto sull'Agricoltura, L'agricoltura tra locale e globale, Distretti e Filiere, Document No. 23, February, CNEL, Rome.

CONSORZIO DEL MARCHIO STORICO CHIANTI CLASSICO (2000),
"Le Cifre del Chianti Classico", Mimeo, S. Casciano V.P., Italy.

CONSORZIO DEL VINO BRUNELLO DI MONTALCINO (1998),
Montalcino, Edizione Cantagalli, Siena.

DELLA CASA, R. "New Economy e Agroalimentare: I Vantaggi e I Rischi" in *Il Commercio elletronico@Inserto*, Agricoltura, Luglio-Agosto.

FABIANI, S. and PELLEGRINI, G. (1997),
"Convergenza e divergenza nella crescita delle province italiane", *Ricerche quantitative per la politica economica* 1997, Banca of Italy-CIDE, 1999, Rome.

FLORIDIA, A. (1994),
"Tuscan culture; between production and consumption" in Leonardi, Robert and Nanetti, Raffaella Y. (eds), *Regional Development in a Modern European Economy: The Case of Tuscany*, Pinter, London.

FLORIDIA, A. (ed.) (2001),
Beni Culturali in Toscana: Politiche, esperienze, strumeti, Franco Angeli, Milano.

FONT, J., GUTIÉRREZ SUÁREZ, R., AND PARRADO DÍEZ, S. (2000),
"Intergovernmental partnerships at the local level in Spain: Mancomunidades and consortia in a comparative perspective", in Löffler, Elke and König, Klaus (eds.), *Managing Accountability in Intergovernmental Partnerships*, Speyer Research Report No. 207, Research Institute for Public Administration (FOEV), Speyer.

FREY, B.S. AND OBERHOLZER-GEE, F. (1997),
"The cost of price incentives: an empirical analysis of motivation crowding-out", *American Economic Review*, 87(4), pp. 746-755.

GARMISE, S. (1994),
"Convergence in the European Community: The Case of Tuscany", in Leonardi, Robert and Nanetti, Raffaella Y. (eds), *Regional Development in a Modern European Economy: The Case of Tuscany*, pp. 22-41, Pinter, London.

GOTTFRIED, H. (1996),
"Corridors of value: rural land in rural life", *Rural Development Perspectives*, Vol. 12, No. 1 (October), pp. 13-18.

GRASLAND, C.
"Organisation de l'espace", Université Paris, Paris.

HOOKER, N.H. AND CASWELL, J.A. (2000),
"Two case studies of food quality management systems", *Journal of International Food and Agribusiness Marketing*, 11(1), pp. 57-71.

IRMEN, E., MILBERT, A. AND PÜTZ, T. (2001),
"Measures of regional accessibility" [DT/TDPC/TI(2001)1], presented at the meeting of the Working Party on Territorial Indicators, Territorial Development Policy Committee, OECD Headquarters, February 15-16, Paris.

IRPET (2001),
Terzo Rapporto sull'Economia Agricola della Toscana, Il Sole 24 ore, Agrisole, Roma.

ISMEA (1995),
Territorio e Struttura Agroindustriale: Un'analisi delle aree ad Alta Vocazione Produttiva, ISMEA, Rome.

ISMEA (2000),
Filiera Olio di Oliva, Il Sole 24 ore AGRISOLE, Rome.

ISSERMAN, A. AND MERRIFIELD, J. (1987),
"Quasi-experimental control-group methods for regional analysis: an application to an energy boomtown and growth pole theory", Economic Geography, Vol. 63, No. 1 (January), pp. 3-19.

ISTAT (1998),
Le aziende agroturistiche in Italia, Rome.

ISTAT (1991),
4^0 Censimento Generale dell'Agricoltura, Rome.

ISTITUTO GUGLIELMO TAGLIACARNE, IRPET, ISTITUTO REGIONALE PROGRAMMAZIONE ECONOMICA TOSCANA (2001),
Osservatorio Economico Provinciale 2000, L'Economia Senese all'inizio del nuovo millennio, Siena.

LATACZ-LOHMANN, U. and HODGE, I. (2001),
"'Multifunctionality' and 'free trade': conflict or harmony?" Eurochoices, Vol. 0, No. 0 (Spring), pp. 42-47.

MANENTE, M. (2000),
"Visitor and mobility management in an urban development strategy" in Tourism, Vol. 48, No. 3/2000/213, Institute for Tourism, Zagreb.

NOMISMA (2000),
Prodotti Tipici e Sviluppo Locale, Il ruolo della produzione di qualità nel futuro dell'agricoltura italiana, VIII Rapporto Nomisma sull'Agricoltura in Italia, Il Sole 24 ore, Bologna.

OECD (1994),
Tourism strategies and rural development, OECD Publications, Paris.

OECD (1997),
"Private sector mechanisms for dealing with price variability: opportunities and issues", Paris.

OECD (2000a),
OECD Territorial Reviews: Teruel, OECD Publications, Paris.

OECD (2000b),
"The role of migration in moderating the effects of population ageing" [DEELSA/ELSA/WP2(2000)6], Working Party on Migration, Paris.

OECD (2001a),
"Appellations of Origin and Geographical Indications: economic and legal implications", Paris.

OECD (2001b),
Bridging the "Digital Divide": Issues and Policies in OECD Countries, OECD Publications, Paris.

OECD (2001c),
Citizens as Partners: OECD Handbook on Information, Consultation and Public Participation in Policy Making, OECD Publications, Paris.

223|

OECD (2001d),
Information and Communication Technologies and their Implications for the Development of Rural Areas, OECD Publications, Paris.

OECD (2001e),
Information Technology Outlook: ICTs, E-commerce and the Information Economy 2000, OECD Publications, Paris.

OECD (2001f),
Innovative People: Mobility of Skilled Personnel in National Innovation Systems, OECD Publications, Paris.

OECD (2001g),
Local Partnerships for Better Governance, OECD Publications, Paris.

OECD (2001h),
Multifunctionality: Towards an Analytical Framework, OECD Publications, Paris.

OECD (2001i),
Policies to Enhance Sustainable Development, OECD Publications, Paris.

OECD (2001j),
OECD Territorial Reviews: Italy, OECD Publications, Paris.

OECD (2002),
OECD Territorial Reviews: Champagne-Ardenne, France, OECD Publications, Paris.

PIMENTEL, D. (ed.) (1993),
World Soil Erosion and Conservation, Cambridge University Press, New York.

PIORE, M. AND SABEL, C. (1984),
The Second Industrial Divide: Possibilities for Prosperity, Basic Books, New York.

PRATT, J.C. (1994),
The Rationality of Rural Life: Economic and Cultural Change in Tuscany, Harwood Academic Publishers.

SALVINI, ANDREA (1999),
Identita e bisogni del volontariato in Toscana, Florence, Italy.

SEN, A. (1999),
Development as Freedom, Knopf, New York.

UNAPROL
La valorizzazione degli oli a denominazione di origine, Aspetti tecnologici e di mercato emersi da uno studio pilota, Pubblicazione non in vendita edita con un contributo del Ministero per le Politiche Agricole.

VAN DEN BROEK, A. AND DEKKER, P. (1998),
"Membership and activity in voluntary organisations – the civil society perspective" in Pharoah, C. and Smerdon, M. (eds), Dimensions of the Voluntary Sector: Key Facts, Figures, Analysis and Trends, 1998 edition, Charities Aid Foundation, West Malling, Kent.

VAN DER BORG, J. (1999),
"Tourism and Culture", paper presented at The World Bank-UNESCO conference Culture Counts: A Conference on Financing, Resources, and the Economics Of Culture in Sustainable Development, 4-7 October, Florence.

VATN, A. (2001),
"Transaction costs and multifunctionality", Paper presented at the OECD Conference Multifunctionality: Applying the OECD Analytical Framework, 2-3 July, Paris, available at www1.oecd.org/agr/mf.

WILLIAMS, A.M. AND SHAW, G. (1998),
Tourism and economic development: European experiences, John Wiley and Sons, Chichester.

WOJAN, T.R. AND PULVER, G.C. (1995),
"Location patterns of high growth industries in rural counties", *Growth and Change* Vol. 26, No. 1 (Winter), pp. 3-22.

WORLD TOURISM ORGANIZATION (1996),
What Tourism Managers Need to Know: A Practical Guide to the Development and Use of Sustainable Tourism, World Tourism Organization, Madrid.

WORLD TOURISM ORGANIZATION (1998a),
Guide for Local Authorities on Developing Sustainable Tourism, World Organization, Madrid.

WORLD TOURISM ORGANIZATION (1998b),
"Tourism and taxation; striking a fair deal", World Tourism Organization, Madrid.

OECD PUBLICATIONS, 2, rue André-Pascal, 75775 PARIS CEDEX 16
PRINTED IN FRANCE
(04 2002 04 1 P) ISBN 92-64-19774-5 – No. 52469 2002